In her book, Beth Erwin dis[
emotional freedom that is ava.
She has experienced the abundant life of Jesus as she has broken
through the traps, lies, and deception of the evil one. Beth shares
her experiences of defeat and victory in a way that encourages you
to embrace the truth that God has a purpose for your life--and that
purpose is full of hope, freedom, love, and joy--promised and granted
by the means of the death and resurrection of our Lord Jesus. After
reading this book, you will be convinced it is never too late to live
for Him and to live for Him is exactly what you were created to do.

Dr. Tom Litteer, *Asst. Dean, GATS*

This is a book about **freedom**--the freedom to overcome what
Beth Erwin describes as "a partnership with death" by which she
means everything that would prevent the follower of Jesus (or
a would-be follower of Jesus) from living a life of Kingdom reality, led by the Holy Spirit, and clearly grounded in the truth and
wisdom of the Word of God. This is not a book of theories. Rather,
Beth writes from her extensive personal experiences and dedicated
study providing practical wisdom and applicable processes that set
the reader on the pathway to experiencing the truth of God. She
demonstrates how such truth can and does create a new way of life,
unrestricted by the bondages of the past, and able to embrace a new
beginning filled with the merciful grace of God, a divine destiny,
forgiveness, a certain hope, and resurrection power. Throughout her
book, Beth shares how God raised her from death to life. She is convinced, and so am I, that God can do the same for you.

Blessings in and through Him,

Randy Clark

D.D., D.Min., Th.D., M.Div., B.S. Religious Studies

Overseer of the apostolic network of Global Awakening

President of Global Awakening Theological Seminary

Beth Erwin, in her new book *Wander No More: Stepping Out of the Wilderness into Abundant Life,* rips the covers off the lies too many of us have believed that wreak havoc on the life God meant for us. Uncovering is only the beginning. Through personal and biblical illustration, Erwin will assure you that you are not alone, it is not your destiny, and you can be free. Each chapter will guide you to freedom by arming you with knowledge of the truth, crafted targeted prayers, and practical direction. Don't wait one more minute to deal a death blow to a spirit of death in your life.

Dr. Kim Maas Founder/CEO Kim Maas Ministries

Author of *Prophetic Community: God's Call For All to Minister in His Gift* and *The Way of the Kingdom: Seizing the Times For a Great Move of God.*

Here is someone who dares to say, "my story is your story." She stories the common pitfalls of our humanity. Beth has written a personal and engaging account of being delivered from the hopeless abyss. There is help for you in these pages. This work is descriptive and prescriptive. It has relevant struggles and practical remedies. It is laced with the balm of scripture and the oil of the testimony of Jesus. You'll laugh and cry and think. Yes, you'll think, then you'll pray and be healed.

Alan Hawkins, Pastor/Teacher

WANDER NO MORE

Stepping Out of the Wilderness into Abundant Life

BETH ERWIN, M.A.

Certain names have been changed to protect the privacy of those whose stories have been shared. However, my name was not changed. This is my story, and my personal dignity has not been spared! This book has been written to facilitate inner healing in those who choose to read the book and apply the principles and prayers within. It is not meant to replace the specialized training or treatment of a health care or mental health professional. Please consult a trained professional before making any decisions regarding medical treatment or care.

ISBN: 979-8-89109-414-7 - paperback

ISBN: 979-8-89109-415-4 - ebook

ISBN: 979-8-89109-416-1 - hardcover

This book is dedicated to Marcia McWhorter,
beloved mentor.
Without you, this book would not be possible.
You were a wonderful teacher and friend. I miss you.

TABLE OF CONTENTS

Chapter Seven: Sloth— Trudging Through the Mire
          of Acedia **235**

Chapter Eight: Conclusion—Dying to Live **279**

Epilogue **303**

PREFACE

This book reflects my personal journey out of the wilderness of a debilitating partnership with death. Put simply, this writing chronicles ways that I rejected the life God had designed for me and how this created within me an inability to live in joy. This unholy and unintentional partnership affected my health, my dreams, and my attitudes.

What is a partnership with death? It is the ways in which we inadvertently reject the life we have been given. It is also the ways in which we reject the principles upon which God encourages us to live our lives. We will explore these "unholy partnerships" in the following pages. For now, let us recognize that one does not have to be nor have ever been suicidal to have embraced death in their lives.

An agreement with death prevents us from living in the unique and amazing identity we have been given in Christ. It inhibits us from being who we really are. Instead we reflect mere shadows of our true selves as the pain and hurt in our hearts take on a life of their own. This book is not about making you a more likable person. God already loves you completely. He couldn't possibly love you more than He already does because His love is perfect.

Therefore, this book is my story of embracing a life that is filled with joy. It is more than one person's story because a theology based only upon one's own experiences is not a sound theology. Our theologies must meet scriptural truths, for it is the Word of God against which we as Christians measure truth. That, with the Holy Spirit, is our beacon.

As the road along this journey unfolded, scriptural truths were revealed to me through prayer, reading books, and the ministry of inner healing. I was also blessed with the counsel of a wise and loving mentor. Through this journey, I learned that we often tend to interpret scripture through our lens of experience. While these personal experiences can help us encounter and understand scripture, we must, however, rise above our experiences and embrace what scripture itself reveals.

For example, scripture teaches that God heals, but if we have not personally received healing from God, does that mean that God no longer heals anyone anymore? If that is true, then should we bother to pray for our sick loved ones?

My experience alone did not form my theology; scripture revealed truths that I could not have personally experienced, truths that spurred my journey to freedom. Scripture teaches us to "be of sober *spirit*, be on the alert. Your adversary, the devil, prowls around like a roaring lion, seeking someone to devour" (I Peter 5:8 NASB). Admittedly, it took a while to understand what this verse looked like in my present-day circumstances.

I read about the children of Israel being delivered from Egypt and how they wandered the desert for forty years before they could enter the Promised Land, a land flowing with milk and honey. On some level, I understood they struggled with personal issues that prevented them from experiencing the promise of abundance. It just did not register with me how that would look in my own life. Slowly, I began to see the connection between my failure to thrive and the wilderness wanderings of Abraham's descendants, the Israelites. Like me, they were going around the same old tree, over and over again, because of their ungodly agreements with death. They had not learned to trust God with their hurts and fears and neither had I.

That is the heart of this book. It is the revelation of how I remained in a dreary and dry desert for much of my life because I had inadvertently embraced deadly partnerships and how I learned to take hold of life, accept my purpose, and enter a land of abundance and joy.

We are reminded in John 10:10 that Jesus came so that we may have life and have it in abundance. As I experienced death's effects on my life, I was not aware of its presence, nor did I realize that the abundance of life was not flourishing in me. It is easy to fall prey to the lie that this is just the way things are this side of Christ's second coming.

Many, like me, have trudged through life accepting meager crumbs rather than dining at the banquet table with joy. However, we don't have to live like this. In fact, God doesn't want us to live like this. Join me in this journey to embrace the incredible, beautiful life that God has given to you. Yes, your life is incredible. It is beautiful and no matter what your experience has been, it is a life worth living.

In the pages that follow, you will see a side of me that doesn't look good. You will see my pride, my bitterness, and more. It isn't pretty. But through it you will see the amazing compassion and grace of God. If you choose to embrace the scriptural truths shared in this book, you will find hope, freedom, and relief. You will experience life. God really is that good.

INTRODUCTION

As previously mentioned, this book was birthed from my journey of learning to choose life and the accompanying realization of the myriad of ways in which I had inadvertently partnered with death. While the agreements I had made with death compare to the desert wanderings of the Israelites, it is not an exposition of their exodus from Egypt. As a matter of fact, we will not even cover those passages of scripture at all. It is, however, my heartfelt offering to share with you what the Holy Spirit taught me through my exodus experience so that you, too, can break free from the effects of death upon your life and dreams.

Scripture exhorts us to "choose life" (Deuteronomy 30:19). While we are born with an innate sense of self preservation, we often make subtle choices to our detriment. Partnering or coming into agreement with death does not always mean that we are suicidal or that we are suddenly going to depart this life. Quite the contrary—it often means that we live out the full number of our days, yet in ways that are significantly less than the life our Creator has called us to live. It means that we get stuck in desert wanderings, failing to step into purpose. This death spirit is content to watch us choose ways that are adversarial to the fullness of life and struggle through the dry and desolate land of discouragement, rejection, bitterness, and the like. We believe that we reap what we sow and that the little bits of sunshine we reap are the rewards of a miserly God sustaining us through the difficulties of life on earth. We remain content to endure in non-flourishing gardens, believing that this is just the way things are in this earth life.

I am reminded of the instructions given to a novice demon, Wormwood, by his uncle in *The Screwtape Letters* by C.S. Lewis. Wormwood was tasked to oppress a certain man's life. This man is referred to as *his patient* throughout the book. Although Wormwood has failed to prevent his *patient's* conversion to Christianity, he is encouraged to not despair and to continue to wage war against his patient for "all the habits of the patient, both mental and bodily, are still in our favor."[1] In a rather tongue-in-cheek manner, God is referred to as the Enemy because the book is written from a demon's perspective. Wormword is told that while patients "sojourn in the Enemy's camp,"[2] many return to the enslavement of evil's dominion.

This all too often reflects the Christian life. Christians must learn to recognize the deathly agreements made with the enemy and break these partnerships in order to live the abundant life Christ has promised. This does not imply a life without difficulty, but it does promise joy and a life that flourishes in all circumstances. It is a life that thrives in the face of evil. It is our inheritance.

What is a Spirit of Death?

In his book, *Storm Warning*, Billy Graham wrote, "Death is an accomplished master of destruction, and his credentials precede him: abortion, abuse, addiction, brutality, conflict, crime, disease, drugs,

---

1   C.S. Lewis, *The Screwtape Letters* (San Francisco CA: Harper One Publishers, 2013), 13. Scribd.
2   Lewis, *Screwtape*, 13, Scribd. (The Enemy in this context is God because it is written from a demon's perspective).

hatred, idolatry, irreverence, jealousy, lies, lust, murder, neglect, pestilence, racial conflict, rape, rebellion, revenge, starvation, suicide, violence, and war. These are Satan's calling cards and his record of achievement swells with each passing year."[3] This description covers a wide range of maladies, and we can see its affects upon the world today. Take a quick scroll through any social media platform and you will find no shortage of conflict, irreverence, hatred and lies. In July of 2021, using data from the FBI's Uniform Crime Reporting System, USA Facts reported that while overall crime rates were down, violent crimes had increased.[4] This reflected a twenty-five percent increase in homicides according to the FBI's site.[5] Often we see in the natural a reflection of what is happening in the spirit: these reports indicate that unnatural death is on the rise.

The Apostle Paul wrote that "the law of the Spirit of life in Christ Jesus has set you free from the law of sin and death" (Romans 8:2 NASB). When we choose Jesus of Nazareth as our Lord and Savior, we become new beings that have been set free from the law of sin and death. While we will explore this in more detail later, it is worth mentioning here because the very function of the spirit of death is its dedication to "keep us ignorant of the rights and promises that have come with that transaction."[6] In other words, the spirit of death is not only something that at times desires to cut your natural life short of its number of days, but it is an entity that desires to suppress the life God has given to you by clouding your perceptions of life

---

3   Billy Graham, *Storm Warning* (Nashville, TN: Thomas Nelson, 2011), 238. Scribd.
4   USA FACTS: Homicides increased by 25% but overall crime rates fell in 2020. July 14, 2021. https://usafacts.org/articles/homicides-increased-by-25-but-overall-crime-rate-fell-in-2020/ (accessed January 26, 2023).
5   Federal Bureau of Investigation: Crime Data Explorer. October 5, 2022. https://cde.ucr.cjis.gov/LATEST/webapp/#. (accessed January 26, 2023).
6   Jonathan Hunter, *Breaking Free From the spirit of death* (Maitland, FL: Xulon Press, 2012), Location 165. Kindle.

through sickness, hurts, shame, and disappointments. It desires to render your life far less than the plans and purposes God designed for you. It robs you of the joy of living.

Death Plays Well with Others

Like any flourishing corporation, Satan's business of destruction is structured with a hierarchy of players. Not all evil entities are given equal status. Scripture reveals a ranking of powers that tells us that "our struggle is not against flesh and blood, but against the rulers, against the powers, against the world forces of this darkness, against the spiritual forces of wickedness in the heavenly places" (Ephesians 6:12 NASB).

Death spirits have a higher rank than your garden variety entities such as lust. This works much like our modern military ranks. The higher the rank a person has, the more power and authority he has. While someone might get away with ignoring a private, they are not going to ignore a captain without repercussions, because the captain has more ability to invoke harm upon the offender, or as Screwtape would say, the "patient." The spirit world works much the same way. The higher-ranking spirits are stronger than the lower-level spirits that are more easily dismissed. Death is one of the higher-ranking spirits.

Each evil spirit works well with others to accomplish its purposes of disempowerment within the lives of its human "patient." Apathy, physical illness, jealousy, and the like are all well-suited partners for this enemy of our souls. This partnering of entities is noted in a myriad of ways. For instance, many assume that all who commit suicide are depressed. In his book, *The Noonday Demon*, Andrew Solomon laments the psychiatrist's focus upon depression assuming that curing one ailment will automatically cure the other; stating that "suicidality is an associated problem that requires its own treatment."[7]

Likewise, dealing with death requires its own treatment. As we walk through these pages together, the partnerships made with death, whether intentional or unintentional, will be broken. We will also address some of the common collaborations death has made with other life sucking powers. While this book is not exhaustive of all such deathly unions, taking a good look at and learning how to deal with these unions will set you free of your entanglement with death and help you learn to identify other such associations as they appear.

Not a Magic Prayer

Each chapter will conclude with a prayer that you are encouraged to pray out loud on your own. The prayers are anointed. They are not magic. This means the prayer is only as powerful as your intention in praying them. Please do a heart check and determine where you are in the process and pray accordingly. In other words, if you are being instructed to forgive someone who has hurt you, but you are not ready to forgive, then start where you are.

In the southern United States, we have a saying, "Who ate the red off your apple?" This is a way of asking, "Who ruined your day?" The point is, rather than praying an insincere, "Lord, I forgive Bubba for eating the red off my apple," pray a more sincere prayer that may sound more like this, "Lord, I am furious with Bubba. He hurt me and I am having a hard time letting it go. I know I am supposed to forgive, but I don't want to, and am asking you to help me want to forgive."

---

7   Andrew Solomon, *The Noonday Demon: An Atlas of Depression* (New York: Scribner Publications, 2011), 390. Scribd.

As you approach the end of each chapter, there will be prayer models that hopefully will fit the stage in healing that best works for you. Feel free to tweak them to reflect the current state of your heart. A sincere prayer is a beautiful prayer and will avail much. An insincere prayer can possibly do more harm than good. Keep it real, ya'll.

Finally, the chapter will conclude with steps to walking it out. Praying this type of prayer often requires some action on our part. It would be rather pointless to unlock the door to your cell only to fail to stand up and walk out of the door.

My Prayer for You

"Father, each person who journeys through these pages will need Your compassion, healing, and love. I pray that You uphold them with Your righteous right hand and guide their steps to commit to choosing life. I pray that You send angels to encamp about them and minister to them throughout the process. I pray that every distraction and hindrance be bound and the tenacity and courage to complete this process and choose life be loosed. Holy Spirit, I ask You to illuminate truths and bring revelation to each heart. I ask that You soften the stony places in their hearts so each person who sojourns these pages may be set free to be more conformed to the likeness of Christ. Father, I ask that You help each reader break free from the life destroying spirit of death and step into the abundant life that You have chosen for them. Jesus, You died that each of us may live. I release a restoration of Your plans for each reader upon their lives. I release a new joy for the life that You have given to them to rest upon them now and forever. Lord, Leif Hetland has prayed for others to love themselves as Jesus loves them. Likewise, I pray that You help each reader learn to love themselves with the love of Christ.

In the name of Jesus. Amen."

Once again, I was awoken not by a noise but more like a feeling. I could tell something was in my room, and the presence of it was strong enough to awaken me from a deep sleep.

It was always the same.

There would be a man made of darkness looming in the doorway to my bedroom. It seemed as if all the dark specks that populate the late-night air would come together to form this giant of a man who would appear in my doorway. He was large and ominous and yet almost transparent at the same time.

It seemed strange that he wore a big cowboy hat. Sometimes I would see him coming down the hall toward my room but he always stopped at the doorway and stared as I trembled uncontrollably in my bed.

I did the only thing I knew to do—hide under the covers. As a child, when I mentioned my nocturnal tormentor, my big brother told me it was just a dream; it could not be real. I decided to believe him.

Until many years later when I was ministering to a young woman who was afraid of a big man made of dark spots that had come into her room since childhood.

He, too, wore a cowboy hat.

CHAPTER ONE

Choosing Life

If you are someone like me who often skips the preface and introduction to get to the good stuff, stop and go back! You will need
the good stuff in both the preface and introduction to fully utilize the
really good stuff in the pages that follow. Also, be sure to check the
footnotes. Some additional explanations are posted there along with
scripture references for your convenience.

You are about to embark upon a journey of discovery. This book
is written to help you realize the ways in which we often inadvertently
partner with death and make a conscious decision to break those
agreements. It is a roadmap for leaving the wilderness and embracing
life which will unlock God's storehouse of abundant living for you.

Now, let's get started. There is an old joke where the grim reaper
stands before an emaciated, wrinkled old man who is clinging to
his walker. Death appears very ominous in his black cloak, holding
a scythe, and booms forth, "I am death!" The decrepit man replies,
"That's okay. I'll talk louder."

Like this gentleman, we often entertain death but are unaware
of its true identity. This brings no offense to death who is content to
watch you wilt and wither with each passing day under his careful

manipulations. It turns everyday pleasures into drudgery, robbing you of joy. He is determined to make you forget who you are.

What are You Thinking?

It is written, "For as he thinks within himself, so he is" (Proverbs 23:7 NASB). This passage describes a stingy man who invites another to dinner. Scripture warns against partaking of this man's supposed delicacies because as Tremper Longman puts it, it will be like a "hair in the throat, so it will be vomited."[8] This means that although the man speaks words of generosity, in his mind he thinks like a miserly person and really has no concern for another. His thoughts dictate what he does, not his words. Ultimately, his actions will follow his thoughts rather than the actual words that he speaks. He will say eat and enjoy but will serve yukky morsels that will make you sick.

Have you ever noticed a person saying one thing but doing another? We all have. The thoughts within our minds determine who we are and how we behave. At any given moment, we are processing thoughts. Our brains unconsciously process inputs from our bodies and send commands accordingly. For example, our gaits change throughout a short walk to prevent pressure from remaining on one part of the foot throughout the stroll, as this would result in unnecessary injury.[9] Just as we are unaware of these bodily "thoughts" that our brains are processing, we are often unaware of the thoughts that find space within our minds. We don't spend time meticulously analyzing every thought; especially those with which we are familiar.

8   Tremper Longman, III, *Proverbs: Baker Commentary on the Old Testament Wisdom and Psalms*. (Grand Rapids: Baker Academic, 2015), 23d. (accessed February 3, 2023. ProQuest Ebook Central).
9   Dr. Paul Brand and Philip Yancey, *Pain: The Gift Nobody Wants* (New York: Harper Collins Publishers, 1993), 119–121.

You see a stop sign and your foot seems to automatically move toward the brake pedal. This is a good thing. But what if all our thoughts are not coming from a healthy source? My daughter bought her husband a t-shirt that had a traffic signal with the yellow light illuminated on it. The caption read, "Challenge Accepted." We all loved this shirt because growing up in a racing family, we could relate. Some of us see a yellow light and begin to slow down. Others see the yellow light and immediately speed up to clear the intersection before the light turns red. But what if a mind was so filled with rebellious thoughts that when seeing a stop sign or a red light, its response was "Heck No! I AM NOT STOPPING FOR NOTHING OR NOBODY!!" How many crashes would it take to rethink those thoughts?

Our minds receive inputs from three different entities: ourselves, the Holy Spirit, and unclean spirits. The problem is that they all sound just like our own voices. The enemy speaking in your mind does not sound like the Wicked Witch of the West while the Holy Spirit gives his best impression of James Earl Jones. No, as these voices are being processed through your brain, they sound just like your own thoughts.

Remember that scripture teaches we are made in the image of God.[10] We are beings that have spirits. Paul prayed that our "spirit and soul and body be kept complete, without blame at the coming of our Lord Jesus Christ" (1 Thessalonians 5:23 NASB). Mark Virkler says that you are "not just a pile of molecules. And if you are a spirit-being, designed to be connected to another, you are designed to be connected to another spirit…either the Holy Spirit or an evil spirit."[11]

---

10   "Then God said, 'Let us make mankind in our image, in our likeness…'" (Genesis 1:26).
11   Mark Virkler, interview by Beth Erwin, February 3, 2023, interview transcript, Virkler, Otter.Ai.

In this same conversation I had with Mark, he commented that there is no chance that we or anyone we know is not connected to spiritual beings whether the connection is with the Holy Spirit, evil spirits, or both. Do not let this alarm you.

Let this reveal to you that not every idea or thought that forms in your mind originates from you. It is important that we learn to hear the sometimes-subtle differences between these voices so that we can discern their origin. Rather than crashing from one bumpy ride to another, coming into agreement with the mind of Christ becomes a new and life-affirming journey. Throughout this book, you will learn how to better identify the origin of your thoughts and break agreements with lies that have formed within your mind. Lies rob you of truth. Truth sets you free.[12]

*See Appendix on How to Hear God's Voice by Mark Virkler

But What if I am a Spirit-Filled Christian?

If you have given your life to Christ, you have the Holy Spirit living within you. Scripture teaches that he leads through a still, small voice. We often hear the earthquakes and the fire alarms but miss that wonderful voice of peace and wisdom that desires to guide our hearts.[13] Some have erroneously said that a Spirit-filled Christian cannot have a demon because the Spirit could not stand to live in a house with an unclean spirit. The Holy Spirit just isn't that easily put off. He is not a wilting flower in the face of evil. If the Holy Spirit could not live in a house with an unclean spirit, then Spirit-filled Christians could not even go to the grocery store because there are unsaved people roaming around the aisles.

---

12 "Then you will know the truth, and the truth will set you free" (John 8:32).

13 "After the earthquake came a fire, but the Lord was not in the fire. And after the fire came a gentle whisper" (I Kings 19:12).

Much of the confusion comes from too much Hollywood and not enough Bible. There is no language in this book that describes or alludes to possession. Having demon troubles doesn't mean that a person projectile vomits, hates priests, and can have their heads spin around like an owl's. (Although that last part could come in handy at times!) That is Hollywood. Pretty scary and not what happens in our everyday lives. Let's use scripture to define our understanding of this issue. The word that is often translated as possessed in scripture is *daimonizomai*, "meaning, literally, 'demonized' or 'having a demon.'"[14]

An example can be found in Matthew's gospel where it is written that "they went out, behold, they brought to him a dumb man possessed with a devil" (Matthew 9:32 KJV). This word would better be translated as a man oppressed rather than possessed. Possession implies that someone has no control over themselves where oppression indicates an unjust or cruel power is being exerted over someone.

Even after receiving much inner healing, there was an area in my life where I seemed to act very much out of character. I would be compassionate and understanding in most circumstances save one: don't leave me waiting on you in a parking lot. My normal laid-back personality would transform, and I would be ready to spew green vomit on the offender. I could not stand to be left waiting. It took a few times of barely avoiding a stroke to recognize that there was a serious issue brewing in my heart. The Holy Spirit reminded me of times as a child where I had been forgotten and left waiting in a parking lot. This had left a gaping wound in my heart which had not been healed. This wound invited an attachment of anger and resentment

---

14   Peter J. Horrobin, *Healing through Deliverance: The Foundation and Practice of Deliverance Ministry* (Grand Rapids, MI: Chosen Books, 2008), 274.

to reside inside my soul. As I forgave those who had forgotten me, my heart began to get free.

Inner healing and especially walking in forgiveness often frees our souls from unholy ties that bind. I was saved. I exhibited the fruits of the Spirit in many areas of my life. But I could not manifest Christ while waiting alone in a parking lot until I was healed and set free. Peter Horrobin sums it up quite beautifully. "Propositionally, it seems unlikely that an evil spirit and the Holy Spirit could dwell within the same person. It seems even more unlikely, however, that the sinless Son of God could come into a broken and demonized world that was under the rule of Satan and governed by an army of evil spirits."[15] Now, with that settled, we are ready to really get down to business.

The Death of Religion

Not only are we made in the image of God, but God also breathed the breath of life into our lungs. It is written, "Then the Lord God formed man of dust from the ground and breathed into his nostrils the breath of life; and man became a living being" (Genesis 2:7 NASB). Do you get that? We are living beings because the breath of God fills our lungs. If we are created in his image according to Genesis 1:26 and filled with His breath, why do we struggle to flourish? Attempting life apart from God is deadly business. Let's look at how that works.

It has often been said that religion is man's attempt to justify himself to God, but Christianity is about relationship. It is about accepting Christ as our source of righteousness. In their book, *Counseled by God*, Mark and Patty Virkler write that "religion brings a heaviness to our spirits…Christianity brings a lightness to our hearts as we accept

15   Horrobin, *Healing Through Deliverance*, 275.

the strength of God to do His will."[16] Mark shares how, although he felt he had come to the Lord in faith, he had begun to strive to live by a set of "Christian" rules and regulations. He wrote about how the more he tried to attain righteousness in his own strength "whole areas of [his] life were cut off and discarded, bringing death to [his] personality and creativity."[17]

The Apostle Paul weighed in on this subject as he strongly admonished the Galatian church against justification through works. He taught that "we may be justified by faith in Christ and not by works of the Law; since by works of the Law no flesh will be justified" (Galatians 2:16 NASB). Craig Keener puts it like this. "Divine righteousness is not a goal to be reached by human effort, but a relational premise that should dictate the new life of faithfulness to Christ…It is a divine gift rather than human achievement."[18]

It was no secret that Jesus was annoyed with the religious leaders of his day. He was frustrated because they placed heavy burdens upon the shoulders of the people while they were unwilling to even lift a finger to alleviate or carry such burdens themselves.[19] Jesus compared himself against these "unfaithful leaders"[20] in John Chapter 10. He said they were like wolves that would devour the sheep and said that their highest ambition was to promote themselves. He said he came to bring life.

---

16   Mark and Patty Virkler, *Counseled by God.* (Buffalo, NY: Lamad Publishing, 2011), 116.

17   Mark and Patty Virkler, *Counseled by God.* (Buffalo, NY: Lamad Publishing, 2011), 115.

18   Craig S. Keener, *Romans* (Eugene OR: Cascade Books, 2009), 40, Kindle.

19   "They tie up heavy, cumbersome loads and put them on other people's shoulders, but they themselves are not willing to lift a finger to move them" (Matthew 23:4).

20   Craig S. Keener, *The IVP Bible Background Commentary: New Testament.* (Downers Grove, Illinois: Intervarsity Press, 2014), 280.

The Passion Translation puts John 10:10 this way, "A thief has only one thing in mind—he wants to steal, slaughter and destroy. But I have come to give you everything in abundance, more than you expect—life in its fullness until you overflow!" That is an exciting verse that gives clear indication of how the enemy works as well as God's intentions toward us. The thief in this passage is the unfaithful religious leaders whose selfish ambitions were killing the people's spirits. This reveals the deathly fruits of our attempts to justify ourselves to God. It keeps us on a continual wheel of frustration where we are either constantly disappointed by others' inability to live up to our expectations (like the Pharisees) or we are in a continual state of repentance and sorrow because we can never measure up. Like Mark, our personalities shrivel and die in the hopelessness of it. It is written that God does not delight in burnt offerings (the works of our flesh) but he takes delight in a remorseful heart.[21]

God spoke to Israel through the prophet Isaiah and said, "For thus said the Lord God, the Holy One of Israel, 'In returning and rest you shall be saved; in quietness and in trust shall be your strength." But you were unwilling, and you said, "No! We will flee upon horses" (Isaiah 30:15-16 ESV). Rather than repenting of their stubborn pride and receiving rest and peace through God's salvation, they chose to trust in their own strength (their own weapons of war and horses), and they were terrified in the end. It is no surprise that we struggle with the tendency to rely upon our strength. Each of us is faced with evaluations at every turn within our culture. We receive reports cards in school that grade our attempts on a scale of perfection. The closer to perfect the work, the higher the grade. We graduate into the workforce, and there we receive performance evaluations. The better

---

21   "You do not delight in sacrifice, or I would bring it; you do not take pleasure in burnt offerings. My sacrifice, O God, is a broken spirit; a broken and contrite heart you, God, will not despise" (Psalms 51:16–17).

we perform, the higher our wages are and the more the boss likes us. Each day we are faced with the idea that we are only as good as the last five minutes. Yesterday's achievements are old news. We are surrounded by a mentality of, "What have you done for me lately?"

What is Killing Us?

While Jesus was speaking specifically about the religious leaders of his time in John 10:10, these religious leaders portray how the enemy works to kill, steal, and destroy. The Greek word that we translate for kill in this passage is *thuo*. It is not the usual word for "kill." It means to sacrifice or to slaughter. Just as the religious leaders were willing to sacrifice those in their charge to their selfish ambitions, the enemy of our souls is willing to sacrifice God's people to his desire to yoke us with burdens too great to carry. He operates on borrowed time with stolen dominion and delights in deceiving mankind into coming into agreement with his lies. Through the burden of performance rather than accepting the grace of the Father, we have often partnered with death and sacrificed our hopes and dreams, allowing our God-ordained purposes to lie dormant. But these seeds of life have not died, they are merely waiting to germinate.

**There is a prayer at the end of the chapter to break agreements with the religious spirit.

Tackled by Blessings

The last part of the verse in John 10:10 reminds us that Jesus came that we might have life in abundance. This is a very real and present reality. Just as the blood of the sacrificial lamb painted upon the doorposts caused the angel of death to passover the families within the house,[22] so the blood of the Perfect Lamb of God in Christ sprin-

---

22   See Genesis 18 to read about the first Passover as it occurred to free the Israelites from Egyptian captivity.

kled upon our hearts causes life to overflow within us. When we receive Jesus as our Lord and Savior, an amazing thing happens—we become new creatures. "Therefore if anyone is in Christ, he is a new creature; the old things passed away; behold new things have come" (2 Corinthians 5:17 NASB). Craig Keener explains that according to Paul this means "believers have already begun to participate in the resurrection life of the coming world."[23] This is powerful language to describe living in the Kingdom of God. Christ came to impart life to us, and the Father has exhorted us to choose that life. In Deuteronomy 30:19–20 (NASB), it is written:

> ...I have placed before you life and death, the blessing and the curse. So choose life in order that you may live, you and your descendants, by loving the Lord your God, by obeying His voice, and by holding close to Him; for this is your life and the length of your days...

Deuteronomy 28 lists a multitude of blessings that will overtake those who follow the ways of the Lord. It describes blessings that will chase you down and overtake you in virtually every area of your life. The good news is we are empowered through faith in Christ to receive those blessings that lead to an abundant life. Note how this passage indicates that life comes by holding close to God. Faith, which is believing God, draws us near to him. When we believe lies, we are choosing death which effectively moves us away from Him. God is not moving away from us: He continues to call us back to himself in repentance. When I was praying over these things, the Lord whispered a phrase to my heart: failure to thrive.

---

23   Craig S. Keener, *The IVP Bible Background Commentary: New Testament*. (Downers Grove, Illinois: Intervarsity Press, 2014), 508.

Failure to Thrive

While this term personally resonated in my spirit, the exact definition of it was unknown to me. It is a term most often used to describe infants whose range of symptoms include: lack of appropriate weight gain, irritability, easily fatigued, excessive sleepiness, lack of age-appropriate social responses such as smiling, failing to make vocal sounds, delayed motor development, and it is associated with learning and behavioral difficulties later in life.[24] Suddenly it began to make sense. Think about these things in your own life. Here are some points of consideration:

- Do you find yourself often getting frustrated or irritated over life's issues?

- Do you find that life simply wears you out, making you feel tired or overwhelmed?

- Do you find it difficult to respond socially or perhaps difficult to exhibit joy or to enjoy your family and friends?

- Is it often hard for you to express yourself?

- Are you accident-prone?

- Have you received a diagnosis of Epstein Barr, Chronic Fatigue Syndrome, or a similar diagnosis? (Spiritual issues can sometimes manifest in our bodies as physical maladies.)

- Have you been diagnosed with asthma or any other breathing difficulty?

- Do you find yourself often short of breath?

---

24   Marissa Selner, "What is Failure to Thrive?" *Healthline*, July 25, 2012, https://www.healthline.com/health/failure-to-thrive.

Thriving did not come naturally to me. I struggled. Despite my abilities, it was difficult for me to attend school regularly. Life often seemed unnaturally hard for me. Even things that should bring joy seemed tedious. Things I wanted to do, even looked forward to doing, would suddenly seem laborious when it came time to do them.

Even after salvation, the struggle continued. It was difficult to find joy when filled with a constant dread of doing. This cloud had hung over me since childhood. I remember seeing in my mind's eye as a little girl a dark cloud hovering over me, waiting for opportunities to oppress me. Perhaps this was the daytime version of the man of darkness wearing a cowboy hat who would awaken me from my sleep. There did not seem much point in describing this to anyone because it would only sound like depression, or something worse and somehow, I knew this dark cloud was not a chemical imbalance in my brain. It was a real entity that was somehow different from depression but every bit as life draining. My hope was in Jesus; my faith was in God. I believed the Word and cherished my salvation. So, what was preventing me from embracing the life God had given to me? Why could I not seem to consistently enjoy it? Why did I feel that somehow my life was darker and uglier than most? Where was the fullness of life that Jesus came to release for me?

On the Blackfeet Indian Reservation

The church I was attending planned a mission trip to hold a weeklong revival meeting on a Blackfeet Indian Reservation. While waiting to board the plane, my fellow passengers, upon hearing my southern accent, would ask where I was headed. When I responded with my destination of Browning, Montana, they all looked at me with surprised expressions and asked the same question: *Why Browning?* Although I did not understand why, no one seemed to think it was worthwhile to visit Browning. While this land held some of the kindest and most generous people I had ever met, their struggle with poverty and oppression was heart wrenching. Looking at the dusty and desolate terrain, one could almost envision the desert in which the Israelites traversed. The land itself seemed to embody the lyrics, "here in this worn and weary land where many a dream has died."[25]

There was a constant breeze that blew across the dust of the earth covering everything with grit. It was easy to tell the ones who lived there from those who did not by the red around their eyes. Visitors could not blend in because they were betrayed by bloodshot eyes! Although my own eyes remained in a constant state of irritation, my heart ached for them. I signed up to do whatever I could that would allow me to interact with these precious people.

As I moved about the community and interacted with the people, there was a young man who continually followed me everywhere I went. He kept a distance from me but stared intently in my direction. It would have been flattering to think that he was infatuated by my profound beauty or effervescent charm, but there was no evidence of attraction coming from him. He simply stared with an intense interest that was a bit disconcerting to say the least.

After a few days of having holes bored through me by his relentless gaze, some of the women from the community took notice and approached me about his behavior. They were very troubled to learn he'd been around for days and wanted to make sure that he had not tried to approach me. When I asked who he was, they replied, "He is bad medicine, please stay away from him." Well, I had no intention of introducing myself to this intense young man, so that was not a problem. The women said that they needed to make the elders

25   Casting Crowns. *Thrive* (Official Lyric Video), December 18, 2013. YouTube Music Video, 5.09, https://www.youtube.com/watch?v=qQ71RW-JhS_M.

aware of the situation and cautioned me against being alone until the matter was settled.

Shortly afterward, the elders and the associate pastor with whom I was traveling questioned me about the young man. The elders appeared equally as troubled by his presence as the ladies had and assured me he would be banned from attending any remaining events. Now, this did not seem like a good idea to me. We were there to bring the Good News of Jesus and he seemed like he could certainly use a big ol' dose of the Holy Ghost! They promised me that they would not ban him unless he tried to approach me. Perhaps they kept this promise, or perhaps they did not. At any rate, the young man never attended another one of our functions. I did not see him again until our second to last night when I was quite alone and unprotected.

The generous people with whom we'd ministered wanted to show their appreciation and threw a party for us. It was my job to write about our time there to share with those who had financially provided for the ministry. I was eager to get my thoughts on paper and wanted to stay behind. This idea did not meet well with the leadership because our motel was in the middle of nowhere, and I would be the only person in the surrounding area while they were gone; even the manager planned to attend the celebration. After promising not to leave the room and to keep the door locked, I was allowed to stay behind and get to work.

Around 11 p.m., there was a knock on my door, and I realized I had indeed forgotten to lock the door. The parking lot was not paved, so I thought I would have heard the distinctive sound tires make on gravel. Expecting my roommate, I jumped up from writing and threw open the door to find a totally empty parking lot and the young man of many stares pacing in front of my door. Realizing my mistake, I made a decision.

Too many things had happened to me in secret. Whatever he planned to do, it would not be in secret. He would have to drag me out of the room and into the graveled lot. He would have to do what he had come to do out in the open, in front of God.[26] I braced myself in the doorway and prepared to fight. He continued to pace and wring his hands. It occurred to me that he was not very good at this assault thing because he was wasting valuable time. Curiosity and fear vied for control over my emotions, but a steely determination won the day. Feet firmly planted, I waited. I have no idea why it did not occur to me to slam the door and lock it tight!

Finally, he spoke. He stammered and said he had been told to stay away from me. I did not assume he meant he had been warned to stay away from me by the tribal elders. It seemed more as if whoever he studied "his medicine" under had told him to leave me alone. Perhaps it only seemed this way to me because of the promises to not ban him from our services. But whoever had warned him did a good job because he did seem very afraid of defying the unofficial restraining order. I continued to watch him pace. After a few seconds that seemed like hours, I forcefully asked, "Then why did you come here?" He told me that he had been watching me. I assured him I had noticed. He said he felt he had to tell me what he saw. He said that the biggest spirit of death he had ever seen was with me all the time. He emphasized that he continually watched, and it never left me. He was clearly overwhelmed by the magnitude of my dark companion.

It was in that moment that I finally knew. Even though he was of bad medicine, the words he spoke were true. Sometimes, you cannot

---

26   I do realize that God could see into the room, but in situations like that the mind thinks a bit differently.

reject the mail simply because the postman has dirty feet. At long last, I understood what that thing that had hovered around me since my earliest memory really was—it was death. Cowboy hat or not, it was a real presence that oppressed me. The Spirit of God rose inside me, and I declared to this troubled young man, "I know what you say is true. But greater is He who is in me than he who is in the world. Whether I live or whether I die, He decides—not that spirit of death."

He stopped pacing. His eyes grew wide as he said to me, "You have big medicine." And with that, he ran away. I have no answer as to how I could have so easily forgotten about this experience, but I did.

I went about my business for another 20 years. It never occurred to me that I could be rid of this pesky thing. I wish I had known. Boy, do I wish I had known.

Back to the Failure

Despite the difficulties of my life, I was a survivor and took great pride in this monumental fact. This pride was a comfort and inspiration to me—that is until I heard the song *Thrive* by Casting Crowns.

Just to know You and to make You known
We lift Your name on high
Shine like the sun, make darkness run and hide
We know we were made
For so much more than ordinary lives
It's time for us to more than just survive
We were made to thrive.[27]

---

27   Casting Crowns. *Thrive* (Official Lyric Video), December 18, 2013. YouTube Music Video, 5.09, https://www.youtube.com/watch?v=qQ71RW-JhS_M

Made to thrive? Survival itself is not the pinnacle of achievement? This required some re-wiring of my thinking process. How had I missed the point of thriving?

According to the Children's Hospital of Philadelphia, some of the possible complications of failure to thrive are shorter height, behavioral problems, developmental delays, thinking problems and difficulties in school.[28] Many of these issues described my daily existence. I had never dealt with this dark companion, and it was having a good time at my expense.

When I was two years old, I went face first into the windshield of my mother's car in the course of a car accident. At the age of thirteen, my appendix burst, and the doctors told my parents they'd do their best, but the poison was throughout my system and my prognosis was grim. I survived countless car accidents and one time a group of young satanists tried to break into my house knowing that I was at home! This is just a short list of my brushes with death.

More Creepy Stares

Eventually, I began experiencing breathing problems. As these issues grew worse, I was diagnosed with asthma. I could not believe I had suddenly acquired asthma at this late stage in life. It did not make sense. Unable to get relief, I reached out to my mentor in inner healing, Marcia McWhorter, to get some answers to help restore my breath. She decided to seek the Lord on my behalf, and we agreed to get together three days later.

She said that the Lord revealed to her that I had a spirit of death. I assured her (really, I argued with her) that I had already been delivered. We will get to that story later, but for now it is enough to

---

28   Children's Hospital of Philadelphia: Failure to Thrive. https://www.chop.edu/conditions-diseases/failure-thrive. (accessed February 4, 2023).

know that I had been delivered of the spirit of death about two years earlier. This deliverance happened more than 20 years after the Man of Many Stares had revealed its presence to me. It was clear to my mentor that my dark companion still lingered. Later I realized that I had not yet learned to change my thinking, and despite having been delivered, I had unintentionally embraced the darn thing right back.

Yet during my conversation with Marcia, my heart remained firm that it was not a death spirit plaguing me. The Holy Spirit intervened and began to coach me by bringing to my mind several weird encounters I had experienced. Having learned to pay attention to the random thoughts that tugged upon my mind when seeking revelation from the Lord, it seemed prudent to share my musings with Marcia.

The reflections were of three disturbing encounters in ministry I had experienced. The first occurred shortly after I had initially received freedom from the spirit of death while at Voice of the Apostles, a conference by Global Awakening. I had received deliverance, and dang it, I wanted the whole world to be free! During an encounter with a disturbed man who attended our church, it was in my heart to get him free, too. He was intellectually delayed in development and although fully grown, would never be able to live on his own. The praise and worship would often disturb him, and he would need to leave the services. He would sit in the vestibule until his turmoil quieted. One morning, I encountered him while he was settling himself and he felt the need to share with me why he was not in the services. Typically, he did not speak to me but this morning he did. I had not yet learned how to appropriately deal with evil entities, but I had recently received deliverance and thought I could handle this guy's issues. Let me assure you that I was not prepared.

After receiving his permission to pray for him, I began to pray and command these tormenting spirits to leave him. His eyes were darting all over the place, he would not look at me and could not seem to find something to settle his focus upon. Freshly back from my conference and filled with the zeal of newfound freedom, I remembered how the person ministering to me had told me to look him in the eye while he prayed. Therefore, I insisted that Melvin look me in the eye. It took several times of firm insistence until he focused his eyes and looked directly into mine. Yikes!

The most creepy, wide-eyed stare in the history of the world met my eyes. It seemed to defy me with total innocence as if saying, "Who, me?" My gut responded the opposite of my command, it revolted screaming, "STOP! Do NOT look at me!" Well, my mom did not raise a dummy. There was no time wasted in telling Melvin that he did not need to look at me after all. That bizarre stare completely freaked me out. Though my prayer for him continued for a bit, my heart had shrunk back. You can probably guess that Melvin did not receive any freedom that day.[29]

This entity revealed itself to me again several months later in Savannah, Georgia. Walking to my hotel after a nice seafood dinner, a homeless man asked for my help. He was hungry and wanted money for food. We talked for a bit, and feeling compelled to help him, I offered to pray for him and to give him enough money to get something to eat.[30] During the prayer, the same intense stare of wide-eyed innocence who studied me from Melvin's eyes challenged

---

29   While we have authority in Christ to do amazing things, sometimes we lack the maturity or understanding to use our authority effectively.

30   Please do not make a theology or a ministry model out of this experience. I felt led to minister to this man and to give him a few dollars. Always follow the leading of the Holy Spirit.

*Melvin is not his real name. The names of the men in these encounters have been changed to respect their privacy.

me from within this man. In both instances, it felt as if the breath was sucked right out of my lungs. Again, though I continued to pray, I am not convinced he received much ministry. Are you starting to catch on? Well, I had not put it together yet. Call me a slow learner, but sometimes it really is hard to see the forest for the trees.

Both Melvin and the Savanah man seemed to be suffering from some sort of mental illness. It was clear that it was the same spirit looking back at me from each of these men, but other than being obviously evil, it was not clear which specific spirit it was. Could it be an entity that took advantage of the mentally ill or developmentally challenged?

Deliverance ministers were unable to identify this spirit based upon the description of my experiences. Eventually, a man dying of cancer called upon me to help him sell his home. We will call him Charles. During the listing process, his grandson revealed to me that Charles was an atheist. It occurred to me that he had probably heard the gospel message many times and he confirmed that this was true. Asking the Lord to help me understand what would pierce his heart with truth, I got an idea. Following the Holy Spirit's lead, I made a bargain with Charles.

We bargained that I would sell his house for more than he expected if he allowed me to pray for him to have a personal encounter with Jesus. The deal was that he had to be willing to sincerely receive the prayer—he had to agree that if Jesus was real, he wanted to know the truth. No magic prayers, right? Typically, prayers require a dose of sincerity. Because God does not violate our free will, we cannot expect Him to answer prayers that we do not mean. That would be a violation. It is God's desire that all men come to salvation knowledge.[31] If Charles accepted the prayer, it would be a step in softening his heart to the Holy Spirit.[32] Charles agreed, and we shook hands on the deal.

While praying, the Lord prompted me to open my eyes. There it was. That same creepy, wide-eyed stare of innocence was intently looking back at me. Daaanng, it was freaky. I continued to pray, but it was difficult. Later, after his home sold, I visited Charles to see if he had met Jesus yet. He agreed to let me pray for him again, and yet again, the stare returned.[33] It was equally as disturbing the second time around as it was the first. Or should I say fourth time around?

As I shared these experiences with Marcia, she was certain this was a spirit of death that was revealing itself to me in others. It must have felt confident of its hold over me to be so bold, but I still was not convinced. Then, I remembered what each person had revealed to me about themselves. While Melvin did not receive any freedom from my prayer, he did find a compassionate heart with whom he felt free to share his dreams and visions. They were stuff of nightmares and he asked for my help because he was really scared.

One vision kept that playing across his mind was about a big, ugly man of darkness trapping people on a bus and viciously murdering them. After realizing that my lack of deliverance training left me woefully inadequate, it was enough to pray God's peace over Melvin which seemed to offer some relief. Savannah Man had asked for my

---

31   "This is good and pleases God our Savior who wants all people to be saved and come to a knowledge of the truth" (I Timothy 2:4).

32   Again, don't create a theology of this one encounter. You can always pray for the salvation of the unsaved whether or not they agree to your prayers. Avoid prayers that say things like, "God, make Charles receive you." We do not pray prayers that violate another person's will. Instead, we pray, "God, soften Charles' heart and help him receive the truth of the Gospel Message."

33   Unfortunately, I did not see Charles again before he died and do not know if he received Jesus. I do know that I prayed a prayer in line with the heart of God and He answered.

help from tormenting visions of death that happened on a military base. He seemed to be reliving an instance of something that had been reported on the news, but it was doubtful he had personally been there. However, the thought was planted in his mind, and he kept seeing the destruction. Charles was being eaten by incurable cancer. All three were being tormented by death. Marcia was right. I needed help, again.

How This Thing Works

Without realizing it, I had embraced death. Though I had been delivered, I had not been set free from the mindset of death. My thoughts were not thoughts of life but of things that stifled and stunted my growth and purpose. When I was a child, my life seemed more lonely and painful than that of my friends. So, I hated my life. I hated parts of my body because kids made fun of my skinny legs. I believed I was ugly.

You will notice a few things that will be repeated throughout this book. It is not because there is a scratch on the record but because through repetition, you will remember. There are things that need to stick with you, and repetition is the glue. Here's one: you do not have to be suicidal to have embraced death. Rejecting the life that God has given to you is embracing death. This will cause us to wander in the wilderness of unfulfillment, never experiencing abundance of life. Failure to really choose life is death. The agreements made with death through trauma and the rejection of my own life had never been broken.

Have you failed to take in the life-giving love and breath of God because you have rejected the life that He has given to you for whatever reason? This means that you, too, are failing to thrive.

22

If shortened height is a complication of failure to thrive in the natural, then would it not stand to reason that in the spiritual realm it would result in our failure to rise to the full stature and position of authority that Christ has given to us?

If behavioral problems are linked to failure to thrive, then would we not struggle to overcome besetting sins?

Failure to Thrive results in developmental delays therefore, would not our growth and maturity in Christ be stagnated?

Failure to thrive is linked to children experiencing problems in school. Would our spiritual failure to thrive not result in an inability to truly take on the mind of Christ?

Can you begin to see why death is happy to plague your life without necessarily needing to outright kill you?

Transformed by the Renewing of Our Minds

Dead men can do nothing for themselves. Just like Lazarus lay bound in grave clothes in a tomb, we are dead in our transgression until Jesus calls us out. Do you hear Him? He is calling you out of the agreements you have made with death.

Jesus told us that we do not need to fear the enemy, and we do not need to get overly excited because the enemy is beneath our feet. Jesus said, "Nevertheless, do not rejoice in this, that the spirits are subject to you, but rejoice that your names are recorded in heaven" (Luke 10:20). Read that again. My heart is leaping with excitement: my name is written in the Lamb's Book of Life! Listen to this good news, "The one who is victorious will, like them, be dressed in white. I will never blot out the name of that person from the book of life but will acknowledge that name before my Father and His angels" (Revelation 3:5 NIV). You are about to choose victory. You are ready to follow Christ and choose life. And nothing can cause your name to be erased. One quick thing first.

Generational Sin

Let's also cover any generational issues that may be a contributing factor. We have all heard sayings like, "the apple doesn't fall far from the tree," and "she is just like her mother" or "he is just like his dad." Our children have an amazing way of acting a lot like us just as we often reflect our own parents, whether or not we intend to. Science calls this genetics. But there is a spiritual element to this phenomenon, and Moses had a conversation with God that sheds some light on how this happens.

"The LORD, the LORD, the compassionate and gracious God, slow to anger, abounding in love and faithfulness, maintaining love to thousands, and forgiving wickedness, rebellion and sin. Yet he does not leave the guilty unpunished; he punishes the children and their children for the sin of the parents to the third and fourth generation" (Exodus 34:6–7).

The first thing to note is how much bigger and encompassing is God's compassion and grace than his punishment. He pours out blessings to a thousand generations and the guilt to only three or four. God is not looking to punish an innocent baby for the meanness of his daddy. That is not what this means. It reveals that there is a propensity to sin in a particular way that runs from generation to generation. Proverbs 22:6 (NKJV) teaches that when we "train up a child in the way he should go…when he is old, he will not depart from it."

Children learn from their parents. What they see in their moms and dads will be what they reflect to the world. If a child sees her dad handle difficult situations with rage, it is likely that the child will learn to use anger to bring control when things feel out of control. Embrace anger long enough and one may very well end up with a spiritual attachment of anger or rage.

Preparing to Pray

The following prayers are general prayers that avail much. The more specific we are in our prayers, the more powerful they are, and we will experience even greater freedom. Before we go to the Lord in prayer, ask the Holy Spirit to reveal to you any way in which you have rejected life in your heart. You will want to jot down any of the ways that he reveals to you in which you have rejected life. Next, you will want to tell the Lord that you no longer choose to agree with the lie or choose to embrace death that God has revealed to you. Also make note of any of the ways you have seen family members reject life through self-hatred, depression, homelessness, or the like. You will want to be specific in both your generational and personal prayers to break agreements with death.

> *Holy Spirit, I ask that You search the heart of this precious reader and reveal any way in which they have rejected the gift of life in their heart.*

Remember, if the first prayer does not resonate with your heart at this time, pick one of the other options as a place to begin your journey to abundant living.

Prayer

Prayer to Break Generational Agreements with Death

Father, in the name of Jesus I choose to forgive my mom, my dad, and all of my ancestors all the way back to Adam for each and every sin whether intentional or unintentional that resulted in the curse or attachment of a spirit of death upon me and my bloodline. (Please mention any of the specific ways you have noticed or the Holy Spirit revealed to you.)

I forgive and release them now and ask that You destroy every evil altar that has been erected to this entity of death in my life and in my bloodline. I release the blood of Jesus to stand as a wall of separation between me and my ancestor's sin and the resulting curse of a spirit of death. Thank You, Jesus for setting me free of this generational attachment of death. I thank You that this freedom is upon my bloodline and that my descendants are free. I ask, Lord that You restore to me and my descendants every blessing that has been stolen from me and my bloodline by this unholy agreement. Holy Spirit, I ask that You fill me with the breath of life. Amen.[34]

Alternate Prayer:

If you do not feel ready to forgive your ancestors, here's a prayer to begin your journey.

Father, I come before You hurt. I want to be free and I want to forgive my ancestors including my mom, dad, and grandparents for the things that they have done that brought a curse of death into my life and bloodline. I am angry and cannot seem to pray to forgive them. Father, help heal my heart and set me free to forgive and

---

34   This prayer model uses elements taken from Dr. Francis Myles, *Battle of the Altars: Spiritual Technology for Divine Encounters!* (Stockbridge, GA: Francis Myles International, 2020).

break free of this generational attachment. Holy Spirit, I ask that You soften the stony places in my heart so that I can walk upon the path of life. In Jesus' name I pray. Amen.

Prayer to Choose Life

Father, in the mighty name of Jesus, I choose life.

I choose life and I break every agreement with death that I have ever made, whether it was intentional or unintentional. (Be sure to specifically break the agreements that the Holy Spirit revealed to you.) I do not agree with death. I receive Jesus Christ of Nazareth, the holy Son of God to be my Lord and Savior from this day forward. Whether this is my first time receiving Him as my Hope or one of many times reaffirming His lordship in my life, I declare Jesus as my Lord.

I repent of every way that I have rejected the life that You, my God and Savior, have given to me. I am sorry that I have not valued the gift of life I have been given and I choose to rejoice in my birth. I ask that You help make this a reality in my life.

This day I declare and decree that I (<u>insert your name here</u>) choose life. I receive the breath of God into my lungs and declare that I will not prematurely die nor will I accept my purpose to be dormant any longer, but that I will live and declare the mighty works of the Lord.

Lord, I ask that you break the power of this spirit off my body and soul. I receive Your healing now. I renounce death and all its partners in the name of Jesus.

Father, I ask right now by Your very own hand that You record my choice to choose life in the Lamb's Book of Life using the blood of Jesus as the ink. In Jesus' name I pray. Amen.

Father, I release the breath of God over this beautiful person who has just prayed this prayer. Lord, I ask that You fill them with joy and purpose. I ask that You begin to rekindle their God-given dreams and desires. I command every cell in their body to come into alignment with this life-affirming choice, in the name of Jesus. Amen.

Alternate Prayer A

Father, I want to choose life, but I am not ready. It scares me to set aside my old patterns of thinking and living and I cannot imagine doing life differently. Honestly, I am not sure that I really want to embrace life; it seems too hard. I am asking You to help me be willing and able to choose life. I want You to heal my heart and deliver me from anything that is blocking me from making this choice to choose and embrace life. I thank You that you will do this. Help my unbelief. In Jesus' name I pray. Amen.

Alternate Prayer B

Father, I know that I should want to choose life, but I don't. I am hurt, angry and not sure that You really do have some great life planned for me. It seems like if You ever did, You certainly don't now. But in case I am mistaken, I am giving You permission to change my heart and help me be willing to choose life. I am only asking that You do this if You honestly have a life and a purpose that has goodness and peace in it for me. If You don't and it is only more and more pain and sorrow, then I am not sure that I want more of that kind of life. So, if there are plans to prosper me and to give me a future and hope, then I am asking that You help me to choose it. In the name of Jesus, I pray. Amen.

> *Father, I pray for You to move upon the hearts of those who have prayed an alternate prayer and bring healing to the woundedness in their soul. Free them from the pain of the past and strengthen them to be willing and able to choose life. Lord, I bind the stronghold of*

death from their lives and loose the love and power of God upon them. In Jesus' name I pray. Amen.

**Feel free to re-word these prayers to match your heart. These are templates and unlike Moses, I did not etch them in stone.

Prayer to Renounce the Religious Spirit

Father, I am so sorry that I have attempted to be righteous through my own efforts. Please help me to more clearly see how this makes a mockery of the sufferings and death of Christ. I believe that only Jesus Christ lived a perfect and sinless life and that He died and rose again on the third day. I come into agreement with scripture that teaches that my righteousness comes through faith in Christ and that my faith is a gift from God the Father. I renounce religion and self-righteousness. Lord, teach me to hate self-righteousness within my heart and to quickly repent of it and return to faith in You.

I repent of every act that came into agreement with a religious spirit. I choose to forgive every religious leader, family member or mentor that taught me to come into agreement with the religious spirit. I renounce the religious spirit and command it to leave my life and my bloodline now and forever more.

Holy Spirit, I ask that you fill me with faith, hope, and love. I ask that you cleanse every part of me that has been stained by the lies of a religious spirit and fill me to overflowing so that I might walk in unity with You.

Thank you, Lord, for setting me free. In Jesus' name I pray. Amen.

Alternate Prayer:

Lord, I do not think that I have a religious spirit. I ask that You search my heart and reveal to me any way that I may be in alignment with this spirit and not know it. If this spirit is influencing my life and relationship with You, I ask that You show me and set me free. I want to walk in relationship with You and I do not want to rely upon my own efforts. In Jesus' name I pray. Amen.

Walking It Out

You have just made a monumental step toward abundant living. There are steps you can take to maintain and build upon what you have begun. Take note of them and embrace them; it will make all the difference in the world.

- *Meditate on a life-affirming scripture verse.* One of my favorites is one with which you are probably familiar: "For I know the plans I have for you," declares the Lord, "plans to prosper you and not to harm you, plans to give you hope and a future" (Jeremiah 29:11). Ask the Holy Spirit to give you additional insight into the meaning of the verse and how He plans to apply it to your life. Write out this verse or any other that speaks life to your heart and tape it on your bathroom mirror. Everyone brushes their teeth twice a day. (If you don't, then you can start now, and your friends will really appreciate it!) This way you will be reminded to ponder the verse for at least four minutes each day.

- *The ways in which you have agreed with a religious spirit and the ways you have partnered with death will begin to be illuminated to you.* You will notice things that you've never paid much attention to before. It may be subtle but acknowledge those thoughts. Scripture says that we should come to agreement with our accuser before going to court. Agree that this is something you have done and repent. Thank the Holy Spirit for showing you this step to freedom. Then let it go! "Settle matters quickly with your adversary who is taking you to court. Do it while you are still together on the way, or your adversary may hand you over to the judge, and the judge may

31

hand you over to the officer, and you may be thrown into prison" (Matthew 5:25).

- *If you keep remembering things for which you have already repented,* say out loud something like this, "Yes, I did that. I am sorry I did but God has forgiven me, and I have chosen to forgive myself, so I do not need to think about this anymore and you have no right to bring it up again." Then let it go.

- *Ask the Holy Spirit to help you recognize your self-talk.* Listen to the voices in your head and begin to identify their source. If the words are condemning, then confront them with truth. You can say things like, "That is a lie that I no longer believe. I do not agree with the lie that I am worthless anymore because God created me for a purpose."

- Journal about what you are experiencing as you travel upon this journey. How has your life or feelings changed since praying this prayer? What are you hoping God will do for you as you choose life? (If you would like to share any of these observations or experiences with me, please feel free to send an email to beth@EzekielTree.com. Your correspondence will be kept confidential and will only be seen by me.)

- If you continue to have problems in this area, please seek the help of someone who knows how to minister additional inner healing. If you do not already have a trusted advisor who can help you find freedom through inner healing, reach out to me at https://ezekieltree.com/ or beth@EzekielTree. com.

- Or Global Awakening has a list of healing ministries around the globe. Here's the link for your convenience. https://healingcertification.com/find-a-certified-healer

If you need help discerning the voice of the Holy Spirit, there is an article by Mark Virkler in the Appendix. There is a book that goes into more depth called, *4 Keys to Hearing God's Voice* that he has written. It is a great resource and has helped many learn to hear God's voice.

Billy Hornsby was an exceptionally smart young man.
He was particularly gifted in math and could do complex
equations in his head.

One day in an eighth-grade math class, his teacher wrote a
problem on the board and called Billy to come to the front
to solve it. Billy solved the problem while walking up to the
chalkboard.

Full of confidence, Billy drew a line on the board and wrote
out his answer. His teacher replied,

"Hornsby, that is not right."

Billy countered that indeed his answer was correct. The
teacher explained that while the answer was right, he needed
to show his work.

Billy disagreed. Full of himself, he argued that it did not
matter. After all, he had gotten the answer correct.

Enraged at this disrespect, the teacher pronounced,

"Hornsby, you will never amount to anything!"

And for some reason, he believed her.

CHAPTER TWO

The Power of Words — The Power of Thoughts

"The tongue has the power of life and death,
and those who love it will eat its fruit."
Proverbs 18:21

Billy's story is true. He was a young man who wholeheartedly embraced the words someone else had spoken about him. He also happened to be the father-in-law of Chris Hodges, lead pastor of The Church of the Highlands in Birmingham, Alabama. Pastor Hodges tells his father-in-law's story as an example of the power of words.[35] The teacher's words were an outburst from an offended heart—but nevertheless, he embraced them and began to live them out.

Billy continued to attend school sporadically, and by the time he was fifteen, he was playing country music in bars. At seventeen, he had left school, and by some people's standards appeared to be

---

35   Chris Hodges, "Week Five: Pastor Chris Hodges – Overflow of the Heart" Church of the Highlands, Birmingham, AL, https://freedom.churchofthe-highlands.com/curriculum.

living the dream—playing tunes in honky-tonks and no longer had homework assignments. The truth is that Billy had taken death by the hand and was led into the land where dreams shrivel up and die right before your eyes. His teen bride was expecting a child and he had the suffocating weight of providing for a family with no education to warrant a decent, paying job.

In need of a better paying gig, Pastor Hodges shares, "he goes where most people in Baton Rouge go to get jobs. They go to the Exxon Chemical Plant there on the Mississippi River."[36] Part of his job application included taking an aptitude test. When Billy Hornsby received a phone call from the plant asking him to come down to talk with them, he refused. He told them to go ahead and tell him that he had flunked the test. Whoever was on the other end of the line convinced Billy to come to the office and talk. During that meeting, the instructor told Billy that no one had ever scored higher on the exam. He said, "You know, Hornsby, if you really put your mind to it, you'll really amount to something someday."[37] And Billy believed him.

Billy got saved a few years later and went on to accomplish much in his life. You can hear the sense of awe and pride in Pastor Hodges' voice as he recounts his father-in-law's accomplishments. He became not only one of the most influential Christian leaders in America but also around the world. He planted churches all over Europe as well as other countries, and he was the founder of Church of the Highlands Arc—a church planting ministry.[38]

One of my favorite things about Billy Hornsby's story is that it shows both the positive and negative power of words upon our life. For some reason, Billy believed his teacher when she told him that he was worthless. But, by the grace of God, he was able to embrace

36   Hodges, Week Five.
37   Hodges, Week Five.
38   Hodges, Week Five.

a new word telling him that he could accomplish great things. His experiences reflect this truth: "There is one whose rash words are like sword thrusts, but the tongue of the wise brings healing" (Proverbs 12:18 ESV). Have you ever heard words like, "I wish you had never been born" or "I am sorry that I ever met you?" Maybe even things like, "You were a mistake" or "You are ugly." Have we let the dagger wounds of harsh words prevent us from receiving wise words of healing? Billy didn't. Neither should we.

Understanding Word Power

Billy was somehow able to receive the healing words that literally reversed the curse he'd received in school. There were times in my life when others spoke words of life over me that I could not accept because I had firmly embraced the lies written upon my heart. Scripture teaches, "Let the words of my mouth and the meditation of my heart be acceptable in Your sight, O Lord, my rock and my redeemer" (Psalms 19:14 NASB). Could it be that unlike Billy, the musings in my heart were the problem? Could the thoughts in your heart be imprisoning you, too?

Words have power. We know that the universe was created by the spoken word of God.[39] God said, "'Let there be light,' and there was light" (Genesis 1:3 NIV). Let's think on this a minute. Do we really think that God said for the earth to form, and it appeared without a thought or plan? Do we think He looked upon what he had just spoken into existence and was surprised by how it turned out? No! We believe that God knew exactly what he was doing when He spoke things into existence. This means He had a picture of what he wanted to create and by His spoken word, the idea in His imagination

---

39   "By faith we understand that the universe was formed at God's command, so that what is seen was not made out of what was visible" (Hebrews 11:3).

became reality. Because we are created in His image, our words also have power. But guess what? We are not God, and our words alone do not have power to create reality.

God and Abraham

Let's look at God's dealing with Abraham. In Genesis 15, God tells Abram (he had not yet been given his new name) that he will have not only a son but many descendants. Look what God does in verse 5 (NIV), "He took him outside and said, 'Look up at the sky and count the stars—if indeed you can count them.' Then He said to him, 'So shall your offspring be.'"

This was not the first time God had told Abram of this promise. In Chapter 12, God had called Abram out of the land of Haran and promised to make him a great nation. Between the events of Chapter 12 and 15, Abram does not always act as a man full of trust in God. Yet, after a bumpy start, it is written, "Abram believed the Lord, and He credited it to him as righteousness" (Genesis 15:6). What happened differently from the promise in Chapter 12 to the confirmation in Chapter 15? Mark Virkler attributes Abram's ability to walk in the promise to the vision of stars the Lord had shown to him.[40]

Abram had a picture to hold in his mind. This picture made the promise a reality to Abram. Just like Billy Hornsby, Abram not only heard words, but he also received them. They became more than a vague and weak, sort-of hope. A picture of a different life began to form in his mind. As his thoughts began to change, he was able to embrace the reality of that picture.

Winston Churchill was a master artist with words. In the preface to his book, *Churchill: The Power of Words,* Gilbert wrote, "Winston

---

40   Mark Virkler, interview by Beth Erwin, February 3, 2023, interview transcript, Virkler, Otter.Ai

Churchill knew the power of words. In speeches, books, and articles, he expressed his feelings and laid out his vision for the future."[41] Churchill envisioned victory, emboldened others to catch his vision with his impassioned words and changed the trajectory of a world war. Are you beginning to see how we can empower words to have a tremendous effect on our lives?

Someone could tell me that I am as dumb as a stump. If in my heart, I know they are wrong, then there's no problem. But I if suspect there might be some truth to the statement, then I will stop learning. It is our thoughts about the words that give them power. The prophet Isaiah asked, "Who has believed our message and to whom has the arm of the Lord been revealed?" (Isaiah 53:1). Do I choose to believe the words of life that God has spoken about me or do I choose to embrace the lies of death?

Thinking Thoughts

Thank goodness Churchill's words flowed from a heart filled with a just and wise vision. Jesus said, "For the mouth speaks what the heart is full of. A good man brings good things out of the good stored up in him, and an evil man brings evil things out of the evil stored up in him" (Matthew 12:34–35). Jesus was teaching about how we speak from the thoughts that are within our minds. Remember the miserly man who invited people for dinner only to make them sick?

If we pay attention to our self-talk, we will discover what is stored within our hearts. We must discover what we are really thinking— what morsels are we feasting our hearts upon? Are we holding onto lies others have said against us or are we embracing the truth of God? Are our minds filled with bitter and resentful mutterings or thoughts

---

41   Martin Gilbert, *Churchill: The Power of Words* (Boston, MA: Da Capo Press, 2012), 13.

of compassion and hope? If we find that the thoughts within our hearts are corrupt, then we will find a place where death has been given a stronghold in our lives. This death is not only spiritual, but it can be physical, too.

The Science of Thinking Thoughts

Put on your lab coat and let's talk science for a minute. My definition of science is this: it is the search and discovery that reveals the amazing way God has put together the universe and designed our bodies to work: it is seeing in the natural the way the supernatural behaves. So don't bug out. This is really cool stuff that will help you see the reality of the effects of your thought life.

The ends of our strands of DNA have caps on them that keep them from becoming frayed or sticking together. These caps are called telomeres and they become shorter each time our cells divide. The length of the telomere determines how fast "your cells age and when they die."[42] This process has an amazing effect on your health and lifespan. Our response to stress can affect the length of our telomeres. This means that how you think about the events in your life can either positively or negatively affect your health, and this biblical truth has been proven under a microscope. Perhaps that is why we are encouraged to "Above all else, guard your heart, for everything you do flows from it" (Proverbs 4:23).

What's Stress Got to Do with It?

Stress has a way of aging people. My mom has always been a beautiful woman who looked younger than her years. But during a particularly

---

42   Dr. Elizabeth Blackburn and Dr. Elissa Epel, *The Telomere Effect: A Revolutionary Approach to Living Younger, Healthier, Longer.* (New York: Grand Central Publishing, 2018), 6, Kindle.

stressful time in her life, she aged tremendously. Overnight, her perfectly smooth completion seemed to wilt before our eyes. Stress, when coupled with worry and fear, can be savage. Sometimes, when I am feeling particularly worked up about something, it feels like I am going to spontaneously combust. Have you ever noticed how someone who is stressed with worry looks as if they are carrying the weight of the world on their shoulders? Sometimes when a friend shares their concerns, we offer sage advice like, "Well, just don't lose any sleep over it," because we all understand the misery of sleepless nights. People's bodies often reveal the burdens they are carrying.

All people deal with varying levels of stress in their lives. But not all people lose sleep over it or look weighed down by it. Some of us view stress the same way my family views yellow traffic lights: a challenge to be accepted. Others experience stress as a threat—and threats are scary. Drs. Blackburn and Epel say that people who feel "overly threatened have shorter telomeres than people who face stress with a rousing sense of challenge."[43] Their point of view dictates the effect of stress on their bodies. How they think about their circumstances can affect them physically as well as emotionally. My marine friend used to always say, "It's mind over matter. If you don't mind, then it don't matter." While that may seem overly simplistic or even callous, there is truth to it.

How Stress as Threat Affects Our Incredible Bodies

When we perceive a situation as a threat our bodies go into fight or flight mode. The levels of cortisol and epinephrine in our bodies begin to rise. Our blood pressure gets higher, and our hearts beat faster. Most of us are familiar with these symptoms. Not all of us know about this thing in our brains called the vagus nerve. It influences

---

43   Blackburn, *Telomeres*, 74, Kindle.

how our bodily functions react to stress. When things in our bodies begin heating up with real or perceived threats, the vagus nerve will stop doing its thing. It "withdraws its activity. That's why it is harder to breathe, harder to stay in control, harder to imagine a world that is a safe place."[44] Consider what your body is experiencing when you constantly think negative and fearful thoughts, when you replay the ugly words over and over in your mind, and when you no longer see the world as a safe place.

I wonder how many times young Billy Hornsby heard his teacher's voice telling him that he'd never amount to anything. This repetitive cycle of negative thoughts causes our bodies to wear out from being in a state of constant vigilance to threats. Studies have shown that the brain responds similarly to worrisome "what if" thoughts as it would if something bad had actually happened.[45] Perhaps this is one of the reasons scripture exhorts us to "Finally, brothers and sisters, whatever is true, whatever is noble, whatever is right, whatever is pure, whatever is lovely, whatever is admirable—if anything is excellent or praiseworthy—think about such things" (Philippians 4:8 NASB). It is noteworthy that Paul wrote these words just after telling his readers not to be anxious about things but to trust God in all things. He said this kind of trust causes our hearts and minds to be guarded by the peace of God![46]

The Recorder

Doesn't that sound amazing? Would you like to set aside the hurtful words that replay throughout your memory and accept the words that

---

44   Blackburn, *Telomere,* 77. Kindle.

45   Blackburn, *Telomere,* 80.

46   "Do not be anxious about anything, but in every situation, by prayer and petition, with thanksgiving, present your requests to God. And the peace of God, which transcends all understanding, will guard your hearts and your minds in Christ Jesus" (Philippians 4:6–7).

God has spoken over you? Sometimes our souls have been wounded by things others have said about us. When deep down inside we are afraid those words could be true in some measure, those words can begin a continuous loop within our minds. During a season when I had received a lot of criticism and was feeling particularly dejected, I began to hear negative words at the weirdest times. I recall while I was browning some ground beef on the stove I actually heard someone who had hurt me saying that I was doing it wrong. Good grief! How does one stir ground beef incorrectly?

The good news is that we can break the cycle and be set free. Our bodies can even heal from the damage of these harmful thoughts that cause so much stress within our cells. Scientists from around the world have made an "extraordinary discovery…that the ends of our chromosomes can actually lengthen, and as a result, aging is a dynamic process that can be accelerated or slowed, and in some aspects even reversed."[47]

Pay attention to your self-talk and the things that you say. We often complain to friends, "Oh, I hate my hair" or "I am so stupid." At the end of this chapter, we are going to deal with the deadly roots of harmful words and stinkin' thinkin.' You will also be shown some steps to help overcome the habit of seeing all negative situations as a threat and learn to view them as a challenge. Before then, let's talk about pythons and ambiguous words.

Pythons and Ambiguous Words

While this may seem to be an odd combination, these two things work together to put a choke hold on your lifeline in the Holy Spirit. We see how this works in Acts Chapter 16. Paul and Silas were going to a place of prayer when they encountered a woman who was said to

---

47   Blackburn, *Telomeres*, 6, Kindle.

have a spirit of divination. She was a slave whose fortune telling made her masters a lot of money. Seeing Paul and Silas she began to cry out, "These men are servants of the Most High God, who are telling you the way to be saved" (Acts 16:17 NIV). According to scripture, she kept this up for days. Eventually, it wore on Paul's nerves, and he cast the spirit out of her. This infuriated her owners who'd just lost their cash cow. They plotted their revenge. Next thing you know, Paul and Silas were beaten and thrown into prison because they had supposedly thrown the city into an uproar.

Let's break this down. First, why did her proclamations, which were true, annoy Paul? She was doing it in a way that drew attention to herself and not to God. Her words were a distraction from their purpose. Roger E. Olson affirms "that the [Holy] Spirit does not draw attention to himself but points to Jesus Christ…"[48] We must be leery of speaking words to glorify ourselves and not God. It is also wisdom to avoid embracing people who speak with a measure of truth but their intentions are to elevate themselves. But what does this have to do with ambiguous words that are not straightforward or clear? And, what in the world does this have to do with pythons?

The Oracle of Delphi

For over one thousand years, people traveled to a temple dedicated to the god Apollo to seek supernatural insight into the issues they were facing. Below the temple was a chasm where, according to Greek legend, the defeated carcass of the snake god, Python, lay rotting. The people would seek a prophecy from a priestess who had dedicated her life in service to Apollo. The priestess was called Pythia

---

48   Roger E. Olson, *The Mosaic of Christian Belief: Twenty Centuries of Unity and Diversity*. 2nd ed. (Downers Grove Il, InterVarsity Press, 2016), 253.

after the snake god from whom she received her so-called prophetic words.

As she perched upon a tripod over the chasm, she'd breathe in the vapors and pronounce an oracle. The prophecy did not come cheap. Michael Scott, who wrote for Princeton University Press on this topic, reports that while the cost varied (apparently the wealthier were charged higher fees), the average price was equivalent to about two days wages plus travel and lodging expenses.[49] This expense did not factor the loss wages of the person seeking the oracle. According to Plutarch, a first century Greek, in previous centuries the temple needed as many as three or four Pythia to serve the needs of the people.[50] By 100 AD, the temple typically required the services of only one priestess. In its prime, however, even the most affluent would seek advice from a medium at Delphi.

One of the most widely memorialized oracles descends from Croesus, a Lydian king of Asia Minor. He traveled to Delphi to find out if he would prevail against Cyrus, King of Persia, should he go against him in battle. He received this Delphic answer, "Croesus, having crossed the river Halys, will destroy a great empire."[51] Croesus, emboldened by this word, gathered his armies and went to war. He was defeated. When he returned demanding an answer from the Pythia, he was told that a great empire had indeed been lost—his own. This was the problem with these oracles. They often did not make sense and were at best ambiguous.

The Pythia was known to give words that were so confusing as to not make sense at all. The best-case scenario for your time and money

49   Michael Scott, "ORACLE." In *Delphi: A History of the Center of the Ancient World*, 9–30. (Princeton University Press, 2014),17. https://doi.org/10.2307/j.ctt5vjv8t.6.
50   Scott, *Oracle,* 12.
51   Scott, *Oracle,* 27.

was to receive a word that had more than one possible interpretation. It is important to acknowledge that while the temple was built to honor a false god and the myth that accompanied him, the events that took place there were actual historical events. Another thought to keep in mind is that myths are stories told about the exploits of gods. Jennifer LeClaire puts it like this: "Myths, in other words, simply worked to describe in natural words the activity of demon spirits whose operations manifested in the natural."[52] This may seem strange to you, but Jesus himself went about casting demons from people. If it was real for Jesus, it is real for me.

Paul's Pythian Problem

According to the NIV translation, the slave girl had a spirit by which she predicted the future. Other translations, such as the KJV and NASB, use the term divination. Both descriptions of this spirit are from the Greek word, python. In describing this woman's condition, Luke linked the spirit upon the slave girl to the same spirit that operated at the Oracle of Delphi. Delphi was located only about 10 kilometers from Corinth. We know that Luke's audience would have been very familiar with this term and would have understood his reference.

It is written that "It is the glory of God to conceal a matter; to search out a matter is the glory of kings" (Proverbs 25:2). This is an awesome verse that describes God's heart in sharing revelation with us. The prophet Jeremiah's words can shed light on the meaning of this passage, "You will seek Me and find Me when you seek Me with

---

52   Jennifer LeClaire, *The Spiritual Warrior's Guide to Defeating Water Spirits: Overcoming Demons that Twist, Suffocate, and Attack God's Purposes for Your Life* (Shippensburg, PA: Destiny Image, 2018), 52, Kindle.

all your heart" (Jeremiah 29:13). [53] There are some things in scripture that are hidden in plain sight and God desires that we mine for the gold within his word. This is a prime example. We can learn a lot from Paul's experience with this slave girl and her unscrupulous owners. When we mine for the gold, we can learn even more. Luke used the term for python spirit because we can learn from the picture it portrays.

Jesus loved to teach in parables, which are pictures drawn with words. We can glean insight into how this spirit works by examining the word picture drawn through its name: python. Pythons are predators who are capable of eating animals larger than themselves. They lure the animal close and then bite it. Then they wrap themselves around the animal and begin to squeeze. With each breath the animal exhales, the python tightens its grip until the animal cannot inhale and it dies. The tasty morsel is then swallowed whole and digested over a matter of days.[54]

Notice that the python does not hunt its prey but tempts it into coming close enough to be caught and wrapped tightly within its coils. It then squeezes the breath out of its victim. Let's see how this overlaps with Paul's encounter with this spirit. Scripture tells us that Paul and Silas were on their way to a house of prayer when they first faced this spirit. It desires to smother your prayer life by cutting you off from the Breath of God, the Holy Spirit! LeClaire says that "Python would rather watch you lick your wounds than pray to a healing God. Python would rather hear you complain or gossip than

---

53   Also: "Ask and it will be given to you; seek and you will find; knock and the door will be opened to you" (Matthew 7:7.
54   Information regarding habits of pythons is taken from the book: Martha E.H. Rustad, *Pythons* (North Mankato, MN: Pebble, 2021), 18–21, Scribd.

take your problems to a miracle-working God."[55] The spirit lured Paul into coming into contact through annoyance.

Simply put, it exasperated him with words. It drew attention to itself using the slave girl to shout words over and over again. The words seemed good but the spirit behind them was not. When the spirit had them close enough, it bit into them with a campaign of false accusations to imprison Paul and Silas to cut them off from their purpose. Not only that, but the attack was accompanied by beatings: this spirit will attack your health.

Think about those telomeres. The stress of this kind of attack can move your brain into a continual state of fight or flight and cause those telomeres to shorten which affects your immune system, your health, and if left unchecked, your lifespan. In this narrative, we are told that their robes were torn off them and they were beaten.[56] LeClaire points out that this is pretty much the same state in which Adam and Eve found themselves after their fateful encounter with a serpent in the Garden. This thing will attempt to humiliate you, and we will talk about this issue in the next chapter.

I was ministering to a lovely young woman who wanted to grow in the Lord but was suffering from a barrage of conflicting thoughts. One part of her would feel overly convicted not to do something while the other part would feel convinced of the opposite. Part of her confusion was a result of the words others had said to her— words that said she was either a goody two-shoes or that she wasn't a good enough Christian. Sadly, both sets of these words were spoken over her through other Christians. They took root in her mind and imprisoned her for years. As we prayed together, I felt impressed that a python spirit was plaguing her. After she received ministry and

---

55   LeClaire, *Water Spirits*, 55, Kindle.
56   "The crowd joined in the attack against Paul and Silas, and the magistrates ordered them to be stripped and beaten with rods" (Acts 16:22).

became free of this spirit, she realized how she had often felt a constriction at her throat as if she were being choked. You can imagine that she was excited to be free. Her freedom would allow her not only to breathe more easily but also to finally draw nearer to God, free of the fear losing friendships and the shame of not being worthy of God's attention.

Uncoiling the Serpent

Is this to say that there is a literal snake lurking around the corner waiting to wrap itself around your chest? Remember, the Lord teaches in word pictures. You are safe to travel to the rainforest without worrying that your prayer life will be devoured. Here's what you can learn:

- A python spirit will attempt to confuse you with words that have multiple meanings. Its purpose is to disorient you and draw you away from God. God is clear and will always give insight to those who seek Him.

- It will use false prophecies to lie to you, thwart your destiny, and make you feel hopeless.

- It will use biting words to sink its teeth into you to begin its stranglehold on your life, causing you to feel like you are continually under pressure, stressed out, and overwhelmed. Think about how anxiety makes you feel as if you cannot breathe.

- It will attempt to wear you down with false accusations. These may come from others or from within your own mind. That is why you must learn to listen to your self-talk. Are you saying things that seem true but are mean-spirited? Are you talking ugly to yourself about yourself?

51

- It seeks to suffocate your prayer life—cut you off from your lifeline in the Holy Spirit, the breath of God.

- In Christ, you are bigger than python!

If we are not connected to the Holy Spirit, we will be rendered helpless and without power because scripture teaches that we are enabled to fulfill our destiny, our calling, through the power of the Holy Spirit.[57] We cannot bear witness of the Gospel of Christ without being connected to the Holy Spirit who testifies that we are children of God.[58] No wonder this spirit wants to kill our life connection to the breath of God.

Sheep Talk

The 23rd Psalm is a fascinating portrait of the goodness of God and His loving protection over every area of our lives. The shepherd, David, writing the psalm rejoices that the Lord anoints his head with oil.[59] Philip Keller, a former shepherd, explains the importance of this passage and the necessity of the sheep's heads being covered in spice-treated oil.[60] During the summertime, sheep are led to the high ground called tablelands where they can eat lush green vegetation. The scene sounds just about idyllic until we learn of a particular problem that plagues the sheep during this season: insects. Of all the pests that annoy the flock, none are more exasperating than the nose fly.

---

57   "But you will receive power when the Holy Spirit comes on you; and you will be my witnesses in Jerusalem, and in all Judea and Samaria, and to the ends of the earth" (Acts 1:8).
58   "The Spirit himself testifies with our sprit that we are God's children" (Romans 8:16).
59   "You anoint my head with oil; my cup overflows" (Psalm 23:5).
60   The information about sheep is gleaned from: W. Phillip Keller, *A Shepherd Looks at Psalm 23* (Grand Rapids, MI: Zondervan, 2015), 102–107.

This insect will lay its eggs inside the nasal passages of the sheep. In a matter of a few days the eggs will hatch into "small, slender, wormlike larvae. They work their way up the nasal passages into the sheep's head; they burrow into the flesh and there set up an intense irritation accompanied by severe inflammation."[61] This becomes so painful and annoying that the sheep will begin to beat their heads against trees, bushes, whatever they can find in an attempt to gain relief. In severe cases, the sheep will end up killing themselves in their efforts to be free of the pain. It is interesting that Baalzebub means "lord of the flies." We can see through this analogy how the enemy can be like a fly that infects our minds!

The beautiful hope within the psalm is that the Good Shepherd anoints his sheep's head with oil to protect them from the infestation of flies. This is not a one-time anointing, but something that needs repeating throughout the season. The Holy Spirit is often likened to oil in scripture. To avoid being consumed by deadly thoughts, we need the anointing of the Holy Spirit. This is not a one-and-done thing. We need fresh infillings to guard our minds and "demolish arguments and every pretension that sets itself up against the knowledge of God, and [to enable us to] take captive every thought to make it obedient to Christ" (2 Corinthians 10:5).

Paul exhorted the Ephesians, "Do not get drunk on wine, which leads to debauchery. Instead, be filled with the Spirit..." (Ephesians 5:18). The Greek word used for filled in this passage is a word that denotes a continuous action. John R.W. Stott compares the word that Paul uses with the word Jesus used while at the wedding feast when he commanded the workers to fill the jars with water.[62] In John 2:7, the word Jesus used for fill meant to fill them up only once. Paul

---

61   Keller, *Psalm 23*, 102.
62   John R.W.Stott, *The Message of Ephesians* (Downers Grove, Il; InterVarsity Press, 1979), 209.

intentionally used a different word. He wanted to ensure that his readers would understand they needed to be continually filled. Stott wrote, "We have been sealed with the Spirit once and for all. We need to be filled with the Spirit and go on being filled every day and every moment of the day."[63] (There is a prayer for you to be filled with the Spirit at the end of this chapter.)

Paul reveals to us the outflow of this continual Spirit-filled life. He says that the words we speak will be pleasant "songs from the Spirit."[64] We will be thankful for what we have been given and will make music for the Lord with the living of our lives.

Wrapping it Up — Pardon the Pun

We have learned how words can have a powerful affect upon our bodies, emotions, and spirits—if we decide to come into agreement with them. Rather than being wrapped in the coils of deadly words, we can live in the truth of God's heart toward us. As we look at the amazing words God our Father has spoken over us, we can be filled with hope and joy.

"For God so loved the world that he gave his one and only Son, that whoever believes in him shall not perish but have eternal life. For God did not send His Son into the world to condemn the world, but to save the world through Him" (John 3:16–17). God loves us. So beautiful are His thoughts toward us that He sent His son to save us not to condemn us.

"See what great love the Father has lavished on us, that we should be called children of God! And that is what we are!" (1 John 3:1) You

---

63   Stott, *Message*, 209.
64   "…speaking to one another with psalms, hymns, and songs from the Spirit. Sing and make music from your heart to the Lord, always giving thanks to God the Father for everything, in the name of our Lord Jesus Christ" (Ephesians 5:19–20).

are God's beloved son or daughter no matter what you have done or what has been said about you.

"But you are a chosen race, a royal priesthood, a holy nation, a people for his own possession, that you may proclaim the excellencies of him who called you out of darkness into His marvelous light" (2 Peter 2:9 ESV). As God's beloved son or daughter, you are royalty set aside for his holy purposes. No matter what has been said about you, or what you have done, you can glorify God with your life.

"Fear not, for I am with you; be not dismayed, for I am your God; I will strengthen you, I will help you, I will uphold you with My righteous right hand" (Isaiah 41:10 ESV). God will always hold your hand and give you strength.

"Be strong in the Lord and the power of His might" (Ephesians 6:10 KJV).

Vacuums and Empty Spaces

Most of us are familiar with Aristotle's words that nature abhors a vacuum. This means that nature does not like empty spaces and will seek to fill them. Scripture puts it like this:

> When an impure spirit comes out of a person, it goes through arid places seeking rest and does not find it. Then it says, 'I will return to the house I left.' When it arrives, it finds the house swept clean and put in order. Then it goes and takes seven other spirits more wicked than itself, and they go in and live there. And the final condition of that person is worse than the first. (Luke 11:24–26)

What Jesus is describing is the need to fill ourselves with the Holy Spirit. As we pray to be free from negative thinking and evil spiritual attachments, we must fill those vacated spaces with pure and holy thoughts and the Spirit of God. You may have noticed elements of this in the prayers in the first chapter and the theme will repeat itself throughout this book. At the end of the chapter is a specific prayer to be filled with the Holy Spirit. No matter your maturity level or if you have been filled before, I pray that you receive this prayer for yourself.

Preparing to Pray

Before we pray to break agreements with deadly thoughts and words, let's pray together: "Search me, God, and know my heart; test me and know my anxious thoughts. See if there is any offensive way in me and lead me in the way everlasting" (Psalms 139:23–24).

Ask the Holy Spirit to reveal to you any ugly words that are stuck within your heart from which he is seeking to set you free. Also, ask the Holy Spirit to uncover any lies that you are believing about who you are. It is a good idea to make note of them so you can pray over them specifically in the prayer models that come next.

Prayer to Break Agreements with Unholy Words and Thoughts

Father, false words can be costly. I see how they can bring such destruction. Your word says "the tongue is a small part of the body, but it makes great boasts. Consider what a great forest is set on fire by a small spark. The tongue also is a fire…It corrupts the whole body, sets the whole course of one's life on fire, and is itself set on fire by hell" (James 3:5–6).

Lord, my life has been set on fire by the consuming words of death spoken over me. (If the Holy Spirit brought to your mind any hurtful words spoken over you, mention them in prayer specifically.) Lord, I choose to forgive those who have spoken hurtful and shameful words over me and my bloodline. I now come out of agreement with every lie of death spoken over me and my bloodline in the name of Jesus. I ask that You send a blessing to those who have cursed me with their words.

Likewise, Lord, I am sorry that I have spoken evil words over others. I am sorry that I used my mouth to sin against you by speaking curses over others. Sometimes I did not even realize that I was cursing, but I now realize that I was. I am sorry. I ask that You bless those that I have cursed whether I did it intentionally or not.

Lord, I need Your help. Please help me hear the words that I am speaking in my mind. Help me discern the source of these words and the content of these words. I want to stop speaking ungodly words in my mind. I do not want them to come out of my mouth either.

Lord, sometimes it feels as if there is a tape recorder in my brain that replays over and over again the hurtful words that others have uttered against me. I have chosen to break agreements with those lies and ask that You bind the recorder from replaying the hurtful sounds in my mind. I ask that You loose the mind of Christ upon me and help me think on things that are pleasing to Your heart.

Lord, I often feel overwhelmed by stress and see it as something that is going to bring great harm to me. I ask that You help me see stressful situations as an opportunity to grow and as a challenge to overcome with the help of the Holy Spirit. Please help me see when my mind is agreeing with the lie that stress is going to kill me. Help me replace this lie with the truth that "I can do all things through Christ who strengthens me" (Philippians 4:13 NKJV).

Lord, infuse me with faith so that my trust in You will guard my mind and fill it with peace.

Lord, I ask that You bring healing to every part of my body that has been affected by unholy words and thoughts. I ask that You restore my telomeres and repair the damage of stress within my body on a cellular level.

Lord, I specifically forgive those who have lobbed false accusations at me. I break agreement with any lie that I chose to believe because of these false accusations and accept Your truth about me and my circumstances. (If the Holy Spirit brought any specific instances to your mind, bring them to the Lord now. Ask the Holy Spirit to show You the truths needed to replace any lies believed.)

Lord, I forgive any religious leaders who confused me, hurt me, or led me astray because they were seeking honor and glory for themselves rather than You. I ask that You send a blessing to them. I repent of every word I have spoken that sought to glorify myself when I should have been honoring You. Lord, help me to discern the imaginations in my heart. Help me see the difference between the dreams You are placing within me from my own vain imaginations.

Lord, I repent of seeking information through unholy channels such as mediums, horoscopes, palm reading, and any other form of divination and witchcraft. I break agreements with these unholy spirits in the name of Jesus. Lord, cleanse me of their influence on my mind and body. Please remove any hooks that they may have in me.

"Let the words of my mouth and the meditation of my heart be acceptable in Your sight, O Lord, my rock and my redeemer" (Psalms 19:14 ESV). I ask these things in the mighty name of Jesus, Amen.

Alternate Prayer A

Lord, I am hurt and upset by the evil words that others have spoken over me, and I want to pray the prayer to forgive ungodly words and thoughts, but I cannot seem to let go. I want to be free from the withering effects of the hurtful words. I ask that You sever the ties that have held me bound and help me break agreements with every lie and every thought that has imprisoned me. I want to be able to forgive but I feel stuck. Lord, I give You permission to unstick my heart so that I come into agreement with the words in the prayer to be free. I want the only fire in my life to be the fire You have set in my soul. Deliver me from the flames of the evil words that have been spoken over me. In Jesus' name I pray. Amen.

Alternate Prayer B

Lord, I am hurt because other people have said some really bad things about me. I hear those words in my mind and I cannot let go. I am angry and want to say things to make them hurt the way they have hurt me. I want them to see how bad it feels to hear such ugly things about themselves. Lord, I do not want to forgive, but I am tired of hurting. If forgiveness really is the pathway to healing, then I ask You to change my heart and help me come into agreement with Your pathway to healing and freedom. In Jesus' name I pray. Amen.

Walking It Out

You may begin to remember hurtful words that have been said to you. Acknowledge that they hurt and ask the Lord to either help you forgive, or pray that you choose to forgive by faith. Remember to pray from a place of sincerity. If you also begin to be aware of some ugly words that have spewed from your mouth, tell the Lord that you are sorry and forgive yourself. Ask the Holy Spirit if you need to apologize to the person you hurt. Follow His lead. You don't want to apologize for something that the person may not be aware of and bring pain where there had been none.

- *Prayer and Praise*: When Paul and Silas were thrown into prison, they began to pray and sing praises to God. Their songs of worship caused a shaking that broke the ties that had held them bound. Honor God with your praises of your lips. Sing like you mean it and watch what happens!

- *Gratitude*: Set your timer for one minute each day and fill that time with gratitude. List things that for which you are grateful. They can be big things or small things. It doesn't matter. Daffodils always make my gratitude list each spring. Don't they look like smiley faces? If you sense an onslaught of negativity entering your mind, stop and purposefully begin to think about things that are a blessing to you: your car, your house, your family—even if they are on your last nerve, there is something about your family that is a blessing. Ask the Lord to help you see it.

- *Listen to Your Own Thoughts*: Ask the Holy Spirit to help you hear what you are saying in your mind. When you hear thoughts that bring feelings of anger, resentment, humiliation, or shame, stop. Listen to the thought and then consider why it is wrong. When the Holy Spirit began to reveal to me how I was talking to myself, I was shocked. I would not talk to my worst enemy the way I was talking to myself. As I became aware of my ugly self-talk, I was able to change. When I heard in my mind, "you are really stupid," I could then consider whether the thought could be true. How can I be stupid if I am created in the image of God and have the mind of Christ?

- *Avoid Gossip*: It is equally important to stop saying ugly things about others. "But I tell you that anyone who is angry with a brother or sister will be subject to judgment. Again, anyone who says to a brother or sister, 'Raca,' is answerable to the court. And anyone who says, 'You fool!' will be in danger of the fire of hell" (Matthew 5:22). How often do we get irritated in traffic and call other drivers names? It really is not beneficial to our lifespans. Let's agree to stop trash talk.

- *Get Out of Your Head and Into Your Life*: Ask the Lord to help you engage in what you are doing. Being present and accounted for in your daily activities will help you find joy in living. Practice really listening to what others are saying. Practice finding something to enjoy in the work before you.

- *Meditate on the Word*: Find scripture verses that speak to your heart and write them down. Ponder the verse and consider the meaning of it. Ask the Holy Spirit how he wants you to apply it to your life. Seek to discover what the original writer of the passage was intending to say to his audience.

Thinking Differently About Stressful Situations

According to Drs. Blackburn and Epel, there are several things that a person can do to think about stressful events differently.[65]

- Think about your problem in the third person. Instead of thinking about what someone just did to you, envision the event as happening to a made-up person. This will enable you to feel "less threatened, anxious, and ashamed."[66] Instead of thinking, "This is making me so mad," turn it around. Consider the situation in terms of what is making Billy Bob or Betty Sue so angry. That helps de-personalize the situation and you will be able to see it less emotionally.

- When faced with a challenge that feels overwhelming and your thoughts birth panic, ask yourself what difference this circumstance will make on your life in the future. What does this mean to your quality of life in five or ten years? This will help you keep things in perspective.

- While this chapter is not specifically about trauma, I would like to mention that Drs. Blackburn and Epel also suggest that when you have experienced a traumatic event, it is a good idea to process the event as if you are watching a movie rather than relieving the event.[67] This will allow you to deal with the trauma without reliving the trauma.

Prayer to Be Filled with the Holy Spirit

Jesus said that it was good that he went to the Father, so that he could send the Holy Spirit to help us. Dr. Randy Clark wrote a beautiful

---

65   Blackburn, *Telomeres*, 97–99.
66   Blackburn, *Telomeres*, 98,
67   Blackburn, *Telomeres*, 98.

prayer to be filled with the Holy Spirit. I would like to pray this prayer over you. If you are willing, tell the Lord that you are ready for the Holy Spirit to fill you to overflowing and for his gifts to be activated within you. Then, receive this anointed prayer.

"Father, in the name of Jesus I ask that You meet the faith and hunger of the person holding this book. I bless this person in the name of Jesus and ask for Your Holy Spirit's fire to come upon him or her. I ask that You release Your compassion and love into this person's heart right now. I ask that You especially impart the gifts of word of knowledge, healing, prophecy, and the workings of miracles through this person in the days ahead. As he or she waits in Your presence, Father, with hands outstretched and palms raised, I ask that Your power would touch these hands. Multiply Your power. Increase Your power. Baptize this reader in Your Holy Spirit and fill this soul with the peace of the Prince of Peace."[68]

And Lord, I come into agreement and release the prayer of Paul upon this beautiful soul, "For this reason I kneel before the Father, from whom every family in heaven and on earth derives its name. I pray that out of his glorious riches he may strengthen you with power through his Spirit in your inner being, so that Christ may dwell in your hearts through faith. And I pray that you, being rooted and established in love, may have power, together with all the Lord's holy people, to grasp how wide and long and high and deep is the love of Christ and to know this love that surpasses knowledge, that you may be filled to the measure of all the fullness of God."[69] It is in the name of Jesus that I pray. Amen.

---

68   Randy Clark, *There is More! The Secret to Experiencing God's Power to Change Your Life* (Grand Rapids, MI: Chosen Books, 2013), 226.
69   Ephesians 3:14–19

Additional Resources

About the Holy Spirit:

The Essential Guide to the Power of the Holy Spirit: God's Miraculous Gifts at Work, by Randy Clark offers balanced and thorough teaching on the infilling of the Holy Spirit.

His book, *There is More! The Secret to Experiencing God's Power to Change Your Life* also contains powerful and transformative teaching.

The Presence & Work of the Holy Spirit by R.A. Torrey

Help Overcoming Negative Thought Patterns:

The Telomere Effect: A Revolutionary Approach to Living Younger, Healthier, Longer by Dr. Elizabeth Blackburn and Dr. Elissa Epel offers techniques to help you learn to manage negative thought patterns. These are found in Part II of the book. This recommendation is not a comprehensive endorsement of every theology that may be represented in the book. However, the book offers understanding of the way we think, how it affects us, and excellent resources to practice overcoming negative thinking habits.

As I lay there, feeling the pounding of my heart, listening to
the blood pulsing through my body, I wondered just what it
took to overdose and had I crossed the line.
I did not want to die.
I wondered how I let myself get to this place.
I felt stupid and wretched.
In my desperation I cried out to God.
He looked upon my degradation and
inhaled the stench of my sin.
He heard my cry.
He answered.

"In the morning, LORD, You hear my voice;
in the morning I lay my requests before You
and wait expectantly."
Psalm 5:3

CHAPTER THREE

Shame— Rejecting the Life God has Given You

"Do not be afraid; you will not be put to shame.

Do not fear disgrace; you will not be humiliated.

You will forget the shame of your youth and remember no more the

reproach of your widowhood."

Isaiah 54:4

At the age of twenty-three, I was divorced and trying to figure out how to raise my beautiful blonde haired, blue-eyed baby girl. She was two. And she was perfect. I wanted her to have a better life than I had known and there was only one way I could think of to give it to her: take her to church.

It was clear in my mind that God did not have much use for me. It made me sad, but what could I do? At an early age, it appeared to me that I had been created to absorb bad things so they would not happen to good little girls. I recall doing laundry and seeing a soiled cloth that had not come clean in the wash. I could identify with that stained scrap that had once been fresh and new. I did not want my perfect little girl to become another dirty rag.

In case you have not noticed, I love to tell stories. I am a bit of a chatter box. But in desperation for a better life for my daughter, a decision was made in my heart. I would dress up, take my baby girl to church every Sunday, and keep my mouth shut. Once my mouth opened, they'd figure out that I was an incorrigible heathen. My hope was that by the time the cat was out of the bag, they would let me keep bringing her to learn about Jesus. God just had to love my girl. She was everything. Surely, He would see that.

I did not know that my identity was clouded with shame. It had always seemed clear that there was something wrong with me. Something that made others not love me. That is what shame does. It attaches to our minds and begins to cause us to see ourselves wrongly. This distorted view entices us to embrace behaviors that bring death to our aspirations, hopes, and relationships. We do not see this as shame, it seems more like an honest evaluation of ourselves. Sometimes this warped view of ourselves is because of things that have happened to us or because of things that we have done. It can come as a result of real or perceived physical deformities. Ronald and Patricia Potter-Efron describe shame as "something more than a feeling. It is a set of physical responses (such as looking down or blushing) combined with predictable actions (such as withdrawal from others), uncomfortable thoughts (such as 'I am a failure in life'), and spiritual despair. [Their] definition of shame is that it is a painful belief in one's basic defectiveness as a human being."[70]

I believed that I was defective. I did not know why I was born undesirable, but it seemed clear that even God could not love

---

70   Ronald T. Potter-Efron and Patricia S Potter-Efron, *Letting Go of Shame: Understanding How Shame Affects Your Life* (San Francisco: Harper & Row, 1989), 1–2.

someone like me.[71] It took a while for this lie to be uncovered within my heart. It took even longer for me to stop believing it. I know this for sure. If God can heal my heart, He can and will heal yours. It may seem unbelievable to you. That's OK. For now, I am going to carry the faith for you until you can hold it for yourself. God loves you, no matter what. By the way, love covers a multitude of sins.[72]

Can Shame Ever Be Good?

While this chapter explores the way shame can be used to bring harm to our souls, it should be acknowledged that it can be used in a positive manner, as well. As a matter of fact, Randolph Richards and Richard James make a point that "Jesus practiced shaming. Jesus shamed those who objected when he healed a suffering woman: 'When he said this, all his opponents were put to shame' (Luke 13:17 NRSV)."[73]

Perhaps this practice is best understood through the verse, "But God chose the foolish things of the world to shame the wise; God chose the weak things of the world to shame the strong" (1 Corinthians 1:27). Calvin explains that "in putting the strong and wise and great to shame, God does not exalt the weak and uneducated and worthless but brings all of them down to one common level."[74]

---

71   In an attempt to numb the pain of shame, I tried a number of things like working hard to excel at work and doing drugs. None of these things helped.
72   "Above all, love each other deeply, because love covers over a multitude of sins" (I Peter 4:8).
73   E Randolph Richards and Richard James, *Misreading Scripture with Individualist Eyes: Patronage, Honor, and Shame in the Biblical World.* (Downers Grove IL: IVP Academic, 2020), 1.
74   David E. Baker, *1 Corinthians: Baker Exegetical Commentary on the New Testament* (Grand Rapids: Baker Academic, 2003) 79.

It is as Richards and James say that "shame was a powerful tool in the biblical world."[75] It can be a powerful tool in today's world as well. Shame can be used righteously as a corrective to usher conviction. It can be used to help each of us acknowledge our desperate need for a Savior. For Scripture assures us that "Indeed, there is no one on earth who is righteous, no one who does what is right and never sins" (Ecclesiastes 7:20). Used well, shame can be a great equalizer for mankind and bring us humbly before the cross of Christ.

However, when used in an ungodly manner, it seeks to bring condemnation. Rather than having a goal to encourage righteousness within us, in the wrong hands it attempts to pollute the way we see ourselves. This is the type of shame we will explore in this chapter. Get ready to remove this ugly fig leaf that seeks to cover who you are in Christ.

Ashamed Because of What Someone Did Not Do

Shame is born from a place of deep rejection and is often a result from not receiving the love and protection we so desperately need. Without that love, we feel exposed. One of the most rarely asked questions is one of the most necessary questions needed to understand the seeds of shame: what did *not* happen? The lack of something good and necessary can be more detrimental to our health than the occurrence of something bad. Think about it, someone deprived of water will fare far worse than the person who has a boss with an aggressively bad personality. One of the most common roots of shame stems from not receiving the love and nurture we need to thrive. Patricia DeYoung wrote that, "a child has to have at least one caregiver who is able to respond in an attuned, consistent way to what the child feels. If this is missing in a major way, the child will

---

75   Richards, *Misreading*, 1.

translate the distress of the mismatch into a feeling like, 'I can't make happen what I need…so there's something wrong with me.'"[76]

It is difficult to be a child with a parent who is unable to connect. The reasons for the disconnect are many and varied but the result is similar: a child riddled with shame. Somehow each little boy or girl understands that moms and dads are supposed to bond with their children and this bond is to be made through love. The bond is woven through communications that go beyond words such as loving eye contact and tender touches. It is created through actions that assure their child that they will always be there for them. It is more than just supplying the basics of food in their mouths and clothes on their backs. It is the assurance that they are going to do life with you—always.

When a child does not feel love, acceptance, and protection from one or both of their parents, they will believe that they are intrinsically broken. Their minds will hear thoughts that they are not loveable and begin to embrace a lie. This lie makes everything in life harder. Life can be challenging. Bad things happen. One who feels loved and valued recovers more easily from the blows of life than one who suffers the deadly effects of shame.

Ashamed of What I Have Done

God is no stranger to our feelings of shame and has the most beautiful way of confronting them. Let's look at the Genesis narrative of God's interaction with Adam and Eve after the fateful snake and fruit event. Eve fell for the oldest trick in the book: doubting God's good intentions toward us. (Or, should I say that it was the first trick in the Book!) The serpent caused her to suspect God and his command to refrain from eating of the Tree of the Knowledge of Good and Evil.

---

76   DeYoung, *Understanding Shame*, 6.

She ate and so did Adam. It was not so yummy after all. Here's what happened:

"Then the man and his wife heard the sound of the Lord God as He was walking in the garden in the cool of the day, and they hid from the Lord God among the trees of the garden. But the Lord God called to the man, 'Where are you?'

He answered, 'I heard you in the garden, and I was afraid because I was naked; so I hid'" (Genesis 3:8–10).

In a nutshell, Adam and Eve did something wrong. It was a pretty bad wrong, too. This caused them to see themselves differently. Suddenly, they were overwhelmed with the desire to hide their most private parts. The efforts they made to cover themselves did not relieve their fear of being seen; especially not from being seen by the Lord. This is a problem on several levels.

Hiding Ourselves from God and Others

Grabbing from the available resources, Adam and Eve made clothes of fig leaves to cover their intimate parts. Up until their moment of defiance, they had been quite comfortable with each other. They could freely "let it all hang out," as the saying goes. Now they felt pain deep within themselves over the wrong they had done. Can you imagine the self-talk that must have ensued within their troubled minds? You can almost hear Eve saying things like, "I am so stupid, how could I have fallen for that?" Adam, on the other hand, appeared to have self-talk that blamed Eve for the problem. But deep down inside, don't you think he thought something like, "Why didn't I stop this from happening?" We blame others hoping that it will relieve our burden of shame. We blame others to prevent ourselves from being seen.

Leon Kass comments, "The story of man's fall inspires in us shame, fear and moral awe...and reveals a different but equally true aspect of human existence."[77] Adam and Eve looked inside themselves and felt as if there were now ugly parts that they did not want others to notice. Dr. Townsend remarks, "Our tendency is to keep the 'unloved' parts of ourselves forever under wraps, with the hope that in time, they will go away and not cause us more pain."[78] Unfortunately, stuffing things down never alleviates the problem. In seeking to isolate from others, we prevent ourselves from being our authentic, relational selves. Exploring the depths of shame, Patricia DeYoung comments, "Sadly, disconnection and isolation don't shut down chronic shame. Even when alone, people prone to shame often continue to treat themselves with suspicion and self-contempt."[79] Our shameful self-talk persists, and we continue to hide.

The self-contempt we feel is revealed in Adam and Eve's choice of covering. Early church father Irenaeus points out there were other leaves available to the couple. Yet, they chose the itchy, discomfort of the fig leaves.[80] Shame often invites a self-loathing that demands punishment. Shame bears the fruit of self-sabotage. At the very least, it produces a discomfort within us that rubs against our souls.

Hiding Because of What Has Happened to Us

Sometimes bad things happen to good people. Attempting to understand this hard truth has been the subject of many sermons and

---

77   Leon R. Kass, *The Beginning of Wisdom: Reading Genesis* (Chicago, IL: Chicago University Press, 2003), 56.

78   Dr. John Sims Townsend, *Hiding from Love: How to Change the Withdrawal Patterns That Isolate and Imprison You* (Grand Rapids, MI: Zondervan, 1996), 27.

79   Patricia A. DeYoung, *Understanding and Treating Chronic Shame: Healing Right-Brain Relational Trauma* (New York, NY: Routledge, 2022), 78.

80   Irenaeus, "Against Heresies" Ante Nicene Fathers, rev. ed. Alexander Roberts, James Donaldson, and A. Cleveland Coxe, trans. Alexander Roberts and William Rambaut, vol 1. (Buffalo NY: Christian Publishing Co., 1885), bk.III, ch. 23, 5, https:www.newadvent.org/fathers/0103.htm.

books. It is easier to believe that we always get only what we deserve. Therefore, bad things happen to bad people. Good folks are exempt. We will not dive into that subject here. Rather, we will accept that bad things have happened that were not our fault. We really did not deserve it. This may feel impossible for some of you to believe. If so, just remember that I am holding faith for you until you can see this truth for yourself. Some have suffered violence and abuse. Others have experienced false accusations or unjust termination of employment. This list of traumas we can experience is long.

Whatever the bad thing is, it can produce feelings of shame within us. When we have been hurt or neglected, we often believe we are or have become defective. It is a pain that permeates all that we think about ourselves and drives our behavioral patterns. Where guilt makes us believe that we have done something wrong, shame believes that we *are* the something that is wrong. This chapter opened with a scripture about the shame of our youth. It seemed impossible that I could ever escape my shame, much less no longer remember it. It was who I believed myself to be.

Families that Cultivate Shame

The Potter-Efrons refer to certain families as "shame-based families."[81] These are families that seem to act as a petri dish for shame. They contain parents who say things to their children that make them feel as if they can never measure up. Perhaps mom always got straight As, or dad never would have dropped that ball. Comments like, "you are always messing up" or "you never will…" flow from the parents' mouths and penetrate the child's soul.

Some children receive signals that they do not quite belong in the family. For example, the musically inclined child in a family of

---

81   Potter-Efron, *Shame*, 74.

athletes. Others get the impression that they should never have been born. Sometimes a parent clearly prefers boys or girls. For example, if you are a boy and mom had issues with males, then you could feel that something was wrong about you because you were a boy. Thinking that the other sex is preferable to your own is a form of self-rejection and creates a death structure with our souls.

When I was young, my parents went through a rough patch in their marriage that seemed to begin about the time that I was born. My birth was the line of demarcation between happy and bad times. While I do not think they meant that I brought the bad times, my young impressionable mind heard that I was the reason things went south in the family. Everything was fine until I came along. In my heart, it was all my fault. I mentioned this because while some of the shameful words that pierce our souls really are directed at us, others are not. Either way, if our little hearts receive the words as directed toward us, our hearts will embrace shame.

Some of you may have been the family scapegoat and really did receive the blame when things went wrong. Remember the point of blame is to hide. Others may blame us to hide the shame they feel in their hearts. We were not created to be scapegoats. Jesus sacrificed himself as the perfect lamb, the ultimate scapegoat. If you were given that mantle, I command it to leave you now in the name of Jesus.

Sometimes it is the way the family, or someone within the family, behaves that causes shame to be birthed into the child's heart. A child who is growing up with a parent who is not appropriately dealing with an emotional or psychological problem such as addiction, depression, or bi-polar disorder can feel humiliation because of the way the parent is acting. Parents struggling with these types of issues often cannot bond with their child nor can they consistently hold things together. The child suffers from the lack of intimacy. The parents' inability to cope causes chaos.

To avoid being "seen," the parent will often train their child in the art of concealment. Remember earlier it was mentioned that people dealing with shame tend to mount a cover up called Operation Fig Leaves? The goal is to protect the family's or the parent's reputation, but the message is clear. There is something wrong with me that needs covering. The child will naturally think because he or she is a part of the family that they are a part of this thing that is terribly wrong. The Potter-Efrons agree that "keeping a lot of secrets can make a family sick with shame."[82] When we tell the truth, the event will, in time, become a part of our past. A lie, however, embeds the event in our future, causing it to stick to us like glue. Lies take on a power of their own and imprison us with the fear of being "seen."

Cultures of Shame

Thinking upon my own experiences as a middle schooler, and then watching my daughter and granddaughter endure it, reminds me of unholy shame-based cultures.[83] School can be a place where we experience the shame of not measuring up. Classmates taunt one another for the way they look, the way they act, or the grades they receive. Unfortunately, church organizations can be similar. Jesus said that it was the sick who needed a doctor, not the well.[84] But, in some churches, people feel the need to hide their diseases for fear of being

---

82   Potter-Efron, *Shame*, 82.
83   There is a difference in Western and Eastern cultures. According to Richards and James, some Eastern cultures see the value of positive shame and are not inclined to immediately recoil from shame as are Western Cultures who tend to only see the unholy type of shame. See their book, *Misreading Scripture with Individualistic Eyes.*
84   "Jesus answered them, 'It is not the healthy who need a doctor, but the sick'" (Luke 5:31).

judged and feeling shame. I have heard too many stories of those who have given up their faith because they felt they could not fit within the culture of a church. They needed healing and discipling, yet they received shame.

"Sometimes American society promotes shame without intending to. We promote achievement so highly that many people feel like failures even when they are quite successful."[85] Despite doing well at what God has created us to do, it is all too easy to see that ladder of success and believe that we have not climbed high enough. Then there are the false images of beauty to which we are exposed through movies and other forms of media. We are confronted with six-pack abs and unblemished skin. Suddenly our ideas of what is attractive is a perfection that does not really exist. These things can produce feelings of inadequacy which is shame.

Abuse

Abuse happens when someone uses either their physical strength or position of power or authority to inflict their will upon another. The abuser uses their upper hand to make another do something they did not want to do. Victims of abuse often feel powerless and may experience feelings of disgust and defilement, particularly in the case of sexual abuse. Abuse plants the lie that we are less than our abuser. Somehow their needs take priority over our own. It is commonly associated with blame, because it leaves us feeling as if we are somehow at fault for what has happened. DeYoung makes a good point that, when someone lives opposite an abusive person, "They will be overwhelmed with shame...Something is terribly wrong and

---

85   Potter-Efron, *Shame*, 98.

because the internalized abuser is shameless, the victim carries all of the shame."[86]

At the end of this chapter, there are prayers to break ties with both the abuse and the abuser. If you have suffered physical, emotional, spiritual, or sexual abuse, I am so very sorry for the hurt and pain you have suffered. You did not deserve it. You are not beyond cleansing. I release the Father's love upon you now. Take a deep breath and receive it. It's OK. Do not be afraid. Just breathe.

If you have not reached out for help, please do it now. If you reached out for help and things did not work out so well, please try again. I promise you that there is recovery. I know this firsthand and would not encourage you if I did not know that God's love really can bring healing from the most horrific pain. If you do not know a qualified counselor or someone gifted in inner healing, check out the websites listed at the end of the first chapter to find healing.

Physical Defects

"But, Beth, you don't understand. I really was a horribly ugly child." This comment came from a woman who shared her story of being ridiculed by her classmates. She was a gangly little girl who wore coke-bottle glasses. She believed that she was hideous. She believed that her classmates had a right to make fun of the way she looked. A young man once shared with me his story of being weaker than most of his classmates. He, too, wore glasses and suffered mockery from his peers. Real or perceived physical malformation in our bodies mark us as different than others. This can breed an outlook of shame if we believe that because something is "wrong" with our bodies then something is intrinsically wrong with who we are as human beings.

---

86   DeYoung, *Understanding Shame*, 79.

The Fig Leaves We Sew

Just like Adam and Eve, we grab hold of whatever is available to mask our pain. These coverings, too, are usually itchy and cause more pain. Kass believes that the story of creation and the fall of man reveals unavoidable truths. The world around us, what he calls the cosmos, is incapable of showing us how to live well.[87] Secondly, "our own native powers of mind and awareness, exercised on the world around us, are inadequate for discerning how to live happily or justly."[88] What he is saying is that these stories teach us that there is not any created thing that will enable us to live well apart from God. And we cannot reason our way through the pain we feel in our hearts.

Pleasers and Performers

Children are quick learners. It does not take long for them to begin to adapt behaviors to get the acceptance they need from their parents. DeYoung calls this "match[ing] the cues coming from their parents."[89] One woman I know had a mother whose addiction to tranquilizers prevented the mom from taking care of her family. One afternoon, craving closeness and affection from her mom, she took one of the pills and crawled into the bed next to her sleeping mother. That attempt proved to be more successful in getting a case of double vision than a dose of much needed nurture.

The point is that shame-based identities can produce people pleasers who are trying desperately to get the acceptance their hearts crave. They will hide their authentic selves in order to avoid rejection. They will try to mirror the person whose approval they are seeking. They think that if they fail to please, then the other person

---

87   Kass, *Genesis*, 57.
88   Kass, *Genesis*, 57.
89   DeYoung, *Understanding Shame*, 7.

will withdraw their love and affection. In cases of abuse, the need to please can be an attempt to avoid being hurt or punished. The lie is, "If someone likes or is pleased with me, then maybe I can feel better and avoid pain." It is rooted in the belief that love and acceptance from others will help us love ourselves.

Performance is a form of pleasing. Where people pleasers want to get people to like them, performance-based personalities need to achieve perfection in order to feel good about themselves. They need that promotion. They need that A+. Without it, they are back to being nothing. In Chapter One, we talked about the dangers of relying upon our own actions and about only feeling as good as your achievement in the last five minutes. This means that you are only as good as your latest performance. If it was bad, you are toast. If it was good, you might feel fine for a bit, but it typically does not last long. "Well-being depends entirely on someone else's response. When the response is good, one feels important and valuable; when not so good, one feels worthless and low."[90]

Perfection is not ours to attain apart from Christ. The religious spirit loves shame-filled people. It perpetuates the shame by masking the pain with the idea that somehow we suddenly became better than others. On the other hand, it will antagonize the shame with relentless guilt.

After reading this chapter, you may see that a religious spirit partnered with shame is keeping you in a constant state of guilt. If you did not pray the prayer to break free of the religious spirit in the first chapter, please go back and embrace the prayer.

---

90   DeYoung, *Understanding Shame,* 7.

Self-Destruction

Self-destructive behaviors are common to those suffering from shame. They can range from drugs and alcohol to unhealthy, even abusive relationships. The need to numb the pain can be great. The draw to those who will treat us with the same contempt we feel for ourselves can be irresistible. What is interesting is that these self-destructive behaviors can quite easily co-exist with high achievements in other areas. Someone may be able to do very well at work or school while nursing an addiction. The high-level executive may go home to an abusive spouse.

I have never been much of an either-or type of person. I am more of a "both/and" girl. Sweet or salty? No, try the sweet and salty combination! As I was graduating from high school, my first love dumped me for my arch-nemesis. My already shame-filled heart had no idea how to find comfort and almost instantly I fell into a life of drugs. There I met a group of people who accepted me. Most importantly, I found oblivion from the relentless pain in my soul. Well, for a while anyway.

Work was another story. I excelled at work during the day and excelled in partying at night. The problem was that no accolades could penetrate the belief of worthlessness in my heart. No amount of drugs alleviated the pain of shame within my soul. I was stuck in a cycle that created increased feelings of shame. I had grown from a sad and lonely little girl into an angry and isolated young woman. Shame will convince us that we will never be more than a pathetic patchwork of every abuse we have endured and every sin we have committed. Shame lies.

The Problem with Hiding

Remember Adam and Eve? They practiced the art of withdrawal. They first began by isolating parts of themselves from each other. We are created to be in relationship with one another. We are created to love and be loved. If we are hiding a part of ourselves from another, can we believe that they really love us? No. What we really believe is that if they truly knew us, they would find us despicable. We believe they love an image but not the person behind the image.

So, we sew itchy, scratchy fig leaves.

The Purple Riviera

When I was in third grade, my dad came home with a new car. He thought it was a black 1966 Buick Riviera. And in a certain light, maybe it was. But most of the time, it was purple. Despite its unusual color, the car had a couple of features that my dad liked: a 465 Wildcat engine and the speedometer. Typically, speedometers are circular in shape with a needle that points to the speed the car is traveling. Most likely, you are familiar with them. But my dad's car had one we had never seen before, nor have I seen since. There was a small window that had a red line in the middle. Behind it was a cylinder of sorts that would spin so the correct speed would be indicated at the red line. My dad liked the unusual configuration, but what I bet he really loved was that this speedometer topped out at 155 miles per hour.

One beautiful afternoon, he decided to take my brother and me to visit relatives several hours away. We loaded into the car, my dad and brother in the front seat and me, being the youngest got the back seat. Hitting the freeway, my dad's foot began to press upon the accelerator, testing to see just what that 465 Wildcat engine would do.

The sun was out. The breeze coming through the open windows was cool but felt good. We had to have been driving faster than the speed of sound. We were flying. Those moments felt like we were on top of the world. It was great to feel wild and free. Until we got to my aunt's house, that is.

We got out of the car, grinning ear to ear from our flight. Overall, we were all feeling pretty good. Then it happened. Someone noticed my hair. See, my dad was bald, and my brother's hair was cut very short. But I was in the back seat with my baby fine hair blowing to kingdom come for well over an hour. It was one tangled mess.

Unfortunately, my cousins were full of ideas about how to fix the problem and swept me away into their laboratory of pain and misery. My older cousins loved to experiment on me, and this was to be no exception. One remembered that she had heard somewhere that vegetable oil was good to remove tangles. When that did not work, another said that she thought it was peanut butter. An hour later, wearing half the kitchen cupboard and devoid of any tears left in my body, I was not only still full of tangles, but I was also a sticky mess with a very sore head.

There are times that we do things to help us feel free from the pain and misery we carry in our hearts. They may even feel pretty good for a while just like I felt pretty good flying down the freeway with my dad and brother without a care in the world. But these things leave our lives in a tangled mess. Our attempts to unravel the mess usually make an even bigger one. We need God.

Where Are You?

While Adam and Eve's efforts to hide parts of themselves from each other may have appeared to bring some degree of relief, those efforts fell far short when faced with their Creator. Rather than hiding only parts of themselves, they hid their entire selves to avoid being known by Him. Adam and Eve have represented us well, as all humanity displays their same tendencies to sin and to hide. When we sew our fig leaves in attempts to solve the problem of shame within our hearts, we hide from the very One who can heal us.

God's response to the couple in disgrace shows us the pathway to healing: "But the Lord God called to the man, '*Where are you?*'" (Genesis 3:9).

Do we think for a moment that God did not know where they were hiding? The psalmist, David wrote, "If I say, 'Surely the darkness will hide me and the light become night around me,' even the darkness will not be dark to you; the night will shine like the day, for darkness is as light to you" (Psalm 139:11–12). God knows. While this seems frightening to shame, it is very good news. God knows what happened. He knew what Adam and Eve had done, yet he came and called out to them. Just as he called out to me and is calling out to you, "Where are you?" That means he is calling you to come to him. He is not calling out to condemn but to give rest to our weary and heaven-laden souls.[91]

How to Find that Rest

God began to ask them questions about what happened. Again, he knew. The point was for them to come to him with their shame and receive his covering rather than their own pitiful and miserable leaves. Scripture records, "And the Lord God made garments of skin for Adam and his wife and clothed them" (Genesis 3:21 NASB). Garments of skin?

---

91   "Come to me, all you who are weary and burdened, and I will give you rest" (Matthew 11:28).

This means that there was a sacrifice of life to cover their nakedness, their shame. Jesus sacrificed himself to cover our shame. Holy Spirit, I ask you to anoint the reading of God's word:

"However, it was our sicknesses that He Himself bore, and our pains that He carried; Yet we ourselves assumed that He had been afflicted, struck down by God, and humiliated. But He was pierced for our offenses, He was crushed for our wrongdoings; the punishment for our well-being was laid upon Him, and by His wounds we are healed" (Isaiah 53:4–5).

"At one time we too were foolish, disobedient, deceived and enslaved by all kinds of passions and pleasures. We lived in malice and envy, being hated and hating one another. But when the kindness and love of God our Savior appeared, he saved us, not because of righteous things we had done, but because of his mercy. He saved us through the washing of rebirth and renewal by the Holy Spirit, whom he poured out on us generously through Jesus Christ our Savior, so that, having been justified by his grace, we might become heirs having the hope of eternal life" (Titus 3:3–7).

While we are dead in our shame, unable to love ourselves and, therefore unable to love others or to love God, God calls out, "Where are you?" because he desires to cover our shame. Before the covering, there is confessing. It is time to confess and be free.

The Playmates of Shame

As we seek to be free from the deadly effects of shame, it is a worthwhile venture to explore some of the fruits of shame and address them specifically. These are shame's friends that help maintain its stronghold on your life to thwart your purpose.

Self-Pity

The term wallowing in self-pity makes perfect sense because it is like being stuck in miry clay. Miry is another word for boggy, and anyone experiencing self-pity certainly feels bogged down with the things that have happened to them or things that should have happened and did not. Self-pity is a preoccupation with one's self. Its vigilant focus is on the things that define us as "poor, pitiful me."

King Ahab had a kingdom. He had just about everything a man could want. That is, until he saw Naboth's field and wanted it for his own. The field was important to Naboth, and he refused to sell. Scripture reports that King Ahab "lay on his bed sulking and refused to eat" (1 Kings 21:4). He became bogged down with an inward focus. History records that Ahab's wife devised a plan that ended in Naboth's death, and Ahab acquired the field. We will look more into this verse when we discuss jealousy in Chapter Six. For now, we can see that Ahab's self-pity had deadly consequences.

Tina Gilbertson talks about the paradox of self-pity. She writes that what often looks like self-pity is an "unconscious attempt to elicit in others that which [we] desperately need but will not provide for [ourselves]."[92] Sometimes others will think that we are wallowing in self-pity when in reality we are trying desperately to get others to give us the pity that we refuse to give ourselves.

Whether we are looking for pity from others because we are too hard on ourselves or are drowning in the pity, we feel for ourselves, we need the Lord's healing. Pity is not the same as love and compassion. One of the most powerful weapons against self-pity is gratitude. If you are not practicing gratitude as outlined in the first chapter, get

92   Tina Gilbertson, LPC., "The Paradox of Self Pity," *Psychology Today*, April 3, 2015, https://www.psychologytoday.com/us/blog/constructive-wallowing/201504/the-paradox-self-pity

started. It will change your life. We will bring our sorrows and perfectionism to the Lord at the end of the chapter.

The Truth of Isolation

When shame drives us to isolate ourselves from others, we are rejecting them. We do not trust them with who we are, and therefore deem them unreliable. Do you often feel you cannot depend on anyone and are better off to just do it yourself?

We were not created to be solitary creatures. Shame makes us want to never need anyone. This is based upon lies and cuts us off from the help we need. When God created Adam, he said, "It is not good for the man to be alone. I will make a helper suitable for him" (Genesis 2:18).

Scripture prompts us to help carry each other's burdens.[93] Townsend teaches that the word for burdens in the Galatians passage depicts a picture of a "gigantic boulder crushing the back of a hurting person."[94] When we face overwhelming hurt, we need others to come alongside us and help. It is written in Ecclesiastes that we should not work alone, for it is a woeful thing for someone to fall and not have anyone there to pick them up.[95] If you are carrying shame because someone did not help you in your time of need, I am sorry. They dropped the ball. You are worthy to receive help and support. But we cannot continue to isolate ourselves because of the failure of others.

On the other hand, scripture tells us that we must carry our own loads. "Each one should test their own actions…for each one should carry their own load" (Galatians 6:4–5). Wait a minute. Scripture

---

93   "Carry each other's burdens, and in this way you will fulfill the law of Christ" (Galatians 6:2).
94   Townsend, *Hiding*, 78.
95   "Two are better than one because they have a good return for their labor; for if either of them falls, the one will lift up his companion. But woe to the one who falls when there is not another to lift him up!" (Ecclesiastes 4:9–10)

says to carry each other's burden then turns around and says carry your own load? What is up with that? Townsend explains this well. He writes that the Greek word for load in this verse could be translated as "knapsack."[96] A person puts what he needs for the day into a knapsack. It is a personal and light load. It differs from the boulder that is too hard for a person to carry on their own. It represents our personal responsibilities. Paul is saying that we help each other with the loads that are too difficult to carry alone, but we must not neglect accepting and carrying our personal responsibilities. Sometimes, we allow shame to excuse us from doing what we are called to do. We begin to see our knapsacks as burdens. We lose joy and we stop living life.

Hiding is Rejecting Yourself

We hide ourselves from others not only because we believe they are jerks that will hurt us, but also because we have judged ourselves as unlovable or unlikeable. Jesus said that the second greatest commandment is "love your neighbor as yourself" (Matthew 12:31). How then can we love others when we hate ourselves? When we believe that God has somehow created us a bit worse than others, we hide. We think that we have been given the short straw in life and that God has treated us unfairly. Rejecting the life that God has given us is partnering with death. It opens the door for more pain and the burden of life becomes even more crushing than before.

The children of Israel were taken from slavery to be delivered into a land flowing with milk and honey. They had seen God perform many miracles of freedom and provision on their behalf. Through the hand of God, they overcame a powerful kingdom.[97] Yet when

---

96   Townsend, *Hiding*, 78.
97   For the full story, see Exodus Chapters 1–12.

they were called to take possession of the promised land, the shame they carried affected their vision. After scoping out the territory, they shrunk back, saying, "We also saw the Nephilim there…and we were like grasshoppers in our own sight, and so we were in their sight" (Numbers 13:33 NASB). Notice how small and insignificant they saw themselves. And, how convinced they were that others saw them the very same way.

I knew a man who was gifted with engines. He could make motors purr and fix about anything. He mentored many young men in his garage with grease up to their elbows. When others spoke about him, it was with awe and appreciation. This fine man never saw that in himself. He had come from a family of medical doctors and felt that he never quite measured up to their academic and professional achievements. Most of his life was clothed in shame because he saw himself for what he was not rather than for what he was. It brought death to his potential every single day of his life. I pray as you embrace these prayers, you are able to see yourself as God sees you. It may sound cliché, but it is a more powerful truth than you can imagine.

Holy Spirit, I ask that you move upon their hearts to help them love themselves as you have called them to love. It will bring life to their bones.

Preparing to Pray

As you consider these things, ask the Holy Spirit to reveal to you any specific issues that he would like to address. Make note of them so you pray and release them in the freedom and healing prayer. If you are having a tough time praying the prayers of forgiveness, you may want to skip to the section on forgiveness in Chapter Four – Offense and come back to this when you are done.

If you are still not sure about your level of shame, there is a quick test to evaluate the level of shame you may be experiencing in the Appendix.

Prayer to Release Shame

Father, I come before You now with hurt in my heart. The burden of shame that I have carried has been a weight too great to carry, and I need Your help. I have seen myself as a grasshopper instead of a mighty warrior in the Kingdom of God. I break agreements with that lie and embrace the reality of who You have created me to be. I ask that You continue to reveal my identity in Christ and help me embrace it as truth.

My heart and soul have been wounded. (Lift up to the Lord any of those wounds that the Holy Spirit has brought to your mind. Be honest with the Lord and tell Him about the things that have hurt you. Yes, He knows, but He wants you to bring them to Him.)

I have often felt like a failure and that my life had no real value. I have wanted to hide myself because I have felt unlovable and unlikable. I am sorry that I failed to pick up my knapsack and embrace my life. I choose now to pick up my knapsack and live my life.

I am asking You to help me forgive those who have hurt me and have helped nurture seeds of shame within my soul. I do not seek to blame them and therefore avoid taking responsibility for my life. I want to be free of the bonds that tie me to the hurt.

I choose by faith to forgive my parents for failing to connect with me in a way that taught me that I mattered; that I was significant and that I was worthy of love. I forgive them for the hurtful things that they did to me (list any specific things that the Holy Spirit brings to your mind). I forgive them for the things that they were supposed to do and did not do. (Again, list any specific instances that the Holy Spirit may bring to your mind.) I forgive them for failing to make me feel safe and secure. I forgive them for the part they played in shame taking hold of my identity.

I choose by faith to forgive and release each person who has hurt me, belittled me, abused me and treated me as if I was not worthy of respect and love. (Again, list any specifics the Holy Spirit brings to mind.) I forgive those who were supposed to come alongside me and help me carry burdens that were too great for me to bear but did not come and offer help.

I forgive those who have judged me and decided that I was less than them in some way. I choose to forgive those who have rejected me. I forgive those who have blamed me and used me as the proverbial scapegoat when things went wrong.

Lord, I am sorry that I believed the lie that there is something inherently wrong with me and that you somehow created me not as good as you created others. I choose to forgive you Lord for all the things that have helped me feel full of shame.

I choose to forgive myself for things that happened that were outside of my control. I choose to forgive myself for the wrong and ugly things that I have done.

I am sorry that I have rejected others before they could reject me. I am sorry for any way that I have dishonored my parents because of the hurt in my heart. I do not want to be a scapegoat, so I will not blame my parents for my shame. Rather, I have chosen to forgive them for the role they played in my embracing shame.

I am sorry that I have hated people who have hurt me and judged mankind as being untrustworthy. I am sorry that I have hid myself from others.

Lord, please forgive me for hating my own life. I choose now, with your help, to embrace and be grateful for the life that you have given to me. I am sorry that I have hated parts of my body and choose now to be grateful for them. I am sorry for any way that I have rejected my sex and believed the opposite sex is better. I embrace who I am as a (male or female).

I renounce the lie that I am unlovable. I renounce the lie that I am unlikable. I renounce the lie that I am ugly. I renounce the lie that my life is insignificant. I renounce the lie that I am dirty and disgusting. I renounce the lie that if someone really knew me, they would be sickened by what they saw. I renounce shame.

I renounce the fig leaves that I have sewn, trying to deal with shame in my own efforts. I renounce hiding. I renounce mind-numbing drugs and activities including escaping through forms of entertainment. I renounce perfectionism and all the ways that I have tried to make people like me.

I choose to embrace the truth. I am loved by God. He loved me first and there is nothing that I can ever do that will make Him love me more or make Him love me less. I am loved. I am created for purpose and God has good plans for me. He has plans to prosper me and to give me peace. I am created in the image of God. Lord, help me to understand the power of this truth. Help me to love me the way Jesus loves me.

I break all ties with humiliating events and those who have shamed and/or abused me. I command all pieces of the humiliating, shaming and abusive events and pieces of the persons linked to them to leave me now, go to the places where they belong and never return to me. I command all parts of me that remained attached to the humiliating, shaming and abusive events and those linked to them to be returned to me now, washed in the blood of Jesus, whole and complete.

Lord, I forgive and release all of my ancestors for each and every sin that released a spirit of shame within my bloodline. I come into agreement with every legitimate claim the enemy has against me and my bloodline that has given him the right to torment me and my family with shame. I ask that you cleanse me and my bloodline, now and forever, of shame.

I renounce shame and everything that comes with it. I command shame to leave me and my bloodline now. In Jesus' name I pray. Amen.

Holy Spirit, I ask that you come now and cleanse every part of this beautiful person's soul, mind, body, and spirit that has been sullied by shame. I ask that you fill them to overflowing and pour a baptism of the Father's love upon them. Holy Spirit, heal them and fill them, in Jesus' name I pray. Amen.

Alternate Prayer A

Lord, I really want to embrace this prayer but I am having a very hard time doing it. I know that it must be true that I am not disgusting and shameful, but something seems to be holding me back. Holy Spirit, will you show me what it is? Will you release me from the thing that is stopping me from embracing the freedom that you are offering?

I am having a hard time forgiving those who have wounded me and need your help to be willing to ask you to work out forgiveness within my heart. I ask this in the name of Jesus. Amen.

Alternate Prayer B

Lord, in the depths of my soul, I hurt. I cannot believe that there will ever be a time when I will feel okay. I feel so dirty and used up that I cannot begin to embrace these prayers. I am afraid to hope only to be shattered again. Holy Spirit, will You heal my heart? Will You touch these deep wounds and set me free?

I am asking you to help me believe that I can be free. I am asking You to help me not to be afraid to be free. I need You to change my heart and help me to be willing to forgive myself and others. If You really are calling out to me, will You give me ears to hear? In the name of Jesus, I pray. Amen.

My Prayer for Each of You

Lord, I pray that You meet each person where they are and bring comfort to the bruised and wounded places within them. Help them embrace the truth of Your love. Give them ears to hear and eyes to see. Holy Spirit, I pray that You seal each of these prayers and bring them to bear much fruit. I pray that You surprise each person that has prayed these prayers with Your touch. You know what they need. I pray that You release to it to them. Bless their socks off, Lord! In the name of Jesus, I pray. Amen.

P.S. More on that Purple Riviera — Example of Generational Sin

In Chapter One, we had a brief discussion on generational sin and prayed to break the power of sins that may have loosed a spirit of death into life through your bloodline. The purple Buick is an example of how this manifests.

My father was an interesting man who loved fast cars and drove them well. If you had had the chance to meet my dad, you would have liked him. Some of you would have loved riding with him, others maybe not. But you would have enjoyed him. While we did not routinely drive in excess of 100 mph, it was not as if it never happened. We never went anywhere that it did not appear as if we were on our way to a five-alarm fire. My family traveled fast. Within days of getting his driver's license, my brother drove the purple Riviera. He had always wondered if you crossed the 155-mph mark on the speedometer if it would begin to spin in circles. About the time he topped 110 mph, a state trooper clocked him and flashed his blue lights. Unbelievably, he did not get a ticket that day. On other days, he was not so lucky.

My adolescence and early adulthood were also marked by an unusual number of speeding tickets. My daughter drives fairly fast and married a man who drives as if he too is on the way to a five-alarm fire wherever he goes. At least two of my nephews have a need for speed. The sin of my father has worked its way down the family line. Yes, it is wrong to ignore the laws of the land, even if they are too slow! It is a generational thing. As I have written this, it occurred to me that this needs to be broken.

If you did not pray the generational prayer in Chapter One, please go back and do so. While you are doing that, I will call my brother. We have some forgiving and repenting to do. Our family might just need to slow down.

Walking It Out

You are making great strides in your journey to abundant living. Please continue to embrace the steps to walking out the healing and freedom you are receiving. Spiritual freedom does not always immediately break our natural habits. These steps are designed to help you overcome the natural habits you've likely formed that are not in alignment with God's truth.

- *Continue to listen to your self-talk.* Are you hearing things in your mind that sound like:

  I feel so stupid! I just can't do anything right.
  I can't believe I just said that.
  I wish I could shrink and be invisible.
  I cannot do this. I am not good enough.
  They probably won't like me, or they really don't like me.

- *Pay attention to your feelings.*

  Are you often feeling a need to clarify what you meant after having a conversation with others?

  Are you often feeling as if you need to apologize but you really are not sure why?

  Do you feel like things are always your fault?

- *Follow up any of these thoughts or feelings with truth talk.*
  - I am loved by God and He created me for a good purpose. "For I am his workmanship, created in Christ Jesus for good works, which God prepared beforehand, that I should walk in them." (Adapted from Ephesians 2:10.)
  - I really can do anything that God asks me to do because He will always help me.

- o "I am part of a chosen race, a royal priesthood, a holy nation, a people for God's own possession, so that I will proclaim the excellencies of my Savior, Jesus Christ, who called me out of darkness into his marvelous light." (Adapted from 1 Peter 2:9.)
- o I am a child of God. I am his and He is mine.

- *Write one of these verses or one of your choosing that uplifts you in your identity in Christ and put it somewhere where you will see it each day.* Meditate upon it and ask the Holy Spirit to give your greater insight into its meaning.

- *Make a practice of choosing to forgive yourself and be quick about it.* If something comes to your mind that you have done wrong, tell the Lord you are sorry, ask him to forgive you, and choose to forgive yourself. Practice saying these things out loud. "Lord, I am sorry that I _____. I choose to forgive myself for _____and I receive your forgiveness. Thank You that it is now washed by the blood of Jesus, and I do not have to think about it anymore."

- *Continue to practice gratitude every day.*

- *Continue to ask God to help you forgive those who have hurt you.*

Additional Resources

The Search for Significance by Robert S. McGee

Hiding from Love by John Townsend

Supernatural Freedom from the Captivity of Trauma by Michael Hutchings

The Supernatural Ways of Royalty by Kris Vallotton and Bill Johnson

Healing the Orphan Spirit by Leif Hetland

It was a stupid argument really.

He was mad. I was mad.

He yelled. I got loud right back.

Wanting to get in the last word,

I made my parting shot as I turned to walk away.

Everything was fine... until he muttered:

"You'd better be glad you weren't standing here

when you said that!"

I spun on my heels and got into his face.

In my fury, I challenged him.

"You think you can take me? You want to try?

Here I am! GIVE IT YOUR BEST SHOT"

I knew he could wipe the floor with me.

He was stronger, much stronger.

But I could not back down.

Chapter Four

Killer Offense

"A person's wisdom yields patience;
it is to one's glory to overlook an offense."
Proverbs 19:11

It would be nice to say that the story you just read was not true. But it is. The warehouse manager had a chip on his shoulder and had become offended. He had felt disrespected much of his life. So it was easy for him to misconstrue the situation. He thought I had usurped his authority by giving an order to someone who worked directly under him. In reality, the nice young man had offered to help me carry something because he said that is how his grandmother taught him to treat a lady. Well, I guess I ended up shooting his lady theory all full of holes, didn't I? Because I certainly acted nothing like a lady.

When the warehouse manager said to me that I should be glad I wasn't standing near him when I lobbed my smart-aleck comment, the chip on my shoulder took control. I was blinded by fury. No one was going to hurt me again. No one was going to even threaten to hurt me and get away with it. In my offense, I needed him to know that he could not mess with me.

As I stood there challenging him, a voice of reason was quietly speaking to me. It reminded me that I was taking on a fight I could not win. Being a woman in a male-dominated industry, I was now faced with another challenge: if I backed down, I would be humiliated. If I did not, I would be beaten *and* humiliated. Stuck between a rock and a hard place, I looked at him full in the eye, and said, "You are not worth it." Rising to my full height, I again spun on my heels. This time, I walked away.

Going straight to my desk, I opened the drawer, pulled out the phone book and looked up a number.[98] Just a few weeks before, I had heard of a Christian counseling ministry. I called the number and made an appointment. This began my inner healing journey. I did not want my beautiful daughter to be raised by an angry woman full of offense. I needed help.

Offense is deadly. It is like a bitter cancer that metastasizes until relationship has been destroyed. It doesn't take much to see that one cannot be aligned with the life-giving power of the Holy Spirit and remain entangled with offense. After all, Jesus was brutally beaten and mocked as he was hung on a cross to die. Yet, he set aside the right to be offended and chose forgiveness. His choice brought life. Our choice to hold onto the hurt and anger turn out much differently. Let's look at a disturbing parallel between offense and death.

---

98   For those of you under a certain age, we really did have big, printed books that held everyone's name and phone number in a certain region. It was quite handy.

An Offended Levite

Offense is a deadly business. The story you are about to encounter is harsh. And —unfortunately, it is real.[99] I pray that the Holy Spirit cover you and guide you through this chapter. It will not be easy. It is, however, very necessary. The Lord spoke this message to my heart several years ago. To be honest, I struggled with releasing it then just as I struggled with sharing it here. There are many stories of offense in the Bible. This is the one the Lord gave to me.

In Judges 19, there was a certain Levite whose concubine had left him and returned to her father's house. Some translations record that she was unfaithful to him and left. Other translations, such as the RSV, indicate that she became angry with him. After an in-depth study of scripture, Robert Boling writes that it was the woman who was the offended party, not the Levite.[100] It is also noteworthy to understand that she was not a prostitute. The term concubine likely meant that she was a secondary wife and did not have full wifely privileges. The story reveals just how few privileges this woman had.

After a few months had passed, he decided to take his servant with him to go and try to persuade her to return to his home. Her father welcomed the Levite and appeared accommodating. Scripture tells us that he remained there for three days, eating and drinking with his father-in-law. On the fourth day, the father-in-law once again tried to get the Levite to remain another day, but this time the Levite loaded his donkeys and left with his concubine.

---

99   George F Moore, *A Commentary on the Book of Judges: A Critical and Exegetical Commentary on Judges* (London: Bloomsbury T&T Clark, 1958), 405. Moore writes that he has no doubt that the civil war that resulted from this event was in fact a historical event.

100   Robert G. Boling ed., *Judges,* 1st ed. (Garden City, N.Y.: Doubleday, 1975), 274.

As it neared darkness, they went into a town called Gibeah which was part of the tribe of Benjamin. There they eventually received the expected hospitality from another who invited them into his home for the evening. But something awful happened. "While they were enjoying themselves, some of the wicked men of the city surrounded the house. Pounding on the door, they shouted to the old man who owned the house, "Bring out the man who came to your house so we can have sex with him" (Judges 19:22).

The story goes downhill fast from here. The wicked men were not easily dissuaded from their vile intentions. Finally, the Levite took his concubine and gave her to the mob.[101] Then, he did a most unusual thing: he simply went to bed. It gets worse:

When her master got up in the morning and opened the door of the house and stepped out to continue on his way, there lay his concubine, fallen in the doorway of the house, with her hands on the threshold. He said to her, "Get up; let's go." But there was no answer. Then the man put her on his donkey and set out for home. When he reached home, he took a knife and cut up his concubine, limb by limb, into twelve parts and sent them into all the areas of Israel. Everyone who saw it was saying to one another, "Such a thing has never been seen or done, not since the day the Israelites came up out of Egypt. Just imagine! We must do something! So speak up!" (Judges 19:27-30).

A Closer Look

Before we move forward in this story, let's take a look at what has happened so far. The Levite had somehow offended his wife. After a

---

101   John H. Walton, Victor H Matthews and Mark W. Chavalas, *The IVP Bible Background Commentary: Old Testament* (Downers Grove, IL: InterVarsity Press, 2000), 274. The writers of this commentary indicate that it was the Levite who gave his concubine to the crowd to save his own life.

while, he decided to try to reason with her to return home with him. On the return trip, wicked men from the Israelite tribe of Benjamin demanded that he be given to them to satisfy their deviant sexual desires. This is truly an offensive situation. His outrage at the offense did not extend to his wife. She became just a means to an end. He gave her to them to save himself and showed no concern for her welfare. His response to the offense is offensive. This Levite certainly did not exhibit the heart of God.

Gathering Sides

The remaining tribes of Israel gathered together to investigate this tragedy.[102] Scripture records, "Then the Israelites said, 'Tell us how this awful thing happened.'

So the Levite, the husband of the murdered woman, said, 'I and my concubine came to Gibeah in Benjamin to spend the night. During the night the men of Gibeah came after me and surrounded the house, intending to kill me. They raped my concubine, and she died. I took my concubine, cut her into pieces, and sent one piece to each region of Israel's inheritance because they committed this lewd and outrageous act in Israel. Now, all you Israelites, speak up and tell me what you have decided to do.'" (Judges 20:3–7)

Did you notice the Levite's story? He left out the self-incriminating parts. He failed to mention that it was he who sacrificed his concubine to save himself. This is typical behavior of offense. It puts all the ugly on the offender while the "victim" remains blameless and innocent of any wrongdoing. It also tends to exaggerate the details to justify the outrage or to ensure others feel sorry for our troubles.

---

102   There were twelves tribes of Israel. Each tribe could be likened to a state within the United States of America. While each tribe had their own leaders, they were all united under Israel which was a nation called by God. To make reading easier, we will call all of the tribes gathered against Benjamin *Israel*.

The Levite needed to ensure that everyone would be on his side. He needed them to see him as blameless so they would gather together to execute vengeance on behalf of his offense. He asked them to tell him what they had planned to do. He clearly expected them to do something. He had carefully crafted a story and delivered it in the severed pieces of his wife to ensure their outrage against his enemies.

The Bad Remedy

The remaining tribes of Israel became so incensed by the wicked men's awful behavior that they demanded justice. We are not told why, but the leaders of the tribe of Benjamin decided against turning the men over to the remaining Israelites to be put to death. Perhaps they did not respond well to the mob mentality that was forming or maybe they did not want to acknowledge the ugly brewing in their own backyard. Their defensiveness is not surprising. We tend to become defensive or self-justifying when confronted with our own offensive behaviors. Whatever the reason, their refusal led to an all-out war.

This war was a disaster. Despite the overwhelming odds against them, the much smaller army of the Benjamites managed to overcome their brothers. Boling reports that the numbers of casualties listed in scripture amount to a catastrophic ten percent loss of life from the larger army of the Israelites.[103] This means that the number of lives lost was an amount that was not typical and was devasting. On the third day of battle, the Israelite army finally prevailed. It had come at a monumental price. How had things gone so wrong?

The Problem

The Benjamites needed some serious correction. It appears they were willing to allow the egregious behavior to go unpunished even

---

103   Boling, *Judges*, 286.

though the Law mandated that homosexuality was punishable by death.[104] Yet, they prevailed against their brothers' much bigger army not once but twice. Let's take a look at scripture to gain insight.

When the Benjamite leaders refused to allow the Israelite army to give the wicked men "what they deserved," the Israelites decided to go to war against their brothers.[105] Notice how they approach the situation with God. "The Israelites went up to Bethel and inquired of God. They said, 'Who of us is to go up first to fight against the Benjamites?' The Lord replied, 'Judah shall go first'" (Judges 20:18).

They asked God who should go first. They inquired of God how to best implement *their* plan. They did not ask God for his plan. In their righteous outrage, they presumed to know the mind of God.

Letting Our Outrage Disengage Our Holy Spirit Connection

Bear with me as we compare this to the situation when the Gibeonites tricked Joshua.[106] The Gibeonites had heard that the Lord had given the land of Canaan into the hands of the children of Israel who were to destroy all of the inhabitants of the land. Wanting to spare their lives, the Gibeonites put on tattered clothing, packed stale bread, and approached Joshua to make a peace agreement. Joshua and his leaders investigated the people's clothes, tasted their bread, and determined that they had indeed traveled from a far land—a land outside the territory of Canaan. They made the agreement. They were deceived. Scripture tells us how this happened. "The men of Israel wanted to know if these men were telling the truth. So they tasted

104   "If a man has sexual relations with a man as one does with a woman, both of them have done what is detestable. They are to be put to death; their blood will be on their own heads" (Leviticus 20:13).
105   "Then, when the army arrives at Gibeah in Benjamin, it can give them what they deserve for this outrageous act done in Israel" (Judges 20:10b).
106   See Joshua 9 for the full story.

the bread—but they did not ask the Lord what they should do" (Joshua 9:14, ERV).

Returning to Connection

It is important to recognize that we continually need the guidance of the Holy Spirit. Joshua and his men did not ask the Lord what they should do. The angry Israelites also did not ask God what to do. We may have heard God correctly. We can know what He has told us to do. And, yet we can still move forward in an ungodly manner. Joshua was deceived by appearances. The Israelites in Judges were deceived by a spirit of offense.

When they asked God who should go first, he replied, "Judah first." Did you know that the name Judah means praise?[107] I believe that God was telling his people to return to him in praise. But they did not hear his message. Just as Balaam heard God from the evil intentions of his heart, so did the children of Israel.[108] They were interested in vengeance. But vengeance always belonged to God. Still does. "Do not take revenge, my dear friends, but leave room for God's wrath, for it is written: "It is mine to avenge; I will repay,' says the Lord'" (Romans 12:19).

---

107   "Then Leah gave birth to another son. She named this son Judah. Leah named him this because she said, "Now I will praise the Lord." Then Leah stopped having children" (Genesis 29:35 ERV).

108   See Numbers 22 for the full story of Balaam and his donkey. God clearly told Balaam that he did not want him to curse the Israelites. Balaam was enticed by what Balak was offering. He craved the prestige and the riches, so he wanted a different answer from God. If we are not interested in hearing God's voice, we will receive answers from the evil within our hearts and deceiving ourselves that we are following God.

Before the third battle, the Israelite army approached the Lord in tears to ask if they should go into battle again.[109] The Lord could not ignore the despicable thing that had happened in Gibeah. It must be dealt with, and he told them they would succeed. Unfortunately, their hearts were still not right. Once they tasted victory, their self-righteous lust for revenge allowed the spirit of offense to reign without restraint. In their zeal for vengeance, they nearly wiped out the entire tribe of Benjamin.

They were sorrowful over their deadly actions. But their sorrow, which could have been avoided by remaining connected to God, could not return their brothers to life. Offense is deadly. They had a right to be outraged. What had happened was horrific. But the Levite was an ungodly man. He incited the spirit of offense within a nation. They took the bait and death reigned. Often our actions of offense can have irrevocable consequences.

Taking the Bait

Rather than seeking God and pursuing Godly justice, the Israelites set out to do what seemed right in their own eyes. This story is a picture of the deadly consequences of failing to follow the heart of God. This story begins with "In those days Israel had no king" (Judges 19:1) and ends with the words, "In those days Israel had no king; everyone did as they saw fit" (Judges 21:25). We cannot handle the hurtful and offensive things that happen to us well, apart from God. When we seek to do what is right in our own eyes, it can have deadly

---

109   "Then all the Israelites, the whole army, went up to Bethel, and there they sat weeping before the Lord. They fasted that day until evening and presented burnt offerings and fellowship offerings to the Lord. And the Israelites inquired of the Lord…They asked, 'Shall we go up again to fight against the Benjamites, our fellow Israelites, or not?' The Lord responded, 'Go, for tomorrow I will give them into your hands'" (Judges 20:26–28).

consequences. We can see in the Levite's story that offense seeks to cut our connection to God and our connection to others.

This is why our enemy seeks to entice us to into holding on to our pain through the spirit of offense. John Bevere explains that the Greek word for offend is *skand-alon*.[110] This refers to the part of a trap that holds the bait. Our enemy baits us into imprisonment by reminding us of the hurts we have endured. He seeks to keep us tied to the events and the persons associated with the events to ensure we remain separated from God and others. Shame seeks to separate us from others by hiding our so-called unlovable parts. Offense seeks to separate us by convincing us to not only annihilate one another but also to build walls to protect ourselves.

Citadel of Offense

"A brother who is offended *is harder to be won* than a strong city, and quarrels are like the bars of a citadel" (Proverbs 18:19 NASB).

Proverbs teaches that offense makes our hearts hard. When we are angry, we close our hearts to the offender. When left unchecked, offense continues its ugly whispers telling us that we must protect ourselves from this type of pain happening again. Bevere observes that "the focus of offended Christians is inward and introspective. We guard our rights and personal relationships carefully."[111] We carefully craft bars around our hearts to make sure that we are not hurt again. Simon and Garfunkel put it like this:

> *I've built walls*
> *A fortress deep and mighty*
> *That none may penetrate.*

---

110   John Bevere, *The Bait of Satan* (Lake Mary, FL: Charisma House, 2014), 26, Scribd.
111   Bever, Bait, 31, Scribd.

I have no need of friendship; friendship causes pains.
It's laughter and it's loving I disdain
I am a rock I am an island…and a rock feels no pain.
And an island never cries.[112]

While these rocks and islands within our hearts may seem prudent, they produce fruits of unrighteousness. These fruits are poison.

Poisonous Fruits

Viewing the rewards of offense will help us learn to not only recognize it but hate it as well. When we see the devasting effects on our lives and the lives of those around us, offense loses its appeal.

Gathering Sides: How Offense Talks

Offense is tricky. It is the sin that declares the sinner as righteous. There are sins, such as lust, that our hearts know are wrong. We seek to hide those types of sins from others. However, when we are offended, we tend to shout it from the rooftops. Why? Because we feel justified. We have been wronged, insulted, and hurt. We often fail to recognize the offense brewing in our hearts. We say things like, "My feelings are really hurt," and fail to recognize that hurt feelings are often a euphemism for offense.

Offense speaks to our wounded hearts. It says things like, "You were disrespected by that person" or "What they did was evil, and people need to know who they really are." We come into agreement with the insult. As we stew on it, we become sure that others need to know the truth about the one who offended us, while we keep the truth about ourselves under wraps. So we run our mouths to make sure those around us can not only commiserate with our pain but

112   Paul Simon, liner notes, *The Paul Simon Song Book* (London: CBS Records, 1965).

presumably, so they can take precautions to avoid being hurt, too. In reality, like the offensively offended Levite, we gather others to exact our vengeance upon those that have hurt us.

Hate's Trash Talk

Our tongues become weapons of mass destruction as we allow our hearts to become embittered. John taught his followers that "Anyone who hates a brother or sister is a murderer, and you know that no murderer has eternal life residing in him" (I John 3:15). I promise you this, if you are holding an offense against someone, you are holding hatred in your heart. *We clean it up and call it other more socially acceptable words, but it is still hatred.* Anita McCall wrote, "The ultimate goal of offense is murder. The enemy seeks an opportunity to gain entry through offense, in order that he can build it into unforgiveness and bitterness with the end result being murder."[113] We malign the other person's character and justify our behavior. We no longer want the offender in our lives. In our hearts, we prefer to no longer acknowledge their existence, if we can help it.

I was sitting in the dentist's office reading a magazine when I heard the words, "You are a murderer." It was so clear that I looked around to make sure no one else had heard it. Gathering my composure as best as I could, I asked the Lord what he meant by that. I knew it had to be the Lord because the words came with no sense of condemnation. Yet, I had never killed anyone. Why did He say that?

Suddenly, I was reminded of how I felt about someone who had deeply hurt my daughter and me. I was way too polite to hate him or wish him dead. I merely fantasized, on occasion, about the world becoming flat for a moment. This guy would get too close to the edge

---

113   Anita McCall, *Overcoming the Spirit of Offense: Understanding How Offense Operates, in Order to Be Able to Overcome It* (Bloomington, IN: iUniverse, 2016), 258, Kindle.

and be sucked out into space. Then my daughter nor anyone else would ever have to suffer his emotional abuse again. I was shocked. I would have never considered that I wished him dead. It still does not feel to me like I wished for his demise. But God says otherwise. We harbor ugly in our hearts and are often unaware of how God views it.

What is worse is that not all offense is real. The more we harbor offense, the more easily offended we become. Becoming hypersensitive to real or perceived insults causes us to become serial murderers. Once you have assassinated one person's reputation among your peers, it becomes easier the next time around. Once we find it acceptable to exile someone to outer space, it is easier to send another floating off into the great blue yonder. Sometimes the desire for vengeance is so great it causes physical harm—to ourselves and to others.

Killing in Your Heart

A woman came to me for prayer for a physical ailment. She actually did not want prayer to be healed but wanted prayer for favor to get disability benefits for which she'd previously been denied. I asked her if she was sure that was how she wanted me to pray. If the government did not feel her issue was severe enough to warrant full-time disability, then perhaps what she was really asking for was to get worse. If her symptoms worsened, she would qualify. I was not keen on praying that way.

I asked her if we could seek God for physical healing instead. She was not receptive to this idea, and as I probed, her story unfolded. She had a mentally challenged little brother who had been in the care of her older brother. The older brother had a lot on his plate and was juggling long-term care for his mother-in-law in addition to caring for his family and his mentally challenged little brother. One afternoon, the little brother, who was in fact a grown man, left the house while the family was dealing with an emergency situation. He wandered off and was not found for several days. Tragically, he had died of exposure. Unfortunately, the woman could not forgive her brother for what had happened. She felt he had been irresponsible with her little brother and was the cause of his premature death.

She wanted her surviving brother to pay for his crime. She prayed every day for God to exact vengeance upon her brother for his sin. Her countenance changed as she shared this. Bitter rage oozed from her. It came as no surprise to me that her physical infirmity began shortly after the death of her little brother. Her hatred and bitterness were eating her alive. It was with much compassion that I held her face in my hands and said to her, "You are the murderer. And you are asking God to be your weapon of destruction every single day. Forgiveness will set you free." She was shocked. The Holy Spirit helped her see the truth of what was within her heart and she agreed to pray for God to help her be willing to forgive. I never saw her again after that, so I do not know how the story ended. I pray it ended in forgiveness and reconciliation.

Victimization

Offense convinces us that we are the victims. As victims, we have no accountability for our embittered responses. We believe that our ungodly responses are warranted because we have been hurt. This woman was carrying a grievance, an offense, against her brother. She felt that an injustice had occurred and needed rectification. The only problem is that it was destroying her. She saw herself, along with her younger brother, as victims. When we see ourselves as victims, we no longer come into agreement with the word of God. God's word says that "No, in all these things we are more than conquerors through him who loved us" (Romans 8:37). We see ourselves as powerless and fail to take responsibility for our actions. This leaves us open to the enemy's vicious attacks.

Bitterness and Resentment

It is like getting a double dose of bitterness and resentment. Offense begets bitterness. When we see ourselves as victims, we blame others and become embittered by the powerlessness and injustice we feel. Bevere points out that often when we are offended, "we believe that we are the only ones who have been wronged. This response leaves us vulnerable to a root of bitterness."[114] Jacob gathered his sons, Joseph and his brothers, together to bless them, but look at what he said to Simeon and Levi. "Cursed be their anger, so fierce, and their fury, so cruel! I will scatter them in Jacob and disperse them in Israel" (Genesis 49:7). Anger left unattended brews into bitterness and resentment. Notice how it scatters. It destroys unity and it destroys our inheritance in the Lord.

In blessing Joseph, who had been the source of bitter jealousy, Jacob said, "With bitterness, archers attacked him; they shot at him with hostility" (Genesis 47:23). Bitterness causes us to even attack God's anointed while feeling justified for our actions. It is brutal. It is no surprise that the Lord instructs us to "get rid of all bitterness, rage and anger, brawling and slander, along with every form of malice" (Ephesians 4:31). Bitterness causes us to be captive to sin.[115]

Betrayal

Because offense causes us to build walls around our hearts, it leads us to protect ourselves at all costs. Not only does it keep others out, Bevere emphasizes that it causes us to betray others to keep ourselves

---

114   Bevere, *Bait*, 36.
115   "For I see that you are full of bitterness and captive to sin" (Acts 8:23).

safe.[116] Let's look at the way scripture portrays this: "And then many will be offended, will betray one another, and will hate one another" (Matthew 24:10 NKJV). The progression is that offense comes, which leads to betrayal and then to hatred. We've already mentioned the link between hatred and murder. So, let us consider this, "Whoever claims to love God yet hates a brother or sister is a liar. For whoever does not love their brother and sister, whom they have seen, cannot love God, whom they have not seen" (I John 4:20).

This is deadly business, and the scary thing is that it can be happening and we do not even realize it. We can harbor these things in our hearts, and because we are offended (or our feelings are hurt), they do not seem like sin. They seem like reasonable responses. Rather than seeing hatred and bitterness for what they are, we merely think that we are suffering from hurt. We do not see how we betray others because we are too preoccupied with the ways we have felt betrayed. Our betrayals against others do not seem like betrayals, rather, they seem like prudent measures to prevent wrongs from happening. We are blinded to the log in our eyes because the speck in our brother's eye has pained us. We get good and stuck.

Stuck in the Past: Legion

Offense causes us to be stuck in the woes of our past. Despite the fact that I typically wore jeans, flannel shirts, and work boots to the office, the day I challenged my coworker to a brawl, I was standing naked, bound in the chains of offense, amongst the tombstones of the wounds of my past. I had been wronged. I was hurt. Somebody needed to care about what had happened to poor, pitiful me.

Most of us are familiar with the story of Legion. Jesus and his disciples crossed the lake and set upon the shore in the region of

---

116   Bevere, *Bait*, 34–25

the Gerasenes. There they were met by a man with an unclean spirit who was so tormented that he often cut himself with stones. The townspeople would chain him, but he would break free and wander amongst the tombs. Seeing Jesus, he ran and fell at his feet. When asked his name, he replied, "'My name is Legion,…for we are many'" (Mark 5:9). Jesus cast the demons from the man, and he returned to his right mind. He also got dressed, for he had been wandering around naked.

Remember how we talked about God speaking to us in pictures? We often talk about Legion and how this word reflects a large number of soldiers in the Roman army. We celebrate that Jesus took it on singlehandedly! It is certainly a story that reveals the awesome authority of Christ which he has shared with us, his followers. There is more to the story, though. Where does scripture tell us that the man wandered? Amongst the tombstones.

We can learn about holding grudges right here. Holding onto offenses ties us to the past. We cannot let go because we are bound and tormented. We can resurrect that story, that wrongdoing, in a New York minute. We dig up the bones of old grievances and suckle them, but they offer no sustenance. We expose the ugly within our hearts to others without realizing our nakedness as we seek to expose another's. We become emaciated fragments of ourselves because we are living in a cemetery of bitterness. Just as this tormented Gerasene man cut himself with stones, we hurt ourselves by living in the pain of the past. Yes, even those offenses that were legitimate hurts brew bitterness if we hold onto them. There is only one way to get free.

Forgiveness

"See to it that no one falls short of the grace of God and that
no bitter root grows up to cause trouble and defile many."
Hebrews 12:15

Did you know that the definition of defile includes to pollute? When
we hold unforgiveness in our hearts, we pollute those around us
with our bitterness and resentments. Just like the Levite loosed a
spirit of offense upon his brothers which incited them to war, we
loose corruption upon those around us with our unresolved offenses.
Think about it. The Israelites were not satisfied with just teaching
their offensive brothers a lesson. Once they got started, they could
not stop until they had annihilated everything. Scripture reports that
only 600 Benjamite men managed to escape into the mountains.[117]
That means even the women and children were killed. It was brutal.

Thousands of deaths could have been avoided on both sides of
the battle had the people sought the face and heart of God in the
matter before rushing into self-righteous vindication. We must learn
to come to the Lord with hearts that forgive and seek his resolution.
Remember, it is written in scripture that we are not to seek our own
revenge.[118] Rodney Hogue asks a pertinent question. "Have you considered that you might be hindering the justice process because you
are attempting to do God's job through your own vengeance?"[119]

---

117   "On that day twenty-five thousand Benjamite swordsmen fell, all of
them valiant fighters. But six hundred of them turned and fled into the wilderness to the rock of Rimmon, where they stayed four months. The men of Israel
went back to Benjamin and put all the towns to the sword, including the animals
and everything else they found. All the towns they came across they set on fire"
(Judges 20:46–48).
118   "Do not take revenge, my dear friends, but leave room for God's wrath,
for it is written: 'It is mine to avenge; I will repay,' says the Lord" (Romans
12:19).
119   Rodney Hogue, *Forgiveness* (Collierville, TN: InstaPublisher, 2008), 17.

What Forgiveness Is Not

Forgiveness is not letting the person off the hook. It is not saying that what happened did not matter. If it did not matter, then there would be no need to forgive, would there? What happened mattered. It probably hurt and maybe even cost you something dear. It was a big deal. We do not, however, want to be bound to another through ties of hatred, resentment, or unforgiveness. We do not want to be forever bound by the things that hurt us. Forgiveness is the key.

Forgiveness does not mean that we have to be reconciled to the offender. There would not have been much good in the Levite being reconciled with the lustful men of Gibeah. Sometimes reconciliation is a necessary part of forgiveness. Sometimes it is not. If you are not willing to be reconciled with your friend who hurt your feelings, you may not have honestly forgiven them. However, if you have been abused by someone who has not repented, then it is not likely that the Lord is asking you to be in a relationship with someone who will continue to abuse you. In this case, the avoidance of relationship is not out of hatred but out of the necessity to keep you safe. The Holy Spirit will guide you in this with wisdom—just ask Him.

What Forgiveness Is

Forgiveness is an act of will that releases the person or people who have hurt or offended us to God. It removes the hook that the enemy can use to torment us with anger, bitterness and even self-pity. It frees us from being yoked with the burden of the painful event. Forgiveness is coming into agreement with the work of the cross. It affirms that we can forgive through the very one who died on our behalf. We have received the ultimate forgiveness. We have been forgiven of all our sins.

We cannot fail to recognize that we have hurt the heart of God. We have rejected Him, ignored Him, and even insulted Him at times. Every one of us has done things that within our hearts we knew were wrong. Yet, He calls out to us with love and compassion, desiring us to return to him in intimacy and love. One of the most beautiful things is that God will empower us to forgive. All we have to do is ask Him. That is why I often pray that I am choosing to forgive by faith, trusting that He will accomplish the work in my heart. While forgiveness is not an emotion, we often feel a release when we earnestly pray to forgive those who have hurt or wronged us.

God desires that we walk freely with Him in peace and righteousness. He desires that we have life. Forgiveness is a key to living an abundant life. It untangles our hearts from the yokes of pain that seek to bring death to our spirits and souls…and even our bodies.

Proving It with Science

In 2008, Australia began working on an act that would require disclosure to patients of any adverse incidents (a mistake or failure to provide the right care) that related to the patients' care. The act mandated that healthcare workers must inform the patients of the effects they could expect to experience as a result of the incident and also what measures they planned to institute to prevent the incident from happening again. Alfred Allan and Diane McKillop set forth to explore the potential effects of these disclosures on the patients. They came to an interesting conclusion.

Not surprisingly, no research could be found that dealt specifically with the impact of an adverse event on the recovery and health of patients. There is, however, a body of psychological literature that indicates that patients' psychological–physiological responses to adverse incidents may impair their recovery and health, especially if the response is prolonged. There is also some evidence that suggests that the patients' forgiveness of the professionals they blame for the adverse event may moderate the effects of the incident on their recovery and health.[120]

This is quite interesting. Their research led them to the conclusion that it was possible that if the patients were able to forgive their healthcare workers for the mistake, then they would likely suffer less adverse effects and experience improved recovery.[121] Conversely, holding a grudge would likely impair their recovery. Holding a grudge is stressful business. We are all familiar with the effects of stress on our health. It is killer.

Dianne Baskevitch explored how unforgiveness played a role in patients with addictions. Let's look at the conclusion of her research.

Either physical injustices or psychological offenses—real or imagined—can result in unforgiveness. Unforgiveness results in chronic stress and leads to a myriad of persistent emotional, physical, and spiritual dysfunction. This is a process that takes time to develop, but what is certain is this: each time an opportunity is missed for forgiveness, a person is less likely to be able to connect his/her dysfunction with the original injustice or offense and is more likely to suffer serious and permanent health consequences (Exline et al., 2004; Harris & Thoreson, 2005; Luskin; 2002).[122]

---

120   A. Allan and D. McKillop, "The Health Implications of Apologizing after an Adverse Event." *International Journal for Quality in Health Care 22*, no. 2 (2010): 126–31. doi:10.1093/INTQHC/MZQ001

121   There appears to be little research in the connection of health and unforgiveness. There has been a bit more research into the aspects of unforgiveness such as anger on the effects of people's health. I pray that science continues to research and discover the truths that the Bible has always revealed.

122   Dianne Baskevitch, "Understanding the Cause, Dynamics and Implications of Unforgiveness: Increasing Compassion for Challenging Patients." Final Forgiveness Thesis, (2010) https://www.academia.edu/34578831/Final_Unforgiveness_Thesis_2010

Her research led her to the conclusion that unforgiveness produced dysfunction within a person's life. Not only that but the more forgiveness is withheld, the less likely the person is able to connect their feelings and responses to current situations to something that happened in the past.

I once asked a receptionist at a doctor's office why she never used the word dollars when she explained the charges. She told me she had learned that money was an emotional trigger for people. If she mentioned that the charge was for forty-five dollars, then it would trigger every thought and emotion that the patient had tied to money and typically cause stress. She noticed that people seemed happier to pay when it was just a number that was not linked to a monetary value and the emotions tied to it. She always said, "That will be forty-five for today."

When we practice unforgiveness, everyday events can trigger the pain of our past and cause us to respond in ways that may far exceed what the situation warrants. Imagine one co-worker asks another to share their apple. This simple request suddenly brought on a tirade from the apple's owner. The anger over the apple stemmed from an incident years earlier. Remember Bubba from the introduction? He is the one who "ate the red off your apple" and apparently, he ate the red off this coworker's apple, too.[123] The point is that one coworker's innocent request knocked against a bruised place in the heart of the other because Bubba had not been forgiven.

But the coworker with the apple doesn't equate his response with Bubba. They were two entirely different circumstances in his mind. He justifies his response by citing how rude the person was to ask for part of his lunch. Perhaps he even believes that they demanded his

---

123   There is a saying in the southern United States, "Who ate the red off of your apple?" This is a way of asking who has upset you.

apple and had no respect for him. Maybe he becomes convinced that the person thinks they are more important than he is. He becomes offended. A relationship is lost. And he does not really understand why. He just knows he has been wronged and his bitterness grows.

The Impossible Repayment Plan

Unforgiveness is held in the idea that somehow, we are going to make the person repay us for the harm they have caused. Imagine that someone borrows a precious family heirloom from you. It is the only kind like it in the world. You trust them and want to bless them, so you loan it to them. They eventually come to you and confess that they cannot return the heirloom to you because it has been lost. You are hurt. You trusted them. They did not value something that meant so much to you and now it is gone, forever.[124]

You just cannot seem to get over it. Every time you see the empty space the heirloom once occupied, your heart grieves and seethes. It feels impossible to forgive. Maybe they did not really even say they were sorry. Forgiving feels like you would lose something. It feels like you would be saying it doesn't matter anymore. If we hold onto those lies, we will become like an army of angry Israelites who become massively destructive to those around us—especially those who offend us.

We already concluded that forgiveness is only needed when what happened really matters. What was lost matters. The reality is this: the person who hurt us cannot restore to us what was lost. The offender cannot restore our dignity, our innocence, our faith, or any other thing that was jeopardized in the offense. Just as the person could never return the lost heirloom because there is not another one

---

124   The premise for this analogy comes directly from Rodney Hogue's, *Forgiveness*, 16-17.

like it in the world, those who have hurt us do not have the power to heal our wounds. Only Jesus can do that.

It has often been said that unforgiveness is like drinking poison and hoping that the other person dies. The Israelites drank the Levite's poison of offense and a catastrophic amount of them died. Sure, some of the Benjamites died, but not nearly as many as did their brothers. It is time to realize that we cannot get what our hearts desperately need apart from letting go and trusting God. Paul wrote, "Get rid of all bitterness, rage and anger, brawling and slander, along with every form of malice. Be kind and compassionate to one another, forgiving each other, just as in Christ God forgave you" (Ephesians 4:31–32).

The Forgiveness Requirement

Wait, did you get that? Paul said we are to forgive as Jesus forgave us. How can we expect Jesus to forgive us for what we have done while we refuse to forgive others? Jesus had something to say about that. He said, "For if you forgive other people when they sin against you, your heavenly Father will also forgive you. But if you do not forgive others their sins, your Father will not forgive your sins" (Matthew 6:14–15).

Forgiving those who have hurt us is not optional. It is a command—from God. If we withhold forgiveness, then it is withheld from us. This is serious business, and we need to get right down to it. It is time to break the cycle of offense in our lives and live.

Love

Scripture exhorts us to love even our enemies. Many will find this difficult to hear. "But to you who are listening I say: Love your enemies, do good to those who hate you, bless those who curse you, pray for those who mistreat you" (Luke 6:27–28). This is imperative

124

to life. Perhaps this is so difficult because deep within our spirits we know that "love covers a multitude of sins"[125] and we are afraid our offenders will not suffer the consequences of their actions. We must remember that our own forgiveness is built upon our willingness to forgive those who have wronged us.

When we seek to see things from God's perspective, everything changes. We begin to see why people behave the way they do. We see that they are hurting and need help not murderous slander or banishment to the outer galaxies. Rather than viewing from a lens of offense, we begin to view through lenses of compassion, and we find peace. As we offer mercy, we will receive mercy.[126]

Let this verse wash over you and refresh your soul. "Love is patient, love is kind. It does not envy, it does not boast, it is not proud. It does not dishonor others, it is not self-seeking, it is not easily angered, it keeps no record of wrongs. Love does not delight in evil but rejoices with the truth. It always protects, always trusts, always hopes, always perseveres" (I Corinthians 13:4-7).

Notice that love rejoices in the truth. We are not to deny the hurt in our hearts. We acknowledge the offense and choose forgiveness and love. Love protects, it does not seek to out the offender because we must always tell the truth. If you must repeat the story, choose your words carefully. The story should likely not be repeated until our hearts have been set free from the offense through forgiveness. We may need to share with a trusted mentor to get help, but that does not mean we share it with every friend we have.

Paul exhorted the Philippians to "Rejoice in the Lord always. I will say it again: Rejoice! Let your gentleness be evident to all. The Lord is near" (Philippians 4:4-5). When we choose to focus on

---

125   "Above all, love each other deeply, because love covers over a multitude of sins" (I Peter 4:8).

126   "Blessed are the merciful, for they will be shown mercy" (Matthew 5:7).

Christ and rejoice in the Lord, we will find our hearts guarded by the peace of God. His peace quiets the whispers of offense.

How to Tell if We are Operating from a Spirit of Offense

- When hurt or offended, we feel the need to gather sides and get others to agree with us against the offender.

- We may have exaggerated our situation to justify our offense or gain the support of others.

- When someone else's truth does not align with our truth, we become defensive and angry.

- We find ourselves making note of all of the faults we can find in the person who has hurt us.

- We are haunted by the pain of our past and can't seem to let go of past hurts and offenses. We relive them over and over again in our minds.

- We are hyper-sensitive to minor grievances. As a matter of fact, all grievances may feel major. (This is a red flag that things happening now are reminding our souls of past wounds even if our minds do not make the connection.)

- We often hear ourselves say things like, "That really hurt my feelings."

- We are mistrustful of others and feel the need to protect ourselves from being hurt again.

- We experience lingering resentful and angry feelings toward those who have hurt us. We feel justified in these feelings because the other person really is a bad human being.

- It is not uncommon for others to feel that you have betrayed them. Or we feel that we have betrayed others because we had no choice.

- We find it difficult to pray for those who have hurt us.

- We want to expose the ugly in someone else's heart.

- We are defensive when faced with our own ugly.

- We see ourselves as victims, often feeling powerless.

- We cannot see that our responses to the negative event may be ungodly. Or we quickly quiet the still small voice of conviction that is trying to set us free.

- We crave vindication.

- Our prayers go unanswered.

The Long and the Short of It

As said earlier, offense is deceptive. It can make us feel justified in our unholy responses to real or perceived wrongs. It causes us to be defensive when confronted with our own actions. We often seek to gain vindication which brings more harm to ourselves than those who have hurt us. If we continue to walk amongst the tombstone of past hurts—reliving the insults—hatred and bitterness will grow. This resentment will cause us to become more aligned with the enemy of our souls than with the God of our salvation. Holding onto offense will affect our prayer life. It will cause us to hear more from the pain than from the God who seeks to heal our pain.

That day in the warehouse, the warehouse manager's pain roared, and my pain roared right back. Surprisingly enough, we became friends. How did that happen? We talked. I understood his pain and he understood mine. We set aside offense and chose compassion. This also meant that we had to tiptoe around each other's issues of pride. In the end, we made a good team and ran that business well. I do wish that I could have dealt with my pride sooner, though. It raised its ugly head and caused problems several years later. As you've probably guessed, offense and pride play well together. Before we deal with the pride side of things, let's dump this mess of offense and take a huge step toward getting our hearts right with God.

Preparing to Pray

Ask the Holy Spirit to open your eyes to see any areas of your heart that are harboring offense toward others. A good place to start is to examine those areas that feel hurt by something someone has said or done to you. By now, you are catching on to the way this works. Make note of anything that comes to your mind so you can be specific in your prayers. Include what the hurt or offense has cost you. When you are ready, head to the prayer section and let's step out of the wilderness of offense.

Father, I pray that You help this soul realize any areas of offense that remain stuck in their hearts and help them be willing to forgive and get off this merry-go-round of bitterness and offense. Help them see that even though the hurt is real and the thing that happened was not right that holding onto the offense is not hurting the offender but is bringing death to their own soul.

I ask that You help them see areas where they have vowed to never again let someone hurt them in a particular way. Show them times where they tried to get others to take sides against the person that offended them. Lord, give them the courage and commitment to step out of this wilderness and into Your Light. In the name of Jesus, I pray. Amen.

Prayer to Release Offense

Father, I am so very sorry that I have partnered with death by holding onto offenses in my heart. Lord, others have hurt me. (This is a good place to list any specific hurts that Holy Spirit is bringing to your mind.) I choose by faith to forgive them. I forgive them for hurting my feelings and for stealing something that was precious to me. (List what you have lost. It can be something like money that was taken from you, or your dignity, harm caused to you, etc. Be specific about who and for what you are forgiving.)

Lord, Your Word says that "an unfriendly person pursues selfish ends, and against all sound, judgment starts quarrels" (Proverbs 18:1). I forgive those who have been unfriendly and started quarrels with me or against me. (Again, list any specific persons and instances that the Holy Spirit brings to mind.)

I repent of every way that in my own hurt and offense that I have brought up quarrels. I ask You to bless and cleanse those I have defiled with bitterness and offense.

I repent of my unholy responses to hurt feelings or offenses. I repent of telling my story to others so they could side with me against the person that had offended me. I am sorry that by doing this I birthed more offense and caused others to be brought into my offense.

I repent of being defensive when faced with my own unholy responses and for the ways I have tried to justify them to myself, to others, and to You, Lord. I repent of holding onto bitterness, malice, resentment, and hatred in my heart. I repent of failing to take responsibility for any part that I played in the offense or maintaining the offense.

I am so sorry that I have ever tried to use You, Lord, as a weapon of mass destruction, hoping that You would hurt those who have hurt me. I repent of seeking vengeance when vengeance belongs to You. Your grace has been poured out upon me so that I have not received what all I deserve. I am sorry that I have not been willing to extend that grace to those who have hurt me. I now turn over those who have hurt and offended me to You. (List them here.)

I am sorry for building walls around my heart to keep others from hurting me again. I ask You to remove these walls and give me the courage to love again.

(This is a good place to ask the Lord to release you from unholy inner vows such as: "I will never again..." Let the Holy Spirit reveal to you if you have ever uttered such things in your heart or with your lips. *)

Help me entrust my heart to You and then I will no longer need these unholy cages to protect my heart. I ask that You remove every unholy cage and replace it with your protection of love.

I repent of self-righteousness. I repent for assuming You were on my side. I am sorry for any way that I have been mad at You because You did not come to my rescue when I was offended. (You may need to forgive the Lord for any way that you have been angry with Him for not protecting you. It's OK. He can handle it. Even though His ways are always right, sometimes we can feel offended with God.)

Lord, in the mighty name of Jesus and by the power of the Holy Spirit I renounce bitterness, unforgiveness, hatred, malice, vengeance, and offense. I break every single agreement I have ever made with offense. I forgive my ancestors for each and every way they partnered with offense and brought the tendency to hold onto offenses into my bloodline. I renounce generational offense. I ask that You send holy angels to destroy every evil altar that has been erected in my heart and in my bloodline to offense. I ask that You blow your breath over the ashes of everything that has been sacrificed upon the unholy altar of offense and scatter them so that they will never come together to form an unholy purpose ever again.

Holy Spirit, I ask that You come and cleanse me and my bloodline of offense. I ask that You cleanse my body, soul and spirit of all agreements with offense and fill me with the Father's compassion and love. I exchange unholy vengeance for divine justice.

In Jesus' name I pray. Amen.

*We make inner vows when we make promises to ourselves. They can be unholy when we say things like, "I will never again trust a man or woman" or "I will never again loan money."

My prayer for you: *Lord, I pray that You touch this person's heart and bring life to every place within their body, soul, and spirit that has been emaciated by deadly offense. In the name of Jesus, I release the breath of life over your bones, over your soul, and over your spirit. Holy Spirit, I ask that You fill them afresh and anew. Fill them now with more! More peace! More joy! More compassion! Thank You, Lord, that you have set this captive free! In the name of Jesus, I pray. Amen.*

Alternate Prayer A

Father, I am hurt. I cannot seem to let go of the pain. I never thought I was offended, and this is coming as a surprise to me. I need time to take this all in and understand what you are speaking to my heart. Holy Spirit, I ask that You move upon my heart and help me be willing and able to forgive those who have wronged me. Help me set aside the offense.

Help me be able to repent of the wrong that I have done. Help me see what I need to repent of and help me see from Your perspective and not just through the lens of my pain. This forgiveness thing is difficult. It still feels like I am losing something. Will You help me to see the truth?

Lord, I want to walk with You and I do not want to be tied to the hurts and offenses that torment me any longer. I ask You for the strength, courage and desire to pray the prayer to be set free. In Jesus' name, I pray. Amen.

Alternate Prayer B

Lord, this is really a difficult pill to swallow. Do You really want me to forgive those who have hurt me so badly? It feels to me like You are saying that it is no big deal that I am hurt. I read about forgiveness, and it says that forgiving someone does not mean that it doesn't matter. I need Your help to believe that. I am so entangled with the hurt that I cannot imagine being free. It is part of who I am. Who would I be without the hurt? Sometimes, it feels like it is all I have left.

I am giving You permission to change my mind and my heart. Help me to be willing to do whatever You are asking me to do to be free from this spirit of offense. I do not want to be a murderer in my heart. Help me, Lord. I am so tangled up in this mess, that I cannot begin to pray what You are asking me to pray.

It is hard for me to ask for Your help since I am a bit upset with You because I am finding it difficult to believe that You really care about what has happened to me. But here goes nothing…Lord, help me let You help me. In Jesus' name I pray. Amen.

If you were unable to pray the prayer to be set free, hear my heart. I am so sorry that you were hurt. I am so sorry that the pain penetrated deep within your soul and torments you. It should never have happened. But it did and I really want you to experience healing and deliverance from the torment. Please accept my prayer for you.

Father, I lift up those who are unable to pray the prayer to be set free and ask You, Lord, to pour out Your compassion on them and woo them with Your love. Help them to see that You are wanting them to be free. Help them be willing and able to let You move upon their hearts and help them be able to say yes to forgiveness. I ask that You change their minds to come into agreement with truth. Set them free from the lies that are holding them bound. Lord, do what You need to do to heal their hearts. They hurt. Heal them. In the name of Jesus, I pray. Amen.

Walking It Out

Taking the steps to walk this out will eradicate this from your life. You do not have to walk amongst the tombstones of past offenses. Here are the steps that can help you remain free!

- Pray for the practical needs of others including those who have offended you. When we begin to pray for the needs of others, compassion develops in our hearts. Praying for the broken leg or the financial needs of someone who has offended you will help you see them not as a monster but as a person who needs God's help. It takes the focus off of ourselves and the shortcomings of those who have hurt us.

- When you are reminded of an offense, immediately go to the Lord and forgive them or at least ask Him to help you to forgive them. Ask the Lord to heal your soul and spirit of the hurt and then move on. If you have already forgiven the person of the offense, do not fall for the enemy's trick to entice you to pick up offense. Say out loud, "I have forgiven (insert name) for doing this or that. I choose to walk in that forgiveness."

- If the memory continues to replay through your mind, go to a trusted friend or mentor for help. Ask the Lord if there is a lie within the offense that you still believe. For instance, I was offended by something someone said to me. It was a very hurtful thing. I struggled to let go of it. I would forgive them, and then BAM! Just like that, I'd be filled with offense again. The Lord revealed to me that deep within my heart, I was afraid something she had said might have a bit of truth to it. I thought maybe I really could be as pathetic as she portrayed me to be. The Lord and I did some business together. I prayed like this: "Lord, I know in my mind that I am not a pathetic loser, but my heart is afraid it is true. By faith, I break agreements with the lies that I am a pathetic loser and always will be. I ask that You help me to embrace the truth that because I am made in your image, I cannot be pathetic. Help me embrace the truth that because I am made with a divine purpose that You will empower me to accomplish it. I cannot be a loser.

• Meditate on one of the verses within this chapter and let the Holy Spirit deposit the truth deep within your spirit.

• Read through King David's story with Saul and notice that he did not let offense take root in his heart. He patiently waited upon the Lord and did not harbor ugly in his heart. (1 Samuel 15–31). (Ugly can be bitterness, resentment, hatred and the like.)

• This is a biggie. Periodically pray for the Lord to search and try you to see if there be any wicked way within you and to create within you a clean and pure heart. It is a game changer when prayed sincerely. I promise you that! (Adapted from Psalms 51:9–10 and 139:23–24.)

Additional Resources

The Bait of Satan by John Bevere

Forgiveness by Rodney Hogue. This book can be found in the Global Awakening Bookstore, online at: https://globalawakening-store.com/product/forgiveness/

Every cell in my body seemed to cry out for water.
But the kitchen was on the other side of the house and
seemed so very far away.
Praying for strength, I managed to get out of bed.
Using the walls for support, I made my way down the
hallway and into the kitchen.
The water felt so good.
As I drank, I began to wonder why God had left me now.
Why was He no longer near when I was desperate for him?
I cried out to him, "God, I have always had faith. I have
always trusted You. Why are You not with me when I need
you the most?"
My cry was met with silence.
Again, I voiced my despair.
"God, I have always had faith…"
Before I could complete my complaint, He finally
responded,
"Really?"
It wasn't the answer that I was expecting.

CHAPTER FIVE

Pride: The Serpent of the Sea

"When pride comes, then comes disgrace,
but with humility comes wisdom."
Proverbs 11:2

Seriously? I mean seriously? There I was an unemployed, single mother too sick and in too much pain to work, and the Lord's response to my cry was, "Really?" Just as I was about to argue the injustice of His comment, the Lord began to reveal to me how wrong I was about myself. He began to show me just how little faith I actually had.

What I learned about myself that day is that I only thought I trusted the Lord. My trust in the Lord mirrored the exact same trust I had in *my* abilities. I had complete confidence in my capacity to get things done. I could earn a good living and could take care of myself and my daughter. I could afford to trust the Lord because I had my life under control. I had things covered. I could work hard and get things done. Then my health failed, and I was lost. My faith was shattered because my faith had only been in myself.

I had to learn to trust in the Lord. I had to learn that it was always Him who met my needs and it had never really been me. It was a long journey. It was not always easy, but I would not trade it for anything. I learned to lean on the Lord and saw firsthand how He not only could but would move mountains for little ol' me. While that was a monumental step toward humility, it turned out that my pride ran deeper than I had imagined. Because I never particularly liked myself all that much, it was difficult for me to see the extent of my pride. Let me shoot straight with you—this is still a journey for me. I am still learning humility. It is not easy, but I know without a doubt it is worth it. Join me as we travel this road together. Let's explore the deadly effects of pride and from where it comes. I just bet that you, like me, will no longer want to partner with this ugliness.

C.S. Lewis made a keen observation about pride. He wrote:

> *There is one vice of which no man in the world is free; which every one in the world loathes when he sees it in someone else; and of which hardly any people, except Christians, ever imagine that they are guilty themselves. I have heard people admit that they are bad-tempered, or that they cannot keep their heads about girls or drink, or even that they are cowards. I do not think I have ever heard anyone who was not a Christian accuse himself of this vice. And at the same time I have very seldom met anyone, who was not a Christian, who showed the slightest mercy to it in others. There is no fault which makes a man more unpopular, and no fault which we are more unconscious of in ourselves. And the more we have it ourselves, the more we dislike it in others.*[127]

---

127   C.S. Lewis, *Mere Christianity* (Durham: HarperCollins Publishers, 2015), 73.

Well, there we have it. Pride is a condition that is known to each of us. As Christians, we are uniquely positioned to overcome it through the power of the Holy Spirit. That does not mean it is easy to see it within ourselves or to admit it to others. It can even be difficult to confess our pride to the Lord. We despise it in others while we excuse it within ourselves. We will discover why in the pages that follow.

Before we explore the unhealthy type of pride that plagues us, let's be reminded that there is a type of pride that is not sinful and indicates a healthy self-assurance that with God's help, we can accomplish what has been put before us to do. This type of pride propels us to do our very best and is the foundation for understanding our value and significance in this world. The focus of this chapter is on the unhealthy pride that goes before a fall.

When Pride Became Ugly

Before there were Adam and Eve, there was a serpent who had previously rebelled against God. His rebellion was evident because as he looked upon the apple of God's eye, mankind, his desire was to pervert them. In Chapter Three, we discussed falling for the oldest trick in the Book—doubting God's good intentions toward us. Now, we will look at one of the consequences of that doubt—the sin of pride.

Scripture records a picture of Adam and Eve living in innocence. They are naked and not ashamed. They have been given a purpose to work and care for the land.[128] Prior to the fall, Kass explains that man "knows no complex or specifically human passions or desires:

---

128   "The Lord God took the man and put him in the Garden of Eden to work it and take care of it" (Genesis 2:15). While this verse refers to man, scripture records that man and woman become one. Therefore, this mandate to care for the earth belonged to both man and woman.

neither shame nor pride, anger nor guilt, malice nor vanity…"[129] At this point, humans are relatively basic in their wants and needs.

Things appeared to be going well until the serpent entered the dialogue and convinced them that God was a liar. We do not know why they decided to doubt God's good intentions towards them, but we can see the fruits of that decision. Notice how the serpent enticed man to fall.

He approached Eve and asked her about eating from the Tree of the Knowledge of Good and Evil. She explained that they could not eat from that tree because if they did, they would die. Look at the serpent's response. "'You will not certainly die,' the serpent said to the woman. 'For God knows that when you eat from it your eyes will be opened, and you will be like God, knowing good and evil'" (Genesis 3:4–5).

Did you see that? He tempted her through pride. By definition, *pride* is "a feeling of deep pleasure or satisfaction derived from one's own achievement."[130] As mentioned, this does not necessarily have to be a bad thing. But perverted pride exalts itself over God and his commands. It is not content to do all things in Christ's strength—it must do all things on its own.[131]

Somehow, the serpent perverted pride and enticed man to no longer be content to be God's beloved child but to crave to be equal to God and no longer subject to Him. Where did he get that idea? While we cannot know for sure, it stands to reason that he tempted her with his own unholy desires. He, too, wanted to be just like God. He was not content with his position. His pride demanded more.

---

129   Kass, *Genesis*, 60.

130   pride. (n.d.) *Random House Kernerman Webster's College Dictionary.* (2010). Retrieved May 1 2023 from https://www.thefreedictionary.com/pride

131   "I can do all this through him who gives me strength" (Philippians 4:13).

Pride from God's Perspective

There are plenty of examples of pride run amuck in the Bible. The prophet Ezekiel depicts an example of man's pride and God's response to it.

> *The word of the Lord came to me: "Son of man, take up a lament concerning the king of Tyre and say to him: 'This is what the Sovereign Lord says: 'You were the seal of perfection, full of wisdom and perfect in beauty. You were in Eden, the garden of God; every precious stone adorned you: carnelian, chrysolite and emerald, topaz, onyx and jasper, lapis lazuli, turquoise and beryl. Your settings and mountings were made of gold; on the day you were created they were prepared. You were anointed as a guardian cherub, for so I ordained you. You were on the holy mount of God; you walked among the fiery stones. You were blameless in your ways from the day you were created till wickedness was found in you. Through your widespread trade you were filled with violence, and you sinned. So I drove you in disgrace from the mount of God, and I expelled you, guardian cherub, from among the fiery stones. Your heart became proud on account of your beauty, and you corrupted your wisdom because of your splendor. So I threw you to the earth; I made a spectacle of you before kings.'"* Ezekiel 28:11–17 NASB*

There are those who believe this passage is talking about Satan. While we should approach this passage with the understanding that this king is representative of someone else, it is not prudent to place the blame on Satan. Wisdom dictates that we must accept this passage as a depiction of the pride of man. Bible scholar John Oswalt does not believe this text refers to the enemy of our souls, and he writes that neither did the leaders of the Reformation.[132]

While some of the early church fathers felt this passage aptly described Satan, there is no reason to argue that the passage only refers to mankind or to Satan. The principles easily can apply to both. We will, however, benefit more greatly from taking the passage in its context and accepting that the pride described here is ours. It is ugly and it causes us to remove ourselves from the presence of God.

Look at what the passage states. There was an exquisite being covered in the finest of gems. This being was anointed for a purpose and walked in the presence of God. The heart of this being became proud of his beauty and this self-exultation caused him to think wisely no longer. This newfound lack of wisdom caused him to fall in disgrace. Sounds a lot like our circumstances, doesn't it?

We have been adorned in more splendor than the lilies of the fields, we have been clothed in royal robes bought by the shed blood of Christ. We have been given the ability to reason and have been endowed with gems of spiritual gifts. Through our relationship with Christ, we have been restored to right relationship with our Creator and can come boldly into the throne room of God.[133]

Look what happens when we begin to trust in our own abilities, the very abilities that are gifted to us by a loving Creator. When we take pride in how God designed us, our haughty thoughts bring us very low. Isaiah records it like this:

---

132   John N. Oswalt. *The Book of Isaiah, Chapters 1-39* (Grand Rapids: Wm. B. Eerdmans Publishing Co., 1986), 119. (I want to show you both sides of the coin on this subject. Many believe this passage to refer to Satan while others do not. Either way, it is a depiction of pride and its destructive nature.)

133   "Let us then approach God's throne of grace with confidence, so that we may receive mercy and find grace to help us in our time of need" (Hebrews 4:16).

How you have fallen from heaven, morning star, son of the dawn!
You have been cast down to the earth, you who once laid low the
nations! You said in your heart, 'I will ascend to the heavens; I will
raise my throne above the stars of God; I will sit enthroned on the
mount of assembly, on the utmost heights of Mount Zaphon. I will
ascend above the tops of the clouds; I will make myself like the Most
High.' But you are brought down to the realm of the dead, to the
depths of the pit (Isaiah 14:12–15).

When we decide that we can live apart from God and stand
upright on our own two feet, we are brought into the valley of the
dead because pride makes us foolish.

Independence of Pride

The serpent tempted man with the same evil desire in his own heart.
Derek Prince explains that the "essence of this temptation is summed
up in one word: independence. It is the desire to be independent
of God."[134] God is our source. He is the One who supplies all of
our needs, and He is not miserly about it. When we seek to live in
any way independent of Him, we are living in pride. Oswalt wrote,
"Pride refuses to brook any rival, including God himself, insisting
that all his prerogatives will be its own."[135]

Whenever we exercise our will over God's, we are walking in
pride. We are saying that what we want or desire is more important
than what He wants. When we choose to walk in our own strength
without leaning upon our Creator, we are partnering with pride.
When we consider this definition, we recognize that every person
struggles with it. Pride says that I cannot witness to my employer

---

134   Derek Prince, *Pride versus Humility* (New Kensington, PA: Whittaker
House, 2016), Location 685, Kindle.
135   Oswalt, *Isaiah*, 119.

because I could lose my job. It convinces us that God cannot really want us to do something that could make us uncomfortable or come at a cost. Pride refuses to forgive those who have hurt us because it insists that our pain is bigger than God's compassion. Pride says that I do not need help, I can do it myself. We must take a long, honest look at ourselves to find the source of pride.

Pride: A Fig Leaf to Cover Insecurity

Typically, when we think of someone who is filled with pride, we think of someone who considers themselves more highly than they ought.[136] Underneath all the bluster, there is usually someone who feels very poorly about themselves. In the above passages regarding the King of Tyre and the King of Babylon, we see kings who exalted themselves over God. We think that we are not like them because we have not become great rulers of our universes. We suspect that we do not suffer from pride because deep inside we do not feel that we are all that and a bag of chips.

However, even when we feel lowly about ourselves, pride can be present. Pride is a fig leaf that attempts to cover the parts of ourselves that feel naked and ashamed. It is a wall of defense to protect us from experiencing pain. Rather than admitting our faults or our sin, we attempt to defend ourselves and deny the truth. We are afraid that if others see our shortcomings, they will reject us. So we deny that we have sinned or have some sort of flaw. It is as if we think that this denial eradicates the truth. We cannot admit to ourselves nor to

---

136   "For by the grace given me I say to every one of you: Do not think of yourself more highly than you ought, but rather think of yourself with sober judgment, in accordance with the faith God has distributed to each of you" (Romans 12:3).

others that we have flaws. "Our self-justification pushes people away because we have to make sure we are right and they are wrong."[137]

It is impossible to have authentic relationships when we are hiding and denying parts of our true selves. All of us have sinned and have fallen short of the glory of God. We are humans with imperfections. Scripture assures us that all of our righteousness is in Jesus and Jesus alone.[138] We don't have it apart from our Lord and Savior. We are all in the same boat in need of the same salvation: Jesus Christ. Pride tries to convince us that we can or have achieved at least some level of justification through our own efforts. This is just not true. None of us have anything to boast about apart from the grace of God. C.S. Lewis proposes that "pride leads to every other vice: it is the complete anti-God state of mind."[139]

Pride's travesty not only separates us from others, but it also separates us from God. Lewis stated, "It is Pride which has been the chief cause of misery in every nation and every family since the world began. Other vices may sometimes bring people together; you may find good fellowship and jokes and friendliness among drunken people or unchaste people. But pride always means enmity—it is enmity. And not only enmity between man and man, but enmity to God."[140]

Pride caused Adam and Eve to cover their private parts from one another, and it caused them to hide from God. The fig leaf of pride prevents us from coming honestly before the Lord to confess our sins and be forgiven. It prevents us from coming before the Lord with our insecurities and hurts to receive healing because we cannot admit

---

137   Heather Bixler, *Breaking Pride: Tearing Down Walls, Walking in Grace* (Indianapolis, IN: Becoming Press, 2021), 25, Kindle.

138   "God made him who had no sin to be sin for us, so that in him we might become the righteousness of God" (II Corinthians 5:21).

139   Lewis, *Mere Christianity*, 73.

140   Lewis, *Mere Christianity*, 74.

that we have a problem. Pride imprisons us. Heather Bixler puts it like this. "When we hide, we live in pride; when we are real, God will heal."[141]

Can you imagine how differently things would have been if Adam and Eve would have refused to admit to God what they had done? God would have stood before them saddened because He would have been prevented from providing a more suitable covering for them because they had shut him out of their misery. If they would have stubbornly and pridefully clung to their painful solutions, they would have blocked God's provision. They would have remained stuck in their leaves and become more and more miserable each moment. With each itch, they would have felt even more pitiful and pathetic. The worse they felt, the more leaves they would need, and they would have continued to spiral away from the Father.

Although it took some coaxing, they managed to set aside their pride and they came before God honestly, admitting what had happened. They did try to pass blame to defend their actions, but God was merciful and ultimately helped them to answer for their part in the disaster. He graciously helped them come to him to receive his mercy.

In pride's prison, we isolate ourselves from one another because we are terrified of our flaws being revealed. We defend ourselves to protect ourselves. Think about this—defensive backs are players on American football fields that provide pass coverage. They try to make sure that the wide receivers for the other team cannot catch a pass, gain yardage (run forward toward the goal) and score a touchdown. When we are defensive, we block others and prevent forward momentum. We are stuck in our pain, covering our flaws. No one wins.

---

141   Bixler, *Pride*, 34.

Taking Off the Fig Leaf

One thing we fail to take into consideration is that when God provided a more suitable covering for his people, they had to do something. They had to remove their self-made fig leaves. For a moment, they had to stand before their Creator naked and aware of their vulnerability. While this can feel utterly terrifying, it is the safest thing that we can do. I am not going to be less than honest here. The depth of my own pride has recently been revealed to me and it has saddened me. I have to ask God for the courage to be vulnerable because I cannot do it on my own. He is helping me. Even though it feels painful to begin with, in the end it feels like freedom. I am anxious for the evil places of pride to be eradicated from my life while often I'm still terrified of exposure!

Jesus taught that those who humble themselves will be exalted.[142] Every single time I have tried to defend myself to avoid being judged or rejected, it has not gone well. Relationships have been damaged. I end up looking small and become more hurt than I was before. Every time that I am honest about my flaws, I am humbling myself. I am not talking about self-deprecating talk where we constantly belittle ourselves to others and even to ourselves. It is saying that I am human, I mess up, and God will and has redeemed me.

Paul wrote to the Philippians urging them to set aside selfish ambition and be united to one another in love.[143] In his message of humility, he used Christ as the perfect example for us to follow. Let's take a look.[144]

---

142   "For those who exalt themselves will be humbled, and those who humble themselves will be exalted" Matthew (23:12).
143   "Do nothing out of selfish ambition or vain conceit. Rather, in humility value others above yourselves, not looking to your own interests but each of you to the interests of the others" (Philippians 2:3–4).
144   The principle for these seven steps to humility is taken from Derek Prince, *Pride versus Humility*, Location 750-807, Kindle.

In your relationships with one another, have the same mindset as Christ Jesus: Who, being in very nature God, did not consider equality with God something to be used to his own advantage; rather, he made himself nothing by taking the very nature of a servant, being made in human likeness. And being found in appearance as a man, he humbled himself by becoming obedient to death—even death on a cross! (Philippians 2:5–8).

Steps to Humility

Step One: A key to success is renewing our minds to think differently. Paul told his readers to take on the attitude of Jesus. We have to be willing to be transformed by allowing our thoughts to come into alignment with God. Often our thoughts seem to take on a life of their own. They run amok with thoughts that are contrary to the heart of God. I am reminded of Gomer Pyle, a character from the Andy Griffith show from the 1960s. Gomer saw the town's deputy make an illegal U-turn. In one of the most country drawls you've ever heard, Gomer flags him down, yelling, "Citizen's arrest! Citizen's arrest!"[145] (It sounded more like Citizen's A-rayest!) We must learn to do this with our unholy thoughts. We must arrest them and make a quick legal U-turn toward Jesus. When we find our minds filled with defensive thoughts that justify ourselves and put all the blame on another, we must recognize the pride, arrest the thought, and get real before God and man.

It can be helpful to ask the Holy Spirit to reveal to us the origin of the thought. "Why am I thinking this way?" is a great question to ask the Lord. If pride is a fig leaf to cover feelings of insignificance,

---

145   Shatner Method. "Gomer Pyle's "Citizen's Arrest!" of Barney Fife - *The Andy Griffith Show* – 1963" September 30, 2021. YouTube Video, 3.25, https://www.youtube.com/watch?v=A1D78Y60gvo

then letting the Lord reveal to us where these feelings began will help us give the hurts to him to heal.

Step Two: Set aside our self-importance. Jesus did not come as a ruler. He came as a servant. This is a significant contrast with the serpent's attitude and the desire he used to tempt Adam and Eve. He wanted to be independent of God and exalt himself. Jesus did not look upon man and think about how much more glorious He is than mankind. He looked upon mankind with compassion and humbled himself to accomplish the greater good of reconciling man to God. When pride rears its ugly head, we want to exalt ourselves and justify our behavior. We want to point fingers at others to hide our imperfections. With amazing compassion, Jesus became a man to bring reconciliation. We must stop pointing out the flaws in others as well as making excuses for our own ugly. Humility means repenting of our sins and mistakes, being willing to forgive the failures of others and choosing compassion both for ourselves and one another.

Step Three: Choose to consider the needs of others as more important than our own. We can do this because we can have full confidence that our Father will supply all of our needs according to his riches in glory.[146] Jesus willfully became a servant. He humbled himself. He did not lord his position over others nor attempt to prove his greatness. He came to help, to heal, and to save. He did not forcefully attempt to prove he was a king. Not only did he come to serve but he did so by taking on the lowly position of a man. He could have presented himself any way he wanted. The prophet Isaiah said, "He had no beauty or majesty to attract us to him, nothing in his appearance that we should desire him" (Isaiah 53:2). Instead, he chose to present himself as ordinary. In getting to know him, we find

---

146   "And my God will meet all your needs according to the riches of his glory in Christ Jesus" (Philippians 4:19).

that he is extraordinary. It is better for us to humbly present ourselves and let others discover the gems God has deposited within us.

Prince notices that because Jesus looked just like everyone around him that his "true identity could not be seen with the normal eyes of the flesh…Only the Holy Spirit could reveal the true divinity of Jesus beneath His veil of flesh, because He was *'found in appearance as a man.'*"[147] Only God sees and knows who we are. There is much wonder and beauty that He has deposited in us as we are created in His image. We cannot look to man to define us—our identities are found in the eyes of our Creator who loves us.

In my life, I found that although I could respond fairly well to constructive criticism in some situations, in other situations I would react defensively. The common denominator for my unholy reactions was a controlling spirit. When someone with a Jezebel-type spirit would come against me, I would not respond well. Despite the person's seemingly good intentions, the spirit behind it would try to control me by insinuating that I was not good enough. It would come disguised as helpfulness. In reality, its goal was to overwhelm and control. It would be easy to say the problem was on the other end, that the problem lay completely in the ugly spirit behind the so-called help. This was not true. I am responsible for my reactions. Pride would demand that I prove myself to them. I would fight the battle by trying to prove myself worthy. Let me assure you, this was highly ineffective.

It has been a long process, but breaking agreements with the lies of insecurity that whispered I was not good enough has gone a long way to help me set aside pride and offense. God sees and knows me. He loves me and says that I am enough. I promise you this—He sees and knows you, too. He loves you and knows that how He created

147   Prince, *Pride vs Humility,* Location 775, Kindle.

you is plenty enough. Perhaps others have indicated to you in word or deed that you are insufficient in some way. They are wrong. At the end of this chapter, you will be given a chance to dump the lie. Take it.

Often the ugly that we hate about ourselves is not really who we are at all. It is our pain rearing its head and acting out. God did not create someone to be a drug addict or a liar or any other such thing. He created us in His image. When we bear an image that does not glorify God, it is often because our hurt is reacting to protect. It really doesn't work, does it?

Step Four: We must die to our selfish ambitions. Jesus died. Becoming a man, Jesus faced the fate of all mankind: death. Jesus did not die just any type of death. He embraced a death that was horrible and did not appear honorable. Dying to self is hard. It may even feel like we are making ourselves look pathetic or criminal. Though they mocked Jesus as he died, his exaltation could only come by dying. Likewise, I must die to myself—my pride and offense. This has been one of the most difficult things I have had to do. It is a process. We will discuss this more in Chapter Seven.

When we are willing to humble ourselves, we become obedient servants of God. It is then that God can do amazing things within and through us. "Pride is a barrier to God working in us."[148] It stops God from doing what he needs and wants to do in our lives. Think back to the alternate Garden story. If Adam and Eve had not removed their self-made fig leaves, then they could not have worn the covering God provided for them.

God will exalt us when we humble ourselves. When we exalt ourselves, we usually end up being humiliated by our actions and responses. God provides opportunities for us to humble ourselves.

---

148   Prince, *Pride vs Humility*, Location 826, Kindle.

Let's ask Him right here and now for the courage and commitment to do it.

Quick Prayer for Humility

Father God, I need your help. I need You to give me the desire, the courage, and the commitment to humble myself. I thank You that you will give me opportunities to practice this. I know You have in the past, and I have not always done a very good job of it. But, with your help, I know that I can learn to die to myself and choose humility. Thank You for helping me. In the name of Jesus, I pray. Amen.

We have learned that the antidote to pride is to humble ourselves. Notice that this is something we choose. It is not something thrust upon us. It is a choice. We are faced with this choice each day. Let's look at what happens when we give ourselves to pride and therefore question the goodness of God.

Leviathan: The King of Pride

Most of us are familiar with Job. He is the guy in scripture that suffered greatly for no apparent reason. It is through his suffering that we are introduced to an epic monster that lives in the sea. This monster or crocodile of sorts has been called by John E Hartley "a primordial creature…[who is] king over all who are proud."[149] He is called Leviathan and causes all sorts of chaos. We will learn that it is only through acknowledging our total dependence upon God, that we can find freedom from this monster.

> "Can you pull in Leviathan with a fishhook
> or tie down its tongue with a rope?"
> Job 41:1

---

149   John E. Hartley, *The Book of Job* (Grand Rapids: Wm. B. Eerdmans Publishing Co., 1988), 346.

Leviathan is mentioned six times in scripture. God told Job, "It looks down on all that are haughty; it is king over all that are proud" (Job 41.34). Biblical scholars notice the similarities between this biblical monster and certain mythological creatures. Both describe a creature that can only be tamed by the ultimate being of superiority which we know is the Most High God. God describes the power of this monster in Job Chapters 41 and 42. He describes a being too powerful to be subdued with human effort. We must submit to God.

The Sea of Pride

In that day, the Lord will punish with his sword—his fierce, great and powerful sword—Leviathan the gliding serpent, Leviathan the coiling serpent; he will slay the monster of the sea.

Isaiah 27:1

Isaiah also calls this serpent a monster, or a dragon as used in some translations, that lives in the sea. Biblical imagery uses the sea to portray several things. One of the most common is chaos. This thing certainly knows how to stir up chaos. The sea, however, is also representative of humanity. You have probably heard the phrase, "the sea of humanity." We have seen that pride dwells in the hearts of humanity and we will see its destructive ways.

Leviathan preys upon the areas within our hearts that seek to be like God. In the Garden, we saw how Adam and Eve were tempted because they wanted to be exalted from their cherished position and be like their Creator. This caused them to lose their earthly position of authority. Pride causes us to elevate ourselves which ultimately causes us to fall. It makes us feel that we are the most important person. In relationships, we will no longer acknowledge the other person's point of view because we are captivated by our own positions. Our actions are always justified in our minds because our pain and hurt is the only priority. We end up acting with pride and causing much damage. We defend ourselves and cover our weakness with pride. We fall.

As previously mentioned, some of us may think that we could not possibly deal with pride because we think so little of ourselves. Unfortunately, that is not so. When we are too shy to go forward for prayer or to step up to what God has called us to do, we are operating in pride. We are making an idol of our reputations over God's commands.

Many Headed

> "It was you who crushed the heads of Leviathan and
> gave it as food to the creatures of the desert."
> Psalm 74:14

Scripture tells us that Leviathan has more than one head. It also teaches that a double-minded man is unstable in all of his ways.[150] When we attempt to give lip service to God but are secretly committed to elevating ourselves, we become tossed to and fro on the sea of pride. Remember that Leviathan is associated with chaos. When we seek to cover our weaknesses and elevate our strengths, we loose chaos into our lives. Additionally, I cannot help but wonder if this speaks of what we often call being two-faced. When we speak insincere words to get people to approve of us, we are partnering with pride. It is something to think about.

---

150   "Such a person is double-minded and unstable in all they do" (James 1:8).

156

Leviathan's Loyal Subjects

This creature is called the king of pride. Each king needs subjects over which to rule. We come under its rule when we choose to walk in pride. We feed it when we choose to give into offense and allow our hurt feelings to fester into resentment and bitterness. When we get upset because we have been misunderstood, we withdraw from relationship and Leviathan has found a loyal subject over whom to rule. It sounds positively horrible, doesn't it?

In the Book of Revelation, there are twenty-four elders laying their crowns at the feet of Jesus. It is written, "They lay their crowns before the throne and say: 'You are worthy, our Lord and God, to receive glory and honor and power, for you created all things, and by your will they were created and have their being" (Revelation 4:10–11). Only God deserves our worship. But when we come into agreement with the king of pride, we give it an allegiance that belongs to God. We submit ourselves to the king of pride that brings destruction instead of the Lord of Lords who brings life.

I hate the thought that I have thrown crowns at the feet of this detestable creature when I have chosen to allow my pride to cause me to withdraw from relationships because my feelings were hurt. It breaks my heart to think that I have taken crowns bought with the sacrificial blood of Christ and given them to the king of pride. But I have done it. I have taken what belonged to the Lord, my submission to him which produces brotherly love, unity, and compassion, and thrown it at the enemy's feet. I have eaten up the bitter morsels Leviathan has served and spewed my pain trying to protect myself. It has only brought more pain. Pain to myself and to others. Lord, I am sorry.

Waking the Dragon: Cursing

> "May those who curse days curse that day,
> those who are ready to rouse Leviathan."
>
> Job 3:8

Scripture teaches that cursing awakens this creature. Job found himself in a bad situation where everything was going very wrong in his life. In his lament, he cursed the day of his birth.[151] He invited those who were experts at cursing, who knew how to rouse Leviathan, to curse the day he was born. If we look closely, we can see the correlation between cursing and complaining. When we continually complain about our circumstances, we are cursing ourselves.

The children of Israel were delivered from slavery and found themselves in an unfamiliar and uncomfortable situation. They felt more vulnerable in the wilderness than they did as slaves in Egypt. It is written, "Now the people complained about their hardships in the hearing of the Lord, and when He heard them, His anger was aroused...and He struck them with a severe plague" (Numbers 11:1, 33b). Reading through the accounts of this story in Numbers Chapter 11, we are shown how the people grumbled and God heard their complaints. He responded to their needs, but they continued to complain. The result is that they were struck with a plague, and many died.

Bible scholars Walton, Matthews, and Chavalas suspect that the plague was a type of food poisoning.[152] Becoming dissatisfied with God's provision, the people complained and began to feast on lust and greed. This brought a terrible sickness into their bodies.

---

151   "After this, Job opened his mouth and cursed the day of his birth" (Job 3:1).
152   Walton, *IVP Old Testament Commentary*, 149.

Those who died were buried at a place the Israelites named, Kibroth Hattaavah. This literally means, graves of lust or graves of desire.[153] Embracing chronic dissatisfaction and complaining is deadly business. It brings a killer plague and invites the king of pride into our midst. We will talk more about this in the next chapter. For now, let's consider how complaining causes us to be embittered toward others and toward God.

Cursing rouses this creature and leaves us vulnerable to his ways because we have moved from God's protective covering choosing instead to abide in the desert of dissatisfaction. We exalt ourselves over God by acting as if we have been given the short straw in life— we are getting less good stuff than we deserve. When we curse, we speak negatively about those who we feel have hurt us, we speak ugly about our circumstances and sometimes even about ourselves. Think about it. When we badmouth others, we are acting in pride. When we complain about the circumstances in our lives, we are accusing God of being miserly toward us. When we decide that there is something seriously wrong with who we are created to be, we become obsessed with ourselves which is a form of pride.

The dark valleys are places where the enemy lurks to capture us. We must be mindful of what we feast upon when we are in the dry and desert seasons of our lives. When we are going through difficult seasons, we must avoid coming into agreement with Leviathan. We must put our focus upon God and trust him.

In *The Screwtape Letters*, Screwtape is advising his demon nephew on the best ways to thwart growth in the human "patient" to whom Wormwood has been assigned. In Screwtape's estimation, Wormwood is unnecessarily giddy over the low feelings the patient

---

153   "H6914 - qiⵣrô⋇ hata'ăvâ - *Strong's Hebrew Lexicon (kjv)*." Blue Letter Bible. Accessed 20 Mar, 2023. https://www.blueletterbible.org/lexicon/h6914/kjv/wlc/0-1/

is experiencing. He explains that as a human being, the patient is prone to highs and lows and that this is part of the way that God has designed them. He cautions his nephew saying, "Our cause is never more in danger than when a human, no longer desiring, but still intending, to our Enemy's will, look round upon a universe from which every trace of Him seems to have vanished, and asks why he has been forsaken, and still obeys."[154]

This is powerful language. It describes the threat to hell itself that a Christian becomes when he decides to obey and trust in the goodness of the Lord despite the seeming hopelessness of his circumstances. During our lives, we will experience highs and lows which we often call desert or wilderness seasons. This is the natural ebb and flow of life. The Israelites struggled in their wilderness wanderings. They often felt sure that God had abandoned them. They experienced feelings that God's provisions were not sufficient, and they engaged in constant complaining. Those of them that roused Leviathan never entered into God's peace and rest. As a result, they died wandering. The same will happen to us if we do not break our partnership with this serpent.

Choking or Savoring: It is a Choice

As said, we all go through seasons of highs and lows. Sometimes we feel the presence of God and other times, like that day in my kitchen, he seems woefully absent. We struggle and may feel lost. But God is always near. His promise to never leave nor forsake us is spoken in

---

154   Lewis, *Screwtape*, 40, Kindle. (In *The Screwtape Letters* the Enemy is God since it is written from a demon's perspective who is trying to keep his human from intimacy in the Lord.

both the Old and the New Testaments.[155] Scripture often speaks of the nearness of God.

> *"Yet you are near, Lord, and all your commands are true" (Psalm 119:151).*
>
> *"The Lord is near to all who call on him, to all who call on him in truth" (Psalms 145:18).*
>
> *"I have set the Lord continually before me; Because He is at my right hand, I will not be shaken" (Psalm 16:8 NASB).*
>
> *"…that they would seek God, if perhaps they might feel around for Him and find Him, though He is not far from each one of us" (Acts 17:27 NASB).*

Notice a common element of these verses. God is always near, but we must acknowledge His presence. We must seek Him to find Him. We must feel around for Him and set Him continually before us. It has often been said that faith is a fact and not a feeling. We must rest in the fact that God is near and speak words of humility that acknowledge this reality. Otherwise, we will rouse the monster in the sea through cursing and complaining. It is a dangerous business.

It is clearly important to consider what we feed upon when we are in desert seasons. We can choose to feast upon the sweet manna the Father provides and thrive. Or we can choose to feast upon the morsels of bitter complaining and unforgiveness that the enemy supplies and die. We choose choking or savoring—pride or humility.

---

155   "Keep your lives free from the love of money and be content with what you have because God has said, "Never will I leave you; never will I forsake you" (Hebrews 13:5).
"Be strong and courageous. Do not be afraid or terrified because of them, for the Lord your God goes with you; he will never leave you nor forsake you" (Deuteronomy 31:6).

Dangerous Disunity

Paul chastised the church at Corinth for coming together in a manner that caused division in the Body. He said because they were not honoring the body of Christ, that they were eating and drinking judgment upon themselves. Paul says that when we cause division through pride, we are bringing judgment upon ourselves. In the Corinthian church, some were gluttonous while others went hungry. There were those in the church that were oblivious to the plight of those who had less than others. They ate and drank their fill while others went hungry. Yet, filled with pride, they were partaking of the Lord's supper and feeling pretty good about themselves. Paul said, "That is why many among you are weak and sick, and a number of you have fallen asleep" (I Corinthians 11:30).

We can see how death is associated with pride when it causes disunity in the Body. When we are overly concerned with ourselves, we cause pain and hurt. When we glory in the blessings that God has bestowed upon us with little to no regard for others who have less, we are walking in pride. Keener explains that "by rejecting or looking down on other members of Christ's body, the church, they also reject the saving gift of his body represented by the bread."[156] When we exalt ourselves over others, we are walking on dangerous ground.

Other times, as mentioned earlier, when we entertain feelings that God created us to be less than others we are also partnering with pride. This form of pride can be linked to self-hatred or rejection. I suspect that this can be a root cause of auto-immune disease. This type of disease causes the body to attack itself as it would a foreign invader. It creates inflammatory responses that bring much harm to the body. When we see ourselves as insufficient, we reject the life that God has given to us. This is a spiritual rejection that I believe can

---

156   Keener, *IVP New Testament*, 484.

manifest as a physical disease. It is allowing pride to twist the truth about who God created us to be to cause us to partner with death. Remember, the words of Screwtape and know that we are dangerous to the enemy when we believe God. We must trust Him enough to be vulnerable. This is rejecting pride and embracing others and ourselves in the love of Christ.

Prime Time Attacks

Listen carefully to what you are about to read. Leviathan does not seek you out. It waits for you to get close and then it bites you with its vicious jaws. Read Job Chapter 41 and see what the Lord had to say about this creature. It is strong. It has impenetrable scales which certainly seem appropriate when colliding with pride. It is resistant to ministry and is a tough nut to crack, but with God's help, we can overcome. Hartley notes that while the identity of this creature has often been disputed, as an "earthly beast, [it is] identified as the crocodile."[157]

How a Crocodile Behaves

Remember we discussed how things in the natural world can paint pictures for us about how things work in the supernatural world? Let's look at how the crocodile attacks to gain an understanding of this wicked creature.[158]

According to Simon Pooley's research, crocodiles tend to attack when it is rainy, during the hot summer months, and during times

---

157   Hartley, *Job*, 339.
158   Much of these comparisons are adapted from Jennifer LeClaire's book *Defeating Water Spirits*.

of breeding.[159] These are the very same times we need to be aware of Leviathan's nearness. Rain is often associated with moves of God. Therefore, using this analogy, we can expect that Leviathan will work to bring division when we are experiencing an outpouring or move of God. The hot summer months represent those times when we are on fire for Jesus. When our enthusiasm is high and we feel as if we are soaring, this creature will seek to drown our faith in chaos and anxiety.

Times of promotion can be opportune for this creature as well. When we are birthing something in the spirit, it will seek to shut us down. A little offense here and a little twist there, and before we know it, we have been blinded by pride's light. It is written that "His sneezes flash forth light, and his eyes are like eyelids of the morning" (Job 41:18 NASB). Jennifer LeClaire says that "Leviathan makes sudden, violent, spasmodic boastful moves against his victims. The light he flashes blinds his victims with pride."[160] Pride often makes us stubborn. This thing sneezes and suddenly we cannot see a single fault of our own but are completely aware of the faults of others. And the cursing ensues.

Are you beginning to see pride's agenda? It wants to devour your relationships with God, with others, and with yourself. It wants you to be separated from others and resistant to ministry. It wants to stop you from promotion and from birthing things of the Spirit. It wants to drown you in the fear and anxiety of exposure. It hates you. It only pretends to protect you while its real goal is to kill your spiritual growth and intimate relationships.

---

159   Simon Pooley, "When and where to Nile crocodiles attack? Here is what we found," *The Conversation*, Simon Pooley, July 15, 2019, https://the-conversation.com/when-and-where-do-nile-crocodiles-attack-heres-what-we-found-119037

160   LeClaire, *Water Spirits*, 80.

Overcoming Leviathan

More on Humility

Rick Warren wrote, "humility is not thinking less of yourself, it is thinking of yourself less."[161] Again, Jesus is our best example. He knew who he was. He knew where he had come from and where he was going.[162] He did not need man to validate him. He had all the approval he needed from his Father. He was so focused upon his Father and his Father's business that he did not have the time nor the inclination to think about himself. When man ridiculed him, he did not defend himself. He knew he was beloved and that he belonged to God. Stop for a moment and consider this. Do you really know this about yourself?

We must clothe ourselves in humility.[163] It is a conscious choice. We are called to be servants. Jesus washed his disciples' feet. This was something that a slave would do. He came to serve rather than be served. Let us endeavor to know who we are in Christ. Let us set our hearts to serve as Jesus served.

Humility does not mean that we engage in self-deprecating talk. When we talk poorly about ourselves, we are coming into agreement with Leviathan because that is a form of cursing. Humility accepts and agrees that we are fearfully and wonderfully made in the image of God. To say that we are worthless or nothing flies in the face of God. It is saying that he made us junk. In the words of Paul, may it never be!

---

161   Rick Warren, *The Purpose Driven Life: What on Earth am I here For?* (Grand Rapids, MI: Zondervan, 2012), 163, Scribd.
162   "Jesus knew that the Father had put all things under his power, and that he had come from God and was returning to God" (John 13:3).
163   "…All of you, clothe yourselves with humility toward one another, because 'God opposes the proud
    but shows favor to the humble" (I Peter 5:5).

Humility admits weakness, readily forgives others for their weaknesses and seeks to bring out the best in others. C.S. Lewis explains that it is fine to appreciate praise from other people when we delight in the fact that we have pleased them. "The trouble begins when you pass from thinking, 'I have pleased him; all is well,' to thinking, 'What a fine person I must be to have done it.' The more you delight in yourself and the less you delight in the praise, the worse you are becoming."[164]

When we put the spotlight on ourselves, then we have begun to walk in pride. Notice the subtle difference. I love it when I cook a meal that delights my family. I enjoy their praise as they push their swollen bellies away from the table. The praise does not tell me that I am the best. It blesses me because I know that I have brought joy to them. A child loves praise from his parents. He experiences happiness knowing that he has pleased them. Likewise, I relish the moments when I feel my Father's delight in me.

Choosing humility is action on our part. This is key to overcoming pride. Remember, Leviathan is the king of pride and as such is a principality. We are no match for Leviathan and need God's intervention. The following steps are ways that we bring ourselves into partnership with the Holy Spirit and abide in the Almighty's shelter.[165]

Repentance

"Repent, then, and turn to God, so that your sins may be wiped out, that times of refreshing may come from the Lord."

Acts 3:19

---

164   Lewis, *Mere Christianity*, 75.
165   The following principles on overcoming pride are taken from Robert Hotchkin's book, *Leviathan Exposed*, Section 3, Strategic Keys to Overcoming Leviathan.

We are refreshed as we walk in forgiveness, freed from the bonds of pride and the wicked jaws of Leviathan. When we believe that we have been wronged, we are often so sure that we are right, and the other person is wrong that we become unable to hear their point of view. We do not hear what they have to say but we durn well expect to be heard. We must ask the Holy Spirit to search our hearts and reveal to us any ways of pride that have been demanding to be heard.

We must no longer hide behind the fig leaves of pride but be willing to acknowledge our sins to the Lord. King David put it best:

When I kept silent, my bones wasted away through my groaning all day long. For day and night your hand was heavy on me; my strength was sapped as in the heat of summer. Then I acknowledged my sin to you and did not cover up my iniquity. I said, 'I will confess my transgressions to the Lord.' And you forgave the guilt of my sin. Therefore let all the faithful pray to you while you may be found; surely the rising of the mighty waters will not reach them. You are my hiding place; you will protect me from trouble and surround me with songs of deliverance. (Psalm 32:3–7.

John put it like this, "If we claim to be without sin, we deceive ourselves and the truth is not in us. If we confess our sins, he is faithful and just and will forgive us our sins and purify us from all unrighteousness" (I John 1:8–9). I urge you to no longer hesitate. Repent and be refreshed.

Love

> "Above all, love each other deeply, because love
> covers over a multitude of sins."
> I Peter 4:8

We have all heard the saying about not bringing a knife to a gun-fight. But in the spiritual realm, bring the big gun to the knife fight! Remember that piercing serpent of pride? Shoot him down with love. It is our mega weapon. Pride and its king are the polar opposite of love. Love covers, pride exposes. Love values relationship and others. Pride seeks to destroy relationship and belittle others.

Pride convinces us that what we have to say is the most import-ant, but love listens and seeks to hear what the other person is saying. I once met a man who was a valued salesperson for a major high-end appliance manufacturer. He had excelled in life. He did not seem to notice his achievements all that much. He was appreciative of them but not boastful. It was amazing to have conversations with him because he listened as if what you had to say was the most important thing in the world. He was not faking it. He was genuinely inter-ested. He loved people. He loved well through seeking to hear what they had to say and placing value on their point of view.

Scripture describes love as being patient, kind, not proud nor dishonoring.[166] It does not demand its own way and is not easily pro-voked. And get this—it does not keep a record of wrongs. How many times have we been upset with someone and suddenly our minds are bombarded with every single thing they have ever done that bothered

---

166   "Love is patient, love is kind. It does not envy, it does not boast, it
is not proud. It does not dishonor others, it is not self-seeking, it is not easily
angered, it keeps no record of wrongs. Love does not delight in evil but rejoices
with the truth. It always protects, always trusts, always hopes, always perseveres"
(I Corinthians 13:4–7).

us. In a flash, our memories are like the elephants' and we can recall with perfect clarity the ugly things they have done against us. This is not love, it is pride. We can see through the biblical description of love that it brings peace instead of the turmoil of pride. "Love never fails" (I Corinthians 13:8a).

Keeping Quiet

"My dear brothers and sisters, take note of this: Everyone should be quick to listen, slow to speak and slow to become angry..."
James 1:19

When seeking to overcome pride, silence is golden. Pride tries to get us to run our mouths in frustration and in defense of our positions. Hearing the other person helps to bring calm to the storm of chaos and confusion that pride seeks to instill. Learning to listen with a prayerful heart will change our lives. Asking the Holy Spirit to help us to truly hear and understand the other person's position will help diffuse anger. We may not agree but a little understanding goes a long way.

One more verse for good measure: "The more the words, the less the meaning, and how does that profit anyone?" (Ecclesiastes 6:11). Silence really can be golden, ya'll.

Speaking the Word

"Gentle words bring life and health; a deceitful tongue crushes the spirit."
Proverbs 15:4 NLT

Subduing our own words is very good and speaking God's word is wisdom. Pride stirs up strife and brings death. Rather than seeking to battle against those who have hurt us, we must step back from the conflict and with sincerity ask the Lord for wisdom. Proclaiming the word over the situation aligns us with God and victory. It is written, "so is my word that goes out from my mouth: It will not return to me empty, but will accomplish what I desire and achieve the purpose for which I sent it" (Isaiah 55:11). God's word is sufficient for every situation we encounter in life. Ask Him for the word you need in your specific situation.

Consider combining the action of love with speaking the word. Chances are that the person who has hurt or irritated you is someone who God loves as much as He loves you. Praying the word over the person whose pride is working against you may help them overcome this evil work in their lives. As destructive as it is in our lives, it is equally destructive in the lives of others.

Take it to the Father

"My help comes from the Lord, the Maker of heaven and earth."
Psalm 121:2

It is not prudent to expect God to intervene in situations into which you have not invited Him. Scripture exhorts us to call upon the name of the Lord. We are called to submit ourselves to the Lord. Robert Hotchkin encourages us that "prayer helps us to get out of our heads and into our hearts."[167] This means that we are to choose to talk to God and trust Him instead of rehashing the situation in our minds. Sharing our hurts, offenses, and battles with God in prayer is paramount. Job suffered troubles and endured insults from his friends. Check out the epilogue to his story. "After Job had prayed for his friends, the Lord restored his fortunes and gave him twice as much as he had before" (Job 42:10).

---

167   Robert Hotchkin, *Leviathan Exposed* (Maricopa, AR: XP Publishing, 2015), 81.

Sing!

> "That my soul may sing praise to You and not be silent. O Lord my God,
> I will give thanks to You forever."
> Psalms 30:12 NASB

The thing that we offer sacrifices to is the very thing that is enthroned in our lives. When we sacrifice unity, brotherly love, and relationship, we empower Leviathan. We must turn from agreeing with this monster of the sea and enthrone God upon the altar of our hearts once again. Job had it rough. He lost everything and all of his children. We are so often appalled at the horror of his great loss that we miss a point of this story. His friends kept insisting that he had done something to deserve the devastation that had come upon him.

Job kept defending himself to them. It was not until he quit defending himself and acknowledged the greatness of God that his situation changed. Scripture records his words, "Then Job replied to the Lord: 'I know that you can do all things; no purpose of yours can be thwarted'" (Job 42:1–2). Once Job voiced his trust in the magnitude of God's perfection, God vindicated him and set his friends straight. Praise brings our circumstances into proper perspective. It dethrones Leviathan and honors God above all things.

Seeking the Mind of Christ

> "Oh, the depth of the riches of the wisdom and knowledge of God! How
> unsearchable his judgments, and his paths beyond tracing out!"
> Romans 11:33

We are taught that there is a way that seems right to us, but it is the way of death.[168] Pride carries a big screwdriver in his tool belt that twists things to make you think you know that things are a certain way but in reality, you may very well be seeing through a polluted perspective. We need the wisdom of God on the issues in our lives, especially those that have hurt or offended us. Have you ever been so sure that things were a certain way, only to find out that you were mistaken? It is important that we pray and ask for the mind of Christ concerning those things and the ones who have caused us pain.

Seeking Council

> "Where there is no guidance the people fall, but in an abundance of counselors there is victory."
> Proverbs 11:14 NASB

When we are upset, we often want to run our mouths to get people on our side. Instead, we should seek wise counsel. We all need someone in our lives who will risk telling us the truth rather than just what we want to hear. We need advisors who will tell us when we are no longer operating in the spirit of God's love and wisdom.

I recall a time when there was no doubt in my mind that I had been wronged and was innocent of wrong on my part. This was a rare feeling for me, and I rather enjoyed the fact that the other party was completely at fault. I shared my hurt with a friend, who quickly pointed out my part in the problem. It was difficult to hear because the feeling of being right was pretty good and the feeling of being even partially wrong was not. The courage of my friend to offer

---

168   "There is a way that appears to be right, but in the end it leads to death" (Proverbs 14:12).

Godly wisdom changed the course of my life. It was a catalyst to my commitment to deal with pride in my heart.

Forgiveness

"But who can discern their own errors? Forgive my hidden faults."
Psalm 19:12 NIV

Pride gives us the eagle-eye vision to see the faults of others but blinds us to those of our own. If you recall our discussion on forgiveness, we are forgiven as we forgive others. Forgiveness is a powerful tool to break the corruption of Leviathan in our relationships. We all have sinned and need forgiveness. We have no right to withhold it from others. Pride says we deserve forgiveness and those who have wounded us do not. Unforgiveness destroys unity.

When God looked upon man coming together for an evil purpose, this is what he observed: "…If as one people speaking the same language they have begun to do this, then nothing they plan to do will be impossible for them. Come, let us go down and confuse their language so they will not understand each other" (Genesis 11:6–7). He was saying that because they were in unity that nothing was impossible for them. If unity, even when united for unholy purposes, is so powerful, we can understand why the enemy of our souls would hope to keep us divided through the pride of unforgiveness.

Getting Ready to Let Go

This chapter may have been challenging for you to get through. It has been a challenge to write, too. I applaud you for reading through to the end. It is time that as God's people we choose to set aside dissension and division. We become divided over so many issues and it glorifies the wrong entity. It is our responsibility to humble ourselves and choose to no longer walk in agreement with pride. Borrowing from Robert Hotchkin's book, *Leviathan Exposed*, we have explored ways that we can partner with God to enable him to remove us from the jaws of pride. We cannot overcome this creature on our own. We need God's help. We need to submit to God and resist the enemy. God will cause him to flee but only if we choose humility. Are you ready? I am. Let's go to our Father and let him begin the work to set us free from these jaws of death and restore life. But, before we do, I'd like to share a quick story with you.

A Personal Story

At the beginning of this chapter, I mentioned being home and unable to work. It was a scary time and I'd like to share with you how I got there. My health had been declining for some time and the doctors were unable to diagnose what was happening to me. I kept putting one foot in front of the other and hoping things would get better. They did not. I felt overwhelming fatigue and pain in my body.

Although I loved the business in which I had worked for over a decade, I had found employment outside the construction industry in obedience to the leading of the Holy Spirit. I was hired to manage a local branch of a company that sold electronic devices. Not only did I enjoy my job, but I was also good at it as well. It turns out that I had an aptitude for finding solutions to problems as they occurred in the field. This eventually led to my being offered a position in sales. While this meant leaving a management position, it was an opportunity to make more money. It was an honor to be noticed and rewarded with the option.

There turned out to be a fly in the ointment. After taking the position, my immediate supervisor began to belittle me when we were in public settings. She was young and I suspect felt intimated by my experience in management. I did not respond well to her passive-aggressive insults. Pride objected to the treatment, and I made a few snarky comments here and there to put her in her place. I suspect I was feeling uncomfortably vulnerable because deep inside I knew that my health was becoming an issue. I was afraid that I would no longer be able to perform well at work.

One morning I awoke to find my bed coverings in utter disarray which was not normal. I was perplexed but needed to get to work so I didn't think any more about it. Oddly enough, the same thing happened the next night. Again, I awoke to sheets and blankets twisted and strewn about the floor. Now this was getting weird.

Things changed the third night. In the early morning hours, I was awakened by hearing myself say, "Ok. I will do it." Not only were the blankets all over the floor, but this time, I was on the floor with them. I realized I had been wrestling with God over some issue and had finally come into agreement with him. Once the agreement was made, peace flooded me. It felt as if the peace completely saturated me.

Although I did not consciously understand what I had agreed to do, I knew in my spirit that I would know when the time came. The next morning, when I arrived at my office and sat at my desk, beloved coffee cup in hand, the understanding came upon my heart. I knew I needed to call my manager and apologize for any disrespect I had shown her. Her response was to fire me.

Opposing emotions came upon me. Both peace and devastation filled my soul. I was shocked and yet not surprised. Deep within me there was an understanding that my mind could not comprehend. As word of my dismissal spread, others in the company were also shocked. Those closest to me questioned why I had confessed disrespect and given her grounds to let me go. I could only say that I had done what I had to do. A few co-workers even contacted their attorneys on my behalf who all agreed that I had a winnable wrongful termination suit. I made it clear that I had no intention of pursuing a suit against the company. God had orchestrated this, and I was not going to fight it.

What happened afterward is something only God can do. I suspect that the higher-ups in the company did not agree with my dismissal and were trying to find a way to rectify the situation. Maybe that was hopeful thinking on my part. Whatever the reason, I was given the opportunity to continue to work while I searched for another job. I was removed from sales and given a menial project. The fall from the golden girl on the rise to doing data entry was painful. Despite the fact that I am not a good typist, it seemed prudent to keep working for a few more weeks so I accepted the offer.

Each day for several weeks, I came to work and input data into the computer. It was grueling but I was determined to do it well. As the project neared completion, I received a call from the president's secretary. She had called on his behalf. He was curious and wanted to know how despite everything that had happened, I could still come to work and do a good job; never once saying anything bad about the company or my former supervisor. They did not understand how I could remain gracious and quiet in the face of the turmoil.

I explained that while the company's name may have been on my paycheck that in my heart everything I did was to honor Jesus. He was my true employer, manager, and provider. I shared with her how I'd felt I had not always honored Him by my defensive attitude toward my manager. Despite that lapse, it was important to me to do the best job I could do no matter the circumstance. She asked me how I could keep silent. My answer was that it was not my place to speak poorly about the company or my former manager because my defense was in the Lord's hands not mine. We ended the call.

The company's president was a proclaimed atheist and likewise, his secretary denied belief in a supernatural Creator. When she relayed our conversation to him, he was impacted because, as she told me, he said that it was the first time he had seen someone live out their faith with sincerity. It touched his heart. She said that they would find something else for me to do until they could figure out how to handle the situation. In my heart, I knew it was time to go. I thanked her and told her that we all needed to accept my dismissal. It had come from a higher place. It was time for me to move into a new season of my life.

Pondering the set of events, here is what I believe had happened. My ego had convinced me to take a position that God did not instruct me to accept. In my heart, I knew that I was not supposed to take that step. I did it anyway because I was proud of the invitation to sales. Additionally, my pride did not take well to this insecure, inexperienced manager making snide remarks about me, and my mouth decided to put her in her place. This all led to a place of death. I lost my job, I lost my dignity, and I was humiliated at my dismissal.

God wrestled with me for three consecutive nights until I released my pride and agreed to embrace humility. I needed to pick up my cross and follow Him. When I embraced humility, the immediate response was not positive. I lost my job. It hurt badly. As I continued to walk in humility and trust God, I was exalted. I gained the respect of the company's president. But more than that, I was a witness for Christ to him. I do not know if he ever gave his life to Jesus. I do know that I planted a seed that could have only been planted by me laying down my pride.

After leaving, the illness in my body continued to rage, and I became unable to work. More areas of pride were uncovered as I was faced with my self-reliance instead of God-dependence. It would be great to tell you that I was able to lay down that pride and never look back. Progress was made. Unfortunately, there were still unhealed places in my heart that clung to the false covering of pride. It took some time to get to the root of it. We are all learning. It is a journey. I am so grateful that the Father's heart toward us is full of tender compassion and He leads us to freedom from the snares that entangle us. "As a father has compassion on his children, so the Lord has compassion on those who fear him; for he knows how we are formed, he remembers that we are dust" (Psalms 103:13–14).

We are beings made from dust formed to bear the image of our glorious Father who has such great compassion. In the face of such amazing truth, pride seems pointless. Let's choose God.

Preparing to Pray

General prayers are good. Specific prayers are amazing. Before we go to the Lord in prayer, let's ask the Holy Spirit to reveal any areas in our lives where we have partnered with pride.

Holy Spirit, please remind me of any specific times or instances where I have grumbled, complained, lied, twisted words for my purposes, attempted to cover the truth, bad-mouthed someone else, disrupted authority, or ushered in disunity. Help me to remember any places of unforgiveness that remain in my heart when others have hurt or wounded me by lying, twisting my words, or saying things that made me feel like I wasn't good enough. Help me be willing to forgive. In the name of Jesus, I pray. Amen.

Remember to add the specific instances that require forgiveness and/or repentance that came to your mind as you pray through the following prayer. It will change your life.

Prayer to Break Agreements with Pride

Father, I come before You, and I no longer want to walk in pride. I no longer want to hurt others and bring more pain to myself by wearing a false covering of pride. I ask You to forgive me for being unwilling to be vulnerable. I need You to bring healing to my heart so I can have the courage to be vulnerable before You and others. I also ask for wisdom so that I will know how to be vulnerable wisely.

I choose to forgive those who have hurt me and said things that I allowed to penetrate my heart and make me feel unworthy. (List any specific instances the Holy Spirit brought to your mind.) I repent of any resentment I held in my heart toward them. I break agreements with the lie that I am not good enough. I am sorry that I have held onto a lie that flies in the face of being Your beloved son or daughter. I renounce the lie that I am unworthy and not good enough. I rebuke it. Holy Spirit, help me to take captive any thoughts that try to build a stronghold of unworthiness in my mind.

Lord, I am sorry for complaining. I am sorry that I have cursed myself by not being satisfied with what You have given to me or the way You created me. I am sorry that I have encouraged others to be dissatisfied by voicing my complaints to them. (List any specific instances the Holy Spirit brought to your mind.) Your word teaches that "…godliness with contentment is great gain" (I Timothy 6:6). Today, I purposefully and willfully choose contentment and renounce complaining and cursing.

I choose by faith to forgive all of my ancestors, from my parents all the way back to Adam, for each and every time that they came into agreement with cursing through complaining. I forgive my ancestors for bringing a curse into the bloodline through chronic dissatisfaction and complaining. I renounce generational complaining and ask the Holy Spirit to cleanse me and my bloodline from cursing and complaining and fill me and my bloodline with contentment.

I am sorry for every time that I have chosen to badmouth myself and to speak negatively of others. I am sorry that I have tried to cover my nakedness by exposing someone else's. I ask that You bring healing to those I have hurt. (Again, list any specifics that have come to your remembrance.) I ask that You heal my body, soul, and spirit of self-rejection.

I am deeply sorry for each and every time that I have not respected the authority You have placed over me. This includes those in governmental positions, teachers, pastors, employers, and my parents. Lord, your word teaches that I am to honor my father and mother that all may go well with me. It specifically teaches, "'Honor your father and mother'—which is the first commandment with a promise— 'so that it may go well with you and that you may enjoy long life on the earth'" (Ephesians 6:2–3). I am sorry for each and every way that I have dishonored them and ask You to cleanse me of this unrighteousness. I choose to forgive them for any way that they have unrighteously provoked me to anger and ask that You bless them. (See Ephesians 6:2–4)

I hate the sin of coming into agreement with Leviathan and am deeply sorry for every time that I have come into agreement with this monster of the sea. I repent of lying and twisting the truth to cover my shame or embarrassment. I choose today to walk in truth and to speak the truth in love.

I am sorry for allowing pride to bring disunity into my relationships and into my community. I break all agreements with disunity and choose the path of peace. Scripture encourages me to give gentle answers that turn away wrath. I choose today to repent of being defensive to cover my insecurities. Again, I choose to walk in truth and I choose to walk in love.

I repent of being more concerned with myself than with the plight of others. I repent of only seeing my point of view and my pain and not choosing to see the pain that is in the hearts of those who have hurt me. I ask that the judgment I have brought upon myself through this pride be crucified in Christ. I ask that the blessings that have been stolen from me through this pride be returned to me and to my bloodline. Help me to see with compassion the hurt that drives others to hurt me and to quickly forgive.

Lord, please help me to know who I am in Christ and what You have planned for me. Help me to understand true humility and to walk in it from this day forward. I ask that my life be a portrait of humility, grace, and love.

Lord, I ask You to set me free from the cords that have entangled me with Leviathan. He is no match for me but he is easy for You to rebuke. I choose today to humble myself. I choose to walk in humility with Your help and trust that You will deal with this principality on my behalf.

In the name of Jesus, I pray. Amen.

Alternate Prayer A

Lord, I can see that there may be instances in my life where pride has gotten the better of me. It feels very scary to admit this, and I need Your help. Please give me the courage to be willing to admit the pride in my heart and be set free. I know that You have created me in Your image and that I am fearfully and wonderfully made, but there are places in my soul that stubbornly remain stuck causing me to feel that I am really not good enough.

I am not sure that little white lies, twisting the truth just a little bit, are all bad. I am sorry for the times that I have outright lied and complained. I often feel exposed and embarrassed. I do not want to feel that way anymore. I really do want to exchange my self-made fig leaf of pride for Your covering of humility. I need Your help to be able to pray.

I need You to cut the yoke Leviathan has on my life and on my relationships. I often feel judged and misunderstood. It feels like if I admit my pride, I will be exposed and judged even more. I feel like I would be crucified and humiliated. Will You help me to see the truth? I really do want to follow You and set aside these things that bring death into my life and my relationships but feel like something is holding me back. Will You cut the ties that bind me and set me free to repent, forgive and come into agreement with You?

In the name of Jesus, I pray. Amen.

Alternate Prayer B

Lord, I can see that Leviathan is an entity that works in the lives of others but I do not see how it works in my life. I feel that I have been abused and wounded by the pride in others. I often feel insignificant, and it doesn't seem like that is anything at all like pride to me.

I feel that others do not choose to be in unity with me unless I agree with everything they say. It feels like I am being asked to set aside any right to have preferences, thoughts, or opinions that differ from those around me. This feels like You are asking me to disappear and let others walk over me even more than they already do or have.

I am hurt and need Your healing. Please heal my heart and set me free from the woundedness that entangles me with lies about myself, others, pride, and especially You.

In the name of Jesus, I pray. Amen.

Walking It Out

- Pray for humility each day.

- When you feel as if you need to defend yourself, take a deep breath and ask the Holy Spirit what is happening. Ask him to help you have a Godly response instead of a defensive response.

- When you are in a situation where you feel defensive or are in conflict, ask the Holy Spirit to help you see the other person's perspective and to have compassion even when you disagree.

- Ask the Holy Spirit to help you be quick to repent. In situations of conflict, ask the Holy Spirit to show you any areas where you may need to apologize, and do not hesitate to do so.

- Ask the Holy Spirit to help you be quick to forgive. When others have offended, wounded, or ticked you off, forgive quickly.

- Ask the Holy Spirit to give you a heart of compassion when in adversarial situations or situations where you feel you are being disrespected.

- Make it a daily choice to choose to walk in love. Ask Jesus to help you.

Additional Resources

If you feel that you could benefit by exploring this subject a bit more, here is a resource that you might find helpful.

Breaking Pride by Heather Bixler

One by one the mothers would call their
children home.
Each child would hang their heads and grumble.
"Ah, Mom, can't I stay outside a little longer?"
The answers were always no.
One by one they would leave.
Looking over their shoulders, they'd say how lucky I was
because nobody made me go inside
to take a nap.
My heart ached for someone who would call me to come
home.
One by one they would leave.
And I would envy them.
I was learning to covet what others had.

CHAPTER SIX

Jealousy—The Seduction that Slays

"Anger is cruel and fury overwhelming,
but who can stand before jealousy?"
Proverbs 27:4

I have a friend who is also an emotional and spiritual healing minister. She is awesome. Because my friend had more experience in spiritual healing, I asked her to sit in on a session with me. It went really well, and as we sat there basking in the amazing healing of God, a thought began to form in my mind. I began to think because my friend was so awesome that my client, whose trust I valued, would like my friend better than me. In my mind's eye, I could see this person continuing a ministry relationship with my friend instead of me. I began to feel pangs of jealousy. Yes, you heard that right. I was experiencing these feelings about a situation that had not even happened.

There, I admitted it. It wasn't easy, but I did. In the previous chapter, we read C.S. Lewis' comment about how everyone deals with pride, but only Christians seem to be able to confess it. As difficult as it is to admit to pride, jealousy is harder to confess. It makes us feel insignificant. Isn't it ironic how something that causes us to feel so small and pathetic empowers us to be so very deadly?

We will cover a lot in this chapter. We will look at envy and jealousy along with covetousness and lust. Often, the terms envy and jealousy will be used in the conventional sense—they will be used interchangeably with one another. We will explore the connection between these things and the spirits behind Jezebel, Athaliah, and Ahab along with the death structures these spirits seek to release in our lives. Let's get started.

Jealousy and Envy: Same or Different?

Right off the bat, we learn that jealousy is no trivial matter. The scripture written at the beginning of this chapter tells us that while anger and fury are dangerous, no one can stand before the power of jealousy. Proverbs reminds us that "A heart at peace gives life to the body, but envy rots the bones" (Proverbs 14:30). Often the words "envy" and "jealousy" are used interchangeably. While both can be deadly, there is, however, a subtle difference. Sarah Protasi explains that "envy is about lack of a good, while jealousy is about the loss of a good."[169]

Both jealousy and envy involve another party. Through envy, we long for what another person has. Jealousy causes us to fear losing what we have to another. It also looks at what another has and desires to take it from them. In small doses, we can envy someone's beautiful new car and be content when we purchase one of our own. When we embrace full-blown jealousy of someone's brand-spanking new SUV, it is not good enough to merely purchase one for ourselves. We do not want the other person to have one and secretly hope that is

---

169   Sara Protasi, "What Is Envy?" In *The Philosophy of Envy*, 6-25 (Cambridge: Cambridge University Press, 2021), section 1.1. doi:10.1017/9781009007023.003.

scratched, dented, or somehow destroyed. We resent what they have and experience feelings of animosity towards them. R.T. Kendall writes that "jealousy is envy manifested."170 During this chapter, we will use both terms and view the ways both envy and jealousy can be sinful and destructive.

Envy Manifested

The Green-Eyed Serpent

In the previous chapter, we discussed how the first expressed sin was pride. Something stuck in that old serpent's craw that caused him to want to be like God. Could it be that what fueled this prideful desire for independence was jealousy toward God? Perhaps he coveted what God had—worship—and he wanted it all to himself.

Although we are not given insight into the divine rebellion, we do have a bit of insight into what happened in the Garden of Eden. St. Augustine believed that because of the serpent's fall from grace, he envied man's righteousness before God.[171] Andrew Louth borrows from another early church father, Ambrose and writes,

> *The cause of envy was the happiness of man placed in paradise, because the devil could not brook the favors received by man because man, though formed in slime, was chosen to be an inhabitant of paradise. The devil began to reflect that man was an inferior creature yet had hopes of an eternal life, whereas he, a creature*

---

170   R.T. Kendall, *Jealousy the Sin that Nobody Talks About: How to Overcome Envy and Live a Life of Freedom.* (Lake Mary FL: Charisma House, 2010), 25, Kindle.

171   Andrew Louth, ed., *Genesis 1-11* (Westmont: InterVarsity Press, 2001), 211. accessed April 4, 2023. ProQuest Ebook Central.

of superior nature, had fallen and had become part of this mundane existence.[172]

Again, we see how things work together in tandem with one another. Pride partners well with envy and with jealousy. The serpent turned green with envy as he looked upon mankind and wanted what he had, he despised them for having something that he had lost in his rebellion fueled by pride. He resented that man possessed what had once belonged to him, the favor of God.

It is written in the Wisdom of Solomon, "but through the devil's envy death entered the world, and those who belong to his company experience it" (Wisdom of Solomon 2:24, NRSVCE).[173] Both jealousy and envy can be deadly. Let's look at how this story of the serpent's envy and jealousy in the Garden is reflected in the lives of Sarah and Hagar.

I Want to Be You Instead of Me

Abram and Sarai were promised a child.[174] The wait was long and extended over 20 years. It must have been difficult for them to be childless and to hold onto the promise in their very late stages of life. Can you image that? Abraham was one hundred and Sarah was ninety when Isaac was born. They waited such a long time for the promise to be fulfilled. Although the story begins with Abram receiving God's promise in faith, we can understand how that faith could have waxed and waned over the long years of waiting.

Eventually Sarai gets the idea that God would provide a child to them through her handmaiden, Hagar. Abram agrees and soon

---

172   Louth, *Genesis*, 212-213.
173   The Wisdom of Solomon is an apocryphal book.
174   God later changes their names to Abraham and Sarah.

enough, Hagar gives birth to a son. Now, we all know how that happened. And we could all guess how that was going to work out.

While this idea seems pretty far-fetched in most of our current cultures, it was not necessarily uncommon during that time. Hagar, as a bondswoman, was considered Sarai's property. As such, it was not out of the ordinary for Hagar to be a surrogate to produce an heir for the family. While something may seem prudent as a practical means to accomplish a desired result, human hearts are a very different matter and seldom remain content to be practical.

Scripture, reports "when she knew she was pregnant, she began to despise her mistress" (Genesis 16:4b). Walton, Matthews, and Chavalas tell us that "women in the ancient world obtained honor through marriage and children. Although Hagar was a servant, the fact that she had conceived a child and Sarai had not caused her to hold her mistress in contempt. Sarai's reaction in abusing Hagar may be based on both jealousy and class difference."175

It is likely that both women experienced jealousy and envy against one another. Each wanted what the other had—Hagar wanted Sarai's position and Sarai wanted Hagar's ability to birth a child. Hagar was a bondservant and considered property. Yet, she could conceive and give birth to a son. Sarai could not. Sarai, however, was considered superior to Hagar in the cultural pecking order. This caused Hagar to resent her situation and to look upon Sarai with derision. I suspect she coveted Sarai's position. Like the serpent, she felt she deserved a favor that rested upon someone else. While it is understandable that Hagar would have longed to no longer be considered a slave, her response to her situation was not godly. She gave in to the resentment that accompanies our agreements with envy and jealousy. I cannot help but wonder if things would have turned out differently

---

175   Walton, *IVP Old Testament Commentary*, 49.

had Abraham, as their spiritual leader, done something to alleviate the rift.

There is no indication in Scripture that he did, so the chasm between the two women widened. Sarai continued to see the resentment in her handmaiden's eyes. It is reasonable to imagine that she must have suffered pangs of jealousy seeing that someone "beneath her" was able to give her husband what she could not. As she likely feared losing her status in Abraham's heart, she witnessed Hagar's hatred. She responded with unkindness, causing Hagar to flee into the desert. The Lord intervened by speaking to Hagar and she returned to her mistress as he instructed.

Jealousy runs deeply and is infectious. Eventually, it drove Hagar and her son Ishmael back into the desert where they would have perished without God's intervention. This time the problem was initiated through Ishmael. Sarai, now called Sarah, did give birth to a son in her old age and this caused animosity in Ishmael's heart.[176] Scripture tells the story plainly.

"The child grew and was weaned, and on the day Isaac was weaned, Abraham held a great feast. But Sarah saw that the son whom Hagar the Egyptian had borne to Abraham was mocking, and she said to Abraham, 'Get rid of that slave woman and her son, for that woman's son will never share in the inheritance with my son Isaac'" (Genesis 21:8–10). No doubt, Ishmael witnessed the green-eyed monster darting between his mother and her mistress. He learned first-hand how to look upon another with derision.

The resentment birthed through jealousy and envy drives wedges that can cause great divisions. One can only wonder how Sarah and Hagar treated one another over the years. It does not appear that they

---

176   Ishmael would have realized that it would not be Isaac and not Ishmael who would be heir to Abraham's vast holdings.

showed concern for each other's welfare. The pain they experienced through coveting what they did not have and being terrified of losing what they did have, caused them to be unable to have compassion for one another. Both Hagar and her son's lives were endangered by being cast out of the safety of Abraham's clan. We can see just how deadly the resentment of jealousy and envy can be in the story of two brothers, Cain and Abel.

Sibling Rivalry

The Bible's first recorded occurrence of one man's jealousy against another is the story of Cain and Abel. It is the age-old tale of sibling rivalry. Both Cain and Abel worked hard and brought the fruits of their labors as an offering to God. Scripture records that God received Abel's offering with favor but not Cain's.177 Cain's offering was based upon self-effort while Abel's was given in accordance with God's command. Yet, Cain became angry and his countenance downcast. Resentment grew and incited Cain to kill his brother.

Rivalry carries with it a connotation of opposition and competition. When rivalry is used in an unhealthy sense, it promotes conflict where one party desires to be superior to another. Sibling rivalry occurs when one child feels that his sibling is receiving more affection or affirmation than he is. This feeling is not limited to family dynamics. It can happen in the workplace, school, friendships, and even in the church. It is the feeling that someone else is receiving the favor that we crave or feel we deserve. The result is a downcast soul that desires to wipe out the competition. Just as Cain desired to

---

177   "In the course of time Cain brought some of the fruits of the soil as an offering to the Lord. And Abel also brought an offering—fat portions from some of the firstborn of his flock. The Lord looked with favor on Abel and his offering, but on Cain and his offering he did not look with favor. So Cain was very angry, and his face was downcast" (Genesis 4:3-5).

kill his brother, we will desire to kill the reputation and position of those who arouse our jealousies. It sounds harsh because it is. When we give into jealousy, we are partnering with a death structure that brings devastation.

Identity Crisis

In both the stories of Sarai versus Hagar and Cain versus Abel, it becomes evident that often something is wrong with the way a person views themselves or their circumstances for jealousy and envy to take root and bear evil fruit. Sarah was belittled in the eyes of her hand-maiden because of her inability to conceive. What she saw in the eyes of her servant reflected her view of herself within her heart. Hagar knew that she would never be the wife of Abraham despite her ability to produce the coveted heir. This touched the painful bruise in her heart that felt like she was somehow less than those who owned her. Cain felt treated unfairly because God did not accept his sacrifice. He could not see the issue in his heart that had caused the problem and his resentment grew.

Likewise, Miriam, and Aaron suffered a problem. They became envious of their brother Moses. As we explore a part of their story as recorded in Numbers 12, David L. Stubbs suspects that we will find that "the sins in the episode involve Aaron's and Miriam's identity, worth, and desire for status."[178]

Aaron had been Moses' right-hand man and had been his spokes-person from the beginning. He was given a significant leadership position over the children of Israel and accompanied Moses in his confrontations with Pharoah. When Moses was only 3 months old, Miriam helped save her brother's life when his mother placed him

---

178   David L. Stubbs, *Numbers* (Grand Rapids: MI, Brazos Press, 2009), 121. accessed March 21, 2023. ProQuest Ebook Central.

in a basket to avoid detection by the Egyptians seeking to kill all Hebrew infant male children.[179] Later, she is "also remembered as a prophet and a musician, singing the song of victory after Israel crosses the Red Sea…her leadership and importance are clearly marked, suggesting her exceptional character and activity."[180] Both Miriam and Aaron played significant roles in the ministry of Moses to lead the Israelites from captivity and through the wilderness.

After leaving Kibroth Hattaavah and traveling to Hazeroth, Miriam and Aaron did a strange thing. They began to talk badly about Moses because of the woman he had married. Now, here is where it gets sticky for them. "'Has the Lord spoken only through Moses?' they asked. 'Hasn't he also spoken through us?" (Numbers 12:2).

Aaron's role fulfilled the role of the high priest for Israel, and Miriam was known as a prophet. Clearly God spoke through them and they were calling attention to this fact to insinuate that there was nothing special about Moses. It was the equivalent of saying that Moses was not all that great and they could do everything that he could do. "At the interpersonal level, Miriam and Aaron are jealous of Moses's status with Israel and with God."181 They pointed out their gifted positions to gain status but it backfired terribly.

God heard the comments and he did not like them one bit. He, in turn, pointed out the humility of Moses in contrast with their lack of it. He also made a very strong point of the special relationship he had with Moses to talk with him "face-to-face" (Numbers 12:8b). We are told that the anger of the Lord burned against them and His presence was manifested as a cloud. When the cloud was lifted, Miriam was found to be leprous. This is interesting because when a person

---

179   See Exodus 1:12-2:10 for full story.
180   Stubbs, *Numbers*, 122.
181   Stubbs, *Numbers*, 123.

was diagnosed with leprosy, they were isolated from others. Miriam, too, was isolated for seven days of cleansing. Instead of being elevated before the people, she was sent out from them in shame.

When we are filled with envy or jealousy, we will often try to gather others to our side and make ourselves appear awesome. But it always has the effect of isolating us and causing us to look small. Aaron and Miriam wanted to be in what C.S. Lewis calls the inner ring.182 We crave the "secret intimacy" of those who are in power.183 Have you ever met someone that just had to be "in the know?" They are tormented when they do not have the inside scoop and will burn with envy to get into the inner circle of those who know what is going on behind closed doors. They crave being in the circle of the elite and feeling elevated over others.

While we are not told why Aaron was not afflicted with leprosy, Aaron did receive a rebuke. He had to ask Moses to beseech the Lord for Miriam's cure. Instead of being elevated over Moses, he had to rely upon Moses for mercy. Stubbs mentions that while it could be a result of the male focused society which caused Miriam to suffer more than Aaron, it is also likely she was the one who murmured against Moses.184 The word used for "talk against" was the feminine singular of the verb, therefore it is possible that she was the one who vocalized their desire to elevate themselves at Moses' expense. This would warrant a more severe punishment for her over Aaron.

We don't know exactly what caused Miriam and Aaron to speak against Moses and to desire to elevate themselves to a position higher than his. Stubbs postulates that it could have been jealousy over their

---

182   C.S. Lewis, "The Inner Ring," in *The Weight of Glory* (New York: Macmillan, 1949), 100.
183   Stubbs, *Numbers*, 123.
184   Stubbs, *Numbers*, 124.

loss of position because of his Cushite wife's influence over him.185 It makes sense they could have felt that her influence was somehow diminishing their value. Perhaps they were concerned they would no longer hold positions of honor. Whatever the case may be, what is interesting to me is where they had been just before envy overtook them.

Kibroth Hattaavah: Lust and Covetousness

Do you remember this place from the last chapter? Kibroth Hattaavah literally means graves of lust or graves of desire. Miriam and Aaron had been in this place before drinking jealousy's deadly poison. It is apparent that they were driven to covet the special position Moses held with God and with man. As we look upon the destruction that is loosed through envy and jealousy, it becomes clear why God instructed mankind to "… not covet your neighbor's house…your neighbor's wife, or his male or female servant, his ox or donkey, or anything that belongs to your neighbor" (Exodus 20:17).

An early church father, Aquinas, offers insight into God's wisdom in commanding us to flee from covetousness. In the Garden, when mankind desired to be like God, it became evident that human desire "has no limits."186 The problem is that we can become enslaved to desires that cannot be fulfilled. As each desire is met, it is accompanied by the craving for more. An idol never gives what it promises. It dangles a carrot in front of our faces to entice us. It says that if we will just do this one thing, then we can get what we so desperately want.

---

185   Stubbs, *Numbers*, 122.
186   Thomas Joseph White Op., *Exodus: Brazos Theological Commentary on the Bible* (Grand Rapids: Brazos Press, 2016) 189. accessed April 4, 2023. ProQuest Ebook Central.

But when we do the one thing, we are not fulfilled. More is required of us until we have become enslaved to our passion. Thomas Joseph White offers this explanation:

> *The human being can become lost in the indeterminate desire for temporal things, wandering indefinitely in the love of a multiplicity of creatures incapable of satisfying the heart's deepest native desire. Covetousness destroys peace of heart, undermines love of neighbor as one's self, obscures justice, and frequently produces wickedness; it is useless to man's true flourishing.*

He is describing to us the futility of coveting. What we covet will never fulfill our deepest longing or heal the void of woundedness within our souls. Instead of loving our neighbors, we grow to resent them and our bones begin to rot. We pervert justice to get what we want. We exchange peace for the wrath of evil desires. We fail to flourish. We fail to thrive. We fail.

Paul counseled all of the churches to "let each one live the life which the Lord has assigned him, and to which God has called him' [for each person is unique and is accountable for his choices and conduct, let him walk in this way]" (I Corinthians 7:17, AMP). Additionally, he wrote to the Philippians about being content in any state in which they may find themselves.[187] It is time that we learn this valuable truth. The life that God has given to each of us has purpose and value. It will look different than the lives of those around us. God will supply all of our needs. He will go above and beyond the basics because he is a generous Father. Here is what is real: "take delight in the Lord, and he will give you the desires of your heart"

---

187   "I know what it is to be in need, and I know what it is to have plenty. I have learned the secret of being content in any and every situation, whether well fed or hungry, whether living in plenty or in want" (Philippians 4:12).

(Psalm 37:4). We must shift our focus to the Lord. When we do, all things become clear. We can weather life's situations with joy, peace, and grace because he will cover us and provide for us.

There was something more in those graves than coveting, there was lust buried there too. Let's talk about it. Lust is described as "intense or unbridled sexual desire and intense longing or craving."[188] Sexual desires are a natural part of the way we are created. Despite puritanical teachings that often had sex seem off-limits, God created sex. When I was a child picking up on the cues of those around me, I was confused about why God created something that we were supposed to do but was considered such an ugly thing. Why had God created something bad and then made that the only way we could have children? It just did not make sense to me.

Sex was designed to foster deep intimacy between a man and woman who are in a lifelong committed relationship of marriage. It is a picture of two becoming one in love and vulnerability. It depicts our relationship with God as he desires to unite with us in intimacy. We have noted, however, that man's desires can be limitless and that this can cause deep cravings that are deadly to our bodies, souls, and spirits. White shares his thoughts on the matter:

> *Sexual passions and instinctual appetites are not intrinsically bad, but they can readily enslave human desires and mar human decision making. As an effect of original sin, fallen human beings frequently experience moral instabilities and failings in this domain (whether in thought, word, or action). This occurs when sexual desires have a negative effect upon the human mind and heart, becoming the occasion for disordered reasoning and action.*

---

188   https://www.merriam-webster.com/dictionary/lust

When we give into lust, we fail to think clearly. Lust fails to count the cost. It demands fulfillment and disregards the feelings of others. Lust is the opposite of love. Love honors, lust devours. Lust objectifies the person who merely becomes a means to gratification. One cannot walk in the lust of the flesh and be unified with God. Scripture teaches, "it is God's will that you should be sanctified: that you should avoid sexual immorality; that each of you should learn to control your own body in a way that is holy and honorable, not in passionate lust like the pagans, who do not know God" (I Thessalonians 4:3–5).

Lust is always attached to pornography. Some justify the use of pornography by claiming that it is just pictures or video and therefore they are not hurting anyone because another person is not involved. It is highly addictive and brings devastation to many lives. Jesus explained that adultery happens in the heart through the eyes. He said, "But I tell you that anyone who looks at a woman lustfully has already committed adultery with her in his heart" (Matthew 5:28). Pornography penetrates our eye gates and deposits addictive lust within our souls. In some ways the person depicted in pornography is not truly real. The person is made up to appear perfect and would not look nor act the same in life. In other ways, the person is a very real person who has been used as a tool to entice others into lust, no longer thinking rationally but spending copious amounts of time and money to feed the idol that enslaves. For a married person, pornography is adultery. As a single person, it is fornication.

Lust defiles. It brings devastation to not only the person who lusts but also the object of their lust. It defiles the marriage bed and inserts a wedge that destroys intimacy. God spoke through the prophet Ezekiel and compared Samaria and Jerusalem to prostitutes who lusted after other nations. Of Samaria, he said, "Therefore I delivered her into the hands of her lovers, the Assyrians, for whom she lusted. They stripped her naked, took away her sons and daughters, and killed her with the sword. She became a byword among women, and punishment was inflicted on her." (Ezekiel 23:9–10). Jerusalem experienced the same fate as her sister, Samaria. Lust not only defiles, it brings death. Lust will cause us to sacrifice things near and dear to us only to be left bereft and destitute, naked and ashamed. It seeks to destroy the person God has created us to be degrading us from children of the King to slaves of the serpent.

There are some spirits attached to lust that we must consider to be able to understand the deadly nature of lust, covetousness, jealousy, and envy. Fasten your seatbelts, this is not going to be pretty. We need to understand just how ugly jealousy and envy can be so that we will learn to hate it and refuse to allow it to fester within our hearts.

I Want That

Let's take another look and Ahab and his desire for something that did not belong to him. Ahab was out for a stroll and came across a lovely vineyard. He wanted it. He does what any reasonable potential buyer would do and approaches the vineyard's owner, Naboth. When he expressed his interest, Naboth refused to sell. Apparently, Ahab was not a reasonable buyer after all. Scripture records that "Ahab went home, sullen and angry because Naboth the Jezreelite had said, 'I will not give you the inheritance of my ancestors.' He lay on his bed sulking and refused to eat" (I Kings 21:4).

What we have here is a king who did not get what he wanted and responded by sulking. He coveted that vineyard and his response to not getting his way was to act like a child. Naboth had licked the red right off Ahab's apple by not giving him the object of his desire. Ahab was a king. He owned much land and lived in a palace. It was not enough. That is the problem with coveting. It tells us that no matter what or how much we have, it is never enough. Envy and jealousy with their partners of lust and covetousness create holes within our souls that cannot be filled.

This story gets worse, much worse. Ahab's wife, Jezebel, decided to take matters into her own hands. This scenario was perfect for someone like Jezebel. It gave her the opportunity to roll up her sleeves and take the reins of power she had coveted. The first thing she did was to write a letter as if it had come from the king himself. She used his seal and sent the letters to set her plan to take Naboth's vineyard into action. While Ahab was wallowing in self-pity, Jezebel seized the opportunity to get what she wanted. She acted as if she were king.

Her plan? Destroy Naboth and get his vineyard. Unfortunately, she was successful. Her false accusations against him resulted in Naboth's death. Ahab got what he wanted by partnering with a controlling, manipulative spirit which is akin to witchcraft. This controlling, manipulative spirit upon his wife was so strong that to this day we refer to this spirit as a Jezebel spirit.

Lord of the Flies

Ahab did a thing. He did several things, actually. As a matter of fact, Scripture tell us that he "did more to arouse the anger of the Lord, the God of Israel, than did all the kings of Israel before him" (I Kings 16:33b). The worst of his evil actions was to align with a foreign wife, Jezebel, and to bring her foreign gods into Israel. Scriptures indicates that Ahab had no fear of the Lord because he considered his sin a trivial thing.[189] His wife's name was a derivative of one of the god's she served, Baal.

Peter Leithart explains that the term Beelzebub or Baalzebub in the Bible can be translated Baal of Flies.[190] Baal means prince, so he is the prince of flies. The word also sounds much like another Semitic word that means dung. Leithart remarks that given her namesake, she is both a "daughter of Baal and dung whose corpse is destined one day to litter the ground."[191]

When we come into agreement with this awful spirit, we are like flies attracted to dung. We feast on the enemy's excrement until we are polluted with corruption. We embrace death and move from the abundant life God has planned for us. We must understand how this spirit works so we can recognize and avoid it in our own lives.

Prophecy Killer

Jezebel was not an ordinary idol worshipper. She was committed to bringing her idolatrous ideas to Israel with her. She made herself busy killing the prophets of the Lord God.[192] This type of spirit will seek to silence of the voice of the Lord within your life. Paul said that he desired that we all may prophesy, but this spirit does not want one

189   "He not only considered it trivial to commit the sins of Jeroboam son of Nebat, but he also married Jezebel daughter of Ethbaal king of the Sidonians, and began to serve Baal and worship him" (I Kings 16:31).
190   Peter J. Leithart. *1 and 2 Kings: Brazos Theological Commentary on the Bible* (Grand Rapids: Brazos Press, 2006), 119. accessed April 9, 2023. ProQuest Ebook Central.
191   Leithart, *Kings*, 120.
192   "While Jezebel was killing off the Lord's prophets, Obadiah had taken a hundred prophets and hidden them in two caves, fifty in each, and had supplied them with food and water" (1 Kings 18:4).

single prophetic utterance from the Lord to be spoken.[193] It wants to shut down any gift that glorifies God and leads others to repentance. Paul continued his exhortation to the Corinthian church about prophesy by teaching them that "…if an unbeliever or an inquirer comes in while everyone is prophesying, they are convicted of sin and are brought under judgment by all, as the secrets of their hearts are laid bare. So they will fall down and worship God, exclaiming, "God is really among you!" (1 Corinthians 14:24). It is clear why prophecy would be so abhorrent to the enemy of our souls.

Rather than hearing from God, this spirit wants you to hear from other demonic spirits. When Ahab died, his son Ahaziah took his place and continued to worship the foreign gods of his mother. Ahaziah was in an upper room of his Samarian home when he fell through some wooden bars. He was badly injured. His solution was to call for messengers, telling them to "Go, ask Baal-Zebub, god of Ekron, if I will recover from my injuries" (2 Kings 1:2 ESV).

God hears all and he was certainly aware of Ahaziah's intent to inquire of false gods. God spoke to the prophet Elijah and sent him to deliver a word to Ahaziah through his messengers. Elijah intercepted the king's messengers and told them to say to him, "'Why are you going to ask questions of Baal-Zebub, god of Ekron? Is it because you think there is no God in Israel?' This is what the Lord says: 'You will never get up from the bed you are lying on; you will die'" (2 Kings 1:3-4).

Idolatry is deadly. Seeking information through demonic means brings devastation and unrest. Why do we act is if God is not aware of our circumstances and only go to him as a last resort? Why do we

---

193   "I would like every one of you to speak in tongues, but I would rather have you prophesy. The one who prophesies is greater than the one who speaks in tongues, unless someone interprets, so that the church may be edified" (1 Corinthians 14:5).

rush to friends, the internet, and other sources of information before asking God to guide us?

In the story we have been exploring, idol worship was not limited to Israel; it had taken root in Judah as well.[194] Eventually, God sends Jehu to deal with this line of ungodly kings in Israel's and Judah's history. When he is met by Joram king of Israel and Ahaziah king of Judah, Joram asked him if everything was alright. Jehu responds by saying, "How can there be peace,' … 'as long as all the idolatry and witchcraft of your mother Jezebel abound?" (2 Kings 9:22). This killer of prophets operates in witchcraft.

Witchcraft and Robbed Inheritance

Part of witchcraft is manipulation and control to get what you want. We have certainly seen that Jezebel was a master of this. Just ask Naboth. She masterminded a diabolical plan to rob him of his inheritance.

When Naboth refused to part with his vineyard, he said, "The Lord forbid that I should give you the inheritance of my ancestors" (I Kings 21:3). Ahab wasn't just asking this man for a parcel of dirt, he was asking for his birthright, for the inheritance passed down from his ancestors to him. This was no small thing. God had forbidden the Israelites to sell the land given to them because it belonged to God.[195] It was to remain in their possession. Simon DeVries points out that Naboth had used this ancestral law as grounds to refuse to

---

194   After Solomon's son took the throne, there was unrest between Northern and Southern Israel. This led to the nations separating and Southern Israel became known as Judah.

195   "The land must not be sold permanently, because the land is mine and you reside in my land as foreigners and strangers" (Leviticus 25:23).

sell his vineyard to Ahab.[196] Ahab would have been well aware of the law.

Remember, jealousy demands what it covets and refuses to count the cost. It wants what it wants. Ahab nor Jezebel cared that they were demanding this man's inheritance against the will of God. They would have been well aware of the story about Esau and Jacob.

Ahab sought to get Naboth to renounce his inheritance—his birthright—by selling him his field. He would have known how much God hated Esau's willingness to sell his birthright. This meant nothing to him nor did it bother Jezebel in the least. As a matter of fact, this spirit seeks to rob its victims of their birthright in Christ. It seeks to destroy your God-given inheritance. We must not come into agreement with this spirit. Those who do will end up like Esau, losing their inheritance in the Lord.

Being unaware of this spirit's agenda can send your blessings and purpose to an early grave like Naboth. But it doesn't need to be that way. John's words declare that "My dear children, you belong to God and have defeated them; because God's Spirit, who is in you, is greater than the devil, who is in the world" (I John 4:4 NCV). You need not fear because it is written, "My Father gave my sheep to me. He is greater than all, and no person can steal my sheep out of my Father's hand" (John 10:29 NCV).

There is more to learn and consider before we go to the Lord in prayer and allow the Spirit of the Lord within us to defeat this evil. Let's continue to explore how this and another spirit operates.

---

196   Simon DeVries, *1 Kings, Volume 12: Second Edition* (Grand Rapids: HarperCollins Christian Publishing, 2015), 342.

Who is Baal?

Not only did Jezebel kill God's prophets, but she also organized and enabled nearly 900 prophets to Baal and to Ashteroh. We've spoken about how she sought to release false prophecies and silence the voice of God through his prophets. We can learn about the spirit of Jezebel by exploring the god she served. Stephen C. Russell and Esther J. Hamori note that not a lot was known about Baal outside of the Bible until about a century ago.[197] We do not have to mine ancient Ugaritic texts to understand the calamity associated with this god. We can see evidence of the fruits of bowing to it in the way the children of Israel responded to Moses' absence in the wilderness and the actions of Jezebel.

When Moses did not come back from the mountain of God in a timely manner, the newly delivered children of Israel became afraid.[198] They could not wait for Moses to return with a word from God. They grew impatient and came up with a plan to gather gold from the people to fashion a golden calf to worship. It just so happens that Baal is often represented as a bull. The people were sure God had deserted them and they needed an answer quickly. When we doubt God and act outside of his commands, we are in rebellion. Guess what scripture says about that? "For rebellion is like the sin of divination, and arrogance like the evil of idolatry" (1 Samuel 15:23).

Fruits of Idolatry

In Deuteronomy 28, God lists a bucket load of blessings that will chase you down and overtake you when you exercise the obedience of faith. This is God's heart towards us—to bless us far beyond what

---

197   Stephen C. Russell and Esther J. Hamori, *Mighty Baal* (Leiden, The Netherlands: Brill, 2020), 1.
198   See Exodus 32 for the full story.

we could imagine.[199] Likewise, we receive the blessings of the enemy when we choose to walk in agreement with him. Those blessings are called curses and they sound like this:

> *The Lord will send on you curses, confusion and rebuke in every-thing you put your hand to, until you are destroyed and come to sudden ruin because of the evil you have done in forsaking him. The Lord will plague you with diseases until he has destroyed you from the land you are entering to possess. The Lord will strike you with wasting disease, with fever and inflammation, with scorching heat and drought, with blight and mildew, which will plague you until you perish. The sky over your head will be bronze, the ground beneath you iron. The Lord will turn the rain of your country into dust and powder; it will come down from the skies until you are destroyed. Deuteronomy 28:20-24.*

Choosing idolatry and coming into agreement with the spirit of Jezebel and the false gods associated with this spirit is costly. At first, it does not appear to be a big deal. It appears to bring insight or comfort. Remember, an idol never gives what it promises. When the children of Israel sought the comfort of a golden calf, they were not comforted at all. Instead, about three thousand men of the people fell that day" (Exodus 32:28 NASB). While these curses may seem harsh, it is important to remember that we serve a merciful God of grace and compassion.

Deuteronomy 28 through 29 constitute a treaty between God and man. God promises to pour out blessings on those who walk in

---

199   "Now to Him who is able to do exceedingly abundantly above all that we ask or think, according to the power that works in us, [21] to Him be glory in the church by Christ Jesus to all generations, forever and ever. Amen" (Ephesians 3:20-21, NKJV).

his righteousness and likewise to withhold his blessing from those who choose not to come to him in the obedience of faith. Walton, Matthews, and Chavalas explored the elements of ancient Near East treaties and found that God's covenant to man in Deuteronomy contained something that these other treaties did not: "a forgiveness clause."[200]

God is not vindictive. He cannot wink at sin because that would be his coming into agreement with it. He is holy. He is righteous. He is compassionate and slow to anger. He provides a way for us to return to him in repentance. He provided righteousness for us because without him, we cannot be righteous. We have a choice. We can choose life and live under a barrage of blessings. Or we can come out of God's protective covenant and walk in the way of Jezebel and her rebellion. Instead of fruitfulness, there will be barrenness. Instead of health, there will be infirmity. As a matter of fact, God promises to put Jezebel on a bed of sickness. He proclaims, "Behold, I will throw her on a bed of sickness, and those who commit adultery with her into great tribulation, unless they repent of her deeds" (Revelation 2:22 NASB).

Not so Sexy Aspect of Jezebel

John penned letters from Jesus to the seven churches while he was in exile on the island of Patmos. To the church at Thyatira, Jesus said, "Nevertheless, I have this against you: You tolerate that woman Jezebel, who calls herself a prophet. By her teaching she misleads my servants into sexual immorality and the eating of food sacrificed to idols" (Revelation 2:20). The spirit of Jezebel is behind sexual immorality.

---

200   Walton, Matthews and Chavalas, *IVP Old Testament Commentary*, 204.

When we come into agreement with this spirit, our moral compass is no longer calibrated to the true north, which is Jesus and the principles of God. Suddenly, sex is taken out of context and becomes something that causes pain rather than pleasure and intimacy. At the end of this chapter, there is a link to a teaching I have posted about God's intention for sexual relations. I encourage you to listen to it, especially if you are single, have children, or work with youth.

Eating foods sacrificed to idols was an issue for Jewish believers. The New Testament talks about some issues that needed to be addressed when adding Gentile converts to Christianity whose foundation was predominately Jewish. A council was formed to make decisions regarding to what degree a Gentile Christian must become "Jewish." They agreed that Gentiles would not be required to undergo circumcision but that they would refrain eating foods that contained blood so as to not offend their Jewish brothers and sisters.

This verse in Revelation indicates that those who followed the spirit behind Jezebel were not adhering to this agreement. They were rebelliously doing as they pleased and "thus endanger[ed] the union of Jews and Gentiles in the church."[201] Unclean spirits seek to stir up discord. They are well aware of the power of unity among believers. We must refuse to feast at their table of gossip, disunity, and disharmony.

We are living in a time when sexual immorality is no longer considered immoral by many. If we look upon the sexually confused and immoral and think in our hearts that those kind of people deserve damnation, then we are not walking in the Spirit of Christ. We are, in fact, coming into alignment with the religious spirit that always brings death. We are called to love the sinner and hate the sin. That

201   Peter J. Leithart, "III.2. In Spirit on Patmos: Messages to Seven Angels—Rev. 2:1–3:21: "In *Revelation 1–11*, 129–208. London: Bloomsbury T&T Clark, 2018. Accessed April 9, 2023.

is a topic too big to cover in this context but I hope that this will stir your heart to seek the Lord about how we can do this in today's world. I hope that it will open your eyes to ways that religion has seeped into our faith and separated us from an intimate relationship with our Savior and caused us to be an exclusionary rather than separate type of people.

Lover of Religion

The spirit of Jezebel hates God but loves religion. This spirit set up false gods in Israel and was zealous about their worship. It will attempt to overcome the still small voice of God with loud cries of false worship to lead others astray. In Chapter One, we discussed the religious spirit and will not repeat that teaching here. It is important to make note of the link between the two spirits and how they work to bring us into a place of performance and works rather than of grace and the obedience that comes through trusting God.

When we love God and trust Him, our obedience is a natural outflow of our hearts. We do not feel the need to do things to gain His attention because we are sure of His promises. We know that when we turn aside from idolatry, He will never leave nor forsake us.[202] On the contrary, idols require a lot of work. When Elijah confronted Jezebel's prophets of Baal, they were trying hard to get Baal's attention. It is written: "They called on the name of Baal from morning till noon. 'Baal, answer us!' they shouted. But there was no response; no one answered. And they danced around the altar they had made" (I Kings 18:26). Isn't it incredible to know that our Father said, "Call upon me and I will answer you…?" (Jeremiah 33:3).

---

202   "Keep your lives free from the love of money and be content with what you have, because God has said, "Never will I leave you; never will I forsake you" (Hebrews 13:5).

Jezebel in a Nutshell

We've spoken about this spirit which takes attributes from foreign gods and manifests itself to bring rebellion and shut down the voice of God. Some things about this spirit may seem quite clear, while others may seem as murky as mud. Let's summarize the qualities of this spirt before we move on and gain a better understanding of what this thing does. Some of these qualities have been mentioned already, others are new. This spirit:

- Seeks to destroy your inheritance in the Lord—your spiritual, emotional and physical inheritance.

- Seeks to incite you to eat forbidden fruit. It defies the mandates of God.

- Seeks to speak false prophecies and to drown out the voice of God.

- Promotes rebellion.

- Hates authority and struggles to submit to those in authority.

- Seeks to gain authority through illegitimate means. (A person motivated by this spirit will come to those in leadership positions under the auspices of helpfulness. The real goal will be to undermine authority to gain recognition and position.)

- Seeks to control. This spirit needs to be in charge. This again can appear as wanting to be helpful but the real need is control.

- Is motivated by jealousy to uproot those who possess what it desires.

- Struggles to forgive and will bring up a past wrong done against them in a blink of an eye. (Now, you knew that we could not go through a chapter without mentioning the need for to walk in forgiveness, didn't you?)

- Does not have an identity of its own. Like Queen Jezebel sought to possess the identity of her husband, the king, this spirit will seek to steal the identity of those in prominent positions.

- Will promise to fulfill your desires. It will offer false prophetic words to flatter or seduce you into craving what you do not have. Just like Jezebel set out to give Ahab a vineyard that he had no right to possess, this spirit will seek to take what belongs to another and make us believe we have a right to it.

- Flatters and maligns at the same time. A person with this spirit will seek influence through flattery but will subtly bring up our flaws and weaknesses. When we respond against this assault, the spirit will not take responsibility but will use our weaknesses to cast the blame on us.

- Is seductive. This spirit will try to seduce you into coming into agreement with it. When Jehu came against Jezebel, this is what she did. "... When Jezebel heard about it, she put on eye makeup, arranged her hair, and looked out of a window" (2 Kings 9:30). She had hoped to seduce Jehu into agreement with her.

- Promotes sexual immorality. This spirit has no problem taking the spouse of another, because it is jealous and wants

213

what it wants. It will lead us to defile ourselves sexually in any number of ways.

Becoming Dung

Remember that Jezebel served the Lord of the Flies or the Lord of Dung? This is what God prophesized about her: "Jezebel's body will be like dung on the ground in the plot at Jezreel, so that no one will be able to say, 'This is Jezebel'" (2 Kings 9:37).

An agreement with this spirit will cause us to become unknown and devalued. We really do become like the object of our worship. Jezebel worshipped at the feet of the Lord of Flies and she became dung on the ground. She was eaten by dogs with nothing left but her skull, feet and hands.[203] We do not want to remain in agreement with this ugliness and become unrecognizable as the persons God has created us to be. We do not want to reflect dung. We want to become more and more conformed into the image of Christ.

As we seek to flee from this dung heap of selfish and jealous ambition, there are a couple more things to consider. Remember that Jesus rebuked the church for tolerating Jezebel. It would appear that this spirit has been too comfortable for too long in our midst. In all the talk we hear about Jezebel, we often forget a very important detail. Jezebel had a daughter.

---

203   "But when they went out to bury her, they found nothing except her skull, her feet and her hands. They went back and told Jehu, who said, 'This is the word of the Lord that he spoke through his servant Elijah the Tishbite: On the plot of ground at Jezreel dogs will devour Jezebel's flesh'" (2 Kings 9:35-36).

Athaliah: Jezebel on Steroids

Scripture teaches that when we sow to the wind that we will reap the whirlwind.[204] This means that there is an exponential growth in what we reap than what we sow. We sow what seems like little seeds, but they grow into much bigger plants. It is interesting that Hosea penned these words in relationship to Baal worship in Israel. This is exactly what happened in the story of Ahab and Jezebel.

They were envious and jealous as they coveted what they did not have. They were impatient and demanded their desires be met quickly. Their daughter, Athaliah, learned from masters of covetousness and rebellion. She saw her father crave a vineyard. What else did she see him go after in ruthless selfishness? She witnessed her mother use witchcraft through manipulation to get what she wanted. How many times did she see her mother flash those painted eyes to seduce another? She feasted at the table of lust for power with her parents and she learned well.

When Ahaziah was twenty-two years old, he became king of Judah and his mother was none other than Athaliah.[205] He was not a king that followed God, it is written that "he too followed the ways of the house of Ahab, for his mother encouraged him to act wickedly. He did evil in the eyes of the Lord, as the house of Ahab had done..." (2 Chronicles 22:3-4a). Leithart writes, "Queen Athaliah, who takes the throne in Judah, comes from the house of Ahab, and she has all the political finesse of her mother Jezebel—or Stalin—killing potential rivals as soon as she takes power (2 Kgs. 11:1; cf. 1

---

204   "They sow the wind and reap the whirlwind" (Hosea 8:7).
205   Scripture calls her a granddaughter of Omri but she is widely considered the daughter of Ahab and Jezebel. There are some scholars who still suspect she was Ahab's sister rather than daughter.

Kgs. 18:3– 4)."[206] Let me tell you, he isn't kidding. This woman was ruthless. She was considered a cannibal because she devoured her own descendants to possess what she wanted—the throne.[207]

When her son died, she looked around and noticed something. This was her grand opportunity to get what her mother always wanted—absolute power. There was only one problem. There were legitimate heirs to the throne. But, if they were to die, then the problem would be solved, right? Yikes. She killed all but one of the male members of the royal household and became an illegitimate queen to the throne of Judah.[208]

This is the product of jealousy and coveting. It will destroy anything that gets in its way. This woman destroyed her own family to fulfill her craving for power. The spirit behind Athaliah seeks to embrace the intentions of Jezebel. This spirit destroyed the destinies of those who had potential to rule and reign. As children of God, we have been called to rule and reign in Christ.[209]

As powerful as these spirits seem to be, God is more powerful. Like her mother, Athaliah came to ruin. We can see the evil fruits of jealousy when it is loosed from those seeking to steal and destroy in vicious power to get what they want. Jezebel and her daughter lusted after power, and worshipped idols who promised what they could

---

206   Leithart, *1 and 2 Kings*, 225. A review of Stalin's atrocities can be found at: https://www.history.com/topics/european-history/great-purge
207   She did not literally eat them but devoured their lives nonetheless.
208   "When Athaliah the mother of Ahaziah saw that her son was dead, she proceeded to destroy the whole royal family of the house of Judah" (2 Chronicles 22:10). 2 Kings 11:2 reveals that one child was safely hidden from Athaliah's destruction.
209   "But you are a chosen people, a royal priesthood, a holy nation, God's special possession, that you may declare the praises of him who called you out of darkness into his wonderful light" (1Peter 2:9). "Here is a trustworthy saying: If we died with him, we will also live with him; if we endure, we will also reign with him" (2 Timothy 2:11-12).

never deliver. But, what about daddy Ahab? He depicts the other side of this coin of jealousy and covetousness.

Back to Ahab and His Not-So-Trivial Sin

We have likely never seen a pout as profound as Ahab's royal pout over Naboth's field. It was a pout steeped in self-pity. He was a poor pitiful king who did not own one little field compared to the kingdom he possessed. We are dangerous when we feel sorry for ourselves. When we indulge ourselves in poor-pitiful-me attitudes, we are partnering with death. Really, we are. Self-pity by nature will not allow its longings to be fulfilled because then it would cease to have a reason for existence. Self-pity can then become a part of our identity. Self-pity by nature prevents fulfillment within our hearts. It is a vicious cycle. We cannot get fulfillment because that would negate the right to feel sorry for ourselves and get others to feel badly for us too. When we are having an affair with self-pity, even when we get what we want, it is never enough.

The other problem is that this woe-is-me attitude invites a Jezebel-type spirit to come and save the day just as Jezebel masterminded a scheme to get Naboth's field. It incites others to get mad or offended on our behalf. This is not a good thing. Jezebel got mad at Naboth because she was offended at his treatment of Ahab. This anger opened the door for her to seize power and wreak havoc.

Despite all of Ahab's accomplishments, he was often passive.[210] Passivity will cause us to avoid conflict and will open the door for us to accept mistreatment rather than risk the pain of confrontation. It is rooted in the fear of man rather than the fear of God. It will cause us to submit our God-given authority to a lesser being—the

---

210   "As for the other events of Ahab's reign, including all he did, the palace he built and adorned with ivory, and the cities he fortified, are they not written in the book of the annals of the kings of Israel?" (1 Kings 22:39).

very thing the Athaliah and Jezebel spirits seek to get us to do. It will cause us to be subservient rather than submissive. Subservient behavior acts as if the other person is better than or somehow more worthy than us. It screams, "I am not enough." Steve Sampson explains that "subservient behavior is giving up one's rights, but submissive behavior is being supportive, agreeable, and willing."[211]

We must learn to walk in submission to those God has placed in authority over us without rebellion or jealousy against them but also without subservience. This brings life. When we walk in passivity or subservience, we are negating our God-given identities. It puts to death who God created us to be and denies the purpose he has for our lives. It accuses God of playing favorites because clearly he has created others more wonderfully than he created us. Steve Sampson defines passivity as "the ultimate expression of spiritual immaturity… along with a refusal to change."[212] He also writes that "it has its roots in demonic blindness, where Satan assaults people's self-worth to the point that it suffocates their ability to stand up for themselves and confront situations and conflicts."[213]

Before we go before the Lord, let's consider how things look when jealousy is being released against us.

When Jealousy is Released Against Us

We often consider jealousy from the viewpoint of our being jealous of another. We have seen through these examples that when someone partners with jealousy against another, the affects can be devasting. I found myself feeling jealous over certain relationships in my life. I was confused by my feelings because in my mind I knew there was

---

211   Steve Sampson, *Discerning and Defeating the Ahab Spirit: The Key to Breaking Free from Jezebel* (Grand Rapids, MI: Chosen Books, 2010), 27, Kindle.
212   Sampson, *Ahab Spirit*, 18.
213   Sampson, *Ahab Spirit,* 27.

enough love in their hearts for all of us. As I pondered my feelings before the Lord, the Spirit revealed to me that someone was jealous of my relationships with these people. I was feeling threatened and misunderstood the source of the feeling of being replaced. It was the first time in my life that I considered that someone might actually be jealous of me.

It is important that we recognize when jealousy is being released against us so that we do not respond in an ungodly manner. Remember when we partner with this spirit, our bones will begin to rot. We can attempt to fight it in the flesh and end up devoured by it. We overcome through forgiveness, compassion, and refusing to come into agreement with the enemy. The Lord will be our shield against this deadly attack when we keep our eyes focused upon him and submit to his ways. Here are some of the ways that we can tell if someone is loosing jealousy upon us.[214]

- They flatter us but also casually and subtly point out our faults.

- We begin to experience feelings of unrest about the relationship.

- They will begin to copy us and try to act like us. This is not the same as someone emulating Godly behaviors that we exhibit. It is more like they try to become us rather than mirror qualities within us that they admire. Or they are trying to be better at being us than we are.

- They may begin to exclude you from social events and relationships.

---

214   Examples are derived from: Harini Natarajan, "How to Tell if Someone is Jealous of You – 14 Signs," reviewed by Dr. Nancy B. Irwin, PsyD, *Stylecraze*, March 6, 2023, https://www.stylecraze.com/articles/signs-of-jealousy/

- They will try to one-up you. Anything you can do; they can do better!

- They will try to create doubt in your mind about your plans and purposes.

- They fail to celebrate your achievements but will amplify your failures or weaknesses.

- They may even begin to deliberately try to steer you in the wrong direction or they will agree with you rather than helping you see the flaw in your plan because they want you to fail.

- They will often talk behind your back so that others will know that you are not all-that-and-a bag-of-chips after all.

The worst thing we can do in situations like this is to fight fire with fire. We cannot fight jealousy with jealousy, nor can we seek to control Jezebel type spirits through our own efforts to gain control. We must recognize what is happening and seek the Lord's wisdom. We may need to remove this person from our inner circle until they receive healing. Let me repeat what was said in the previous paragraph. *We must forgive them and walk in compassion rather than judgment, jealousy, and resentment.* We will need the Spirit's help, but He is always there when we seek Him.

Can These Things Ever Be Good?

Just like we talked about regarding pride, a little envy and jealousy can be used in a positive manner. Perhaps I notice how kind Sally Sue and Billy Bob treat one another and think that I would like that kindness to be better reflected in my own marriage. This is not a bad thing, unless I approach this desire from a lie of lack. In my ugly thinking, I may suspect that there are a limited number of good marriages allowed and that somehow by having a good marriage, Billy Bob and Sally Sue are keeping me from my fair share of goodness in my own marriage.

If, however, I go to the Lord with a sincere heart and share with Him my desire to have some of the same kindness in their marriage in my own, He can begin to move on my behalf. I have opened the door to the Holy Spirit to bring healing and maturity into my life and my marriage. It is important to note that my kind, healthy marriage may not look exactly like Billy Bob and Sally Sue's. For instance, my husband kisses me each morning before he leaves for work. If he were to come into our bedroom and say, "Good morning, honeybuns, I wub, wub, wub you, my little flower of blossoming beauty," I might be more inclined to vomit than to wub, wub, wub him right back. Some people might just melt at such words, I am not one of them.

Preparing to Pray

Let's take a look at the ways we have seen how jealousy and its cohorts manifest and how they seek to devour our lives so we will know specifically how to pray and be set free. Please ask the Holy Spirit to read through the list with you to highlight any areas that are specific to your life and make note of them. If there are any specific people or circumstances that require forgiveness and/or repentance, please make note of them as well.

Remember that specific prayers are more powerful than generic ones.

Holy Spirit, I ask that you move upon this beautiful heart and open their eyes to see where they have been stuck wandering around the same old tree because their hearts have been stuck in any of these areas. Lord, I ask that you give them courage and conviction to break free and step into life. In the name of Jesus, I pray. Amen.

- Resents the blessings of others.

- Like Ishmael, will mock others that appear to have what we covet.

- Desires status and resents those who have it. Will seek to get us to try to elevate ourselves at the expense of others.

- Destroys our peace.

- Prevents us from walking in the love of Jesus.

- Creates division, tries to gather sides pitting others against the object of our envy.

- Prevents us from walking in humility.

- Blocks repentance. Incites us to be stubborn (like a bull) and refuse to change.

- Drowns out the voice of God in our lives.

- Impairs our ability to rightly reason and discern.

- Births confusion.

- Causes us to doubt God.

- Seeks to destroy our inheritance in the Lord.

- Pushes us to act outside of God's timing.

- Causes us to adopt a pessimistic point of view.

- Promotes infirmity. (Remember God said Jezebel would be put on a bed of sickness.)

- Instills self-pity.

- Causes us to adopt either passive or aggressive behaviors rather than Christ-like assertiveness.

- Promotes sexual immorality.

Each segment of this chapter could be a book in itself. There are many layers of jealousy and the things associated with it. Some parts may have resonated with you, while others did not. After you have gone through the above list and noted with the help of the Holy Spirit the parts that are specific to you, be sure to also take note of the issues that may run in your family. Even if they have not had a stronghold on your life, you do not want these things in your bloodline to pass on to future generations or to have the opportunity to pop up unexpectedly later in your life.

When you are ready, proceed to the prayer section. Feel free to leave out any parts of the prayer that do not pertain to you or your family line. But please fill in specific areas of unrepented sin that the Holy Spirit has highlighted to you. For example, if you are praying over the issue of control, then repent of things that you have done to control others and forgive those who have done things to control you. Again, be specific. It is time to get free!

Prayer to Break Free of Jealousy and Its Partners

Lord, I come before You and I am so sorry that I ever came into agreement with jealousy and envy. I am sorry that I looked at what others had and resented them for it, wanting to possess what they had. I am sorry for resenting the blessings of others rather than being grateful for my own blessings.

I am sorry that I was overly protective of what You have given to me because I was afraid someone would take it from me. I am sorry that I have mocked others and for any way that I have tried to elevate myself over them. I am sorry for trying to make myself look better by demeaning others.

Lord, I deeply regret doubting You and for the things doubt drove me to do such as acting outside of your timing and taking matters into my own hands when I should have left them up to You. I am sorry for ever doubting that You have my best interests at heart and that You will always be generous and good to me. I am sorry that I have looked upon my life as less than others and break agreements right now with that lie.

I also break agreements with the lie of lack that told me that there were limited resources. Because I believed this lie, I thought because someone else had something, that it somehow took something from me. I could not be loved in areas where they were loved or could not excel in areas where they excelled and things like that. Lord, You have unlimited resources and do not play favorites, so I choose today to rejoice in the successes and blessings of others as if they were my own. Help me to do this and to appreciate what You have given me.

Lord, I renounce self-pity and break all agreements with it in the name of Jesus. I cancel this cycle of feeling sorry for myself and break the power of this sin off of my life.

Lord, I renounce all stubbornness and unwillingness to change the ugly in my heart. I hate it and refuse to partner with it anymore. I give You permission to bring conviction to my heart and help walk in repentance.

Lord, I renounce the fear of man and repent of all the ways that I have operated in it through either passive or aggressive behaviors. I am so sorry for any and all ways that I have come into agreement with the spirits of Jezebel and Athaliah. I am sorry for every time that I have tried to control, dominate, or manipulate to get my way. I am sorry for pitting people against each other and creating division. I repent of rebellion and stubbornness. (Remember to list the specific ways you have done this.)

Lord, I also repent of those times where I have partnered with an Ahab spirit and invited Jezebel to operate in my life to take control and get me what I wanted. I am also sorry for agreeing with this spirit in being childish and resentful when I did not get my way. (Again, be specific.)

I forgive and release all of my ancestors from my mom and dad, all the back to Adam for every sin of jealousy, envy, covetousness, and lust. I come into agreement with every legitimate claim the enemy has against me and my bloodline for agreeing with these ugly spirits of jealousy, envy, lust, and covetousness. Furthermore, I come into agreement with every legitimate claim the enemy has against me and my bloodline for partnering with spirits of Jezebel and Athaliah. I also come into agreement with every legitimate claim the enemy has against me and my bloodline for embracing an Ahab spirit. I ask for Your forgiveness for these unholy alliances and ask that You destroy every evil altar erected to these ugly spirits. Please destroy them permanently from me and my bloodline.

Lord, I am sorry for every indecent act of sexual immorality that I have ever embraced and that my ancestors committed. (Remember to be specific.) I repent of personal and generational lust including any fornication, adultery, pornography, sexual addictions, sexual deviances and any way that I or my ancestors have used our bodies in sexually impure ways. I choose to forgive those who used my body in unholy ways and break all soul ties with them. I command these ties to be broken and all pieces of them that remained in me to be returned to them right now. I command all pieces of me that have been stuck within that person or those persons to be returned to me now, washed in the blood of Jesus, whole and complete.

I renounce jealousy and generational jealousy. I renounce envy and generational envy. I renounce covetousness and generational covetousness. I renounce lust and generational lust. I renounce the spirit of Jezebel and all of its underlings including but not limited to witchcraft, rebellion, manipulation and control, both personally and generationally. I renounce the spirit of Athaliah and all its underlings both personally and generationally. I renounce the spirit of Ahab and all of its underlings both personally and generationally. I command these spirits to leave me and my bloodline now and never to return.

Holy Spirit, please come and wash me and my bloodline, cleansing me and my bloodline from all the effects of these spiritual attachments. I ask that You restore to me all the blessings stolen from me and my bloodline due to these unholy partnerships. I cancel any and all assignments of jealousy, covetousness, lust, spirits of Jezebel, Athaliah, and Ahab released against me or my bloodline.

Holy Spirit, I ask that You restore my health and remove all infirmity from me now. I ask that You restore my mind and remove all confusion from me now. I ask that You restore peace and remove all fear, anxiety, and unrest from me now. I ask that You give me the mind of Christ and restore my ability to hear the voice of God. I ask that You teach me to walk in the assertiveness of Christ, forsaking all aggressive or passive behaviors. Help me to walk in humility and trust, accepting Your timing as perfect, choosing to be content in what you have given to me.

I love You, Lord. You are good and You alone are worthy of all praise, honor, and glory. I celebrate the life You have given to me and look forward to deeper intimacy and partnership with You. In the name of Jesus, I pray. Amen.

Alternate Prayer A

Lord, I love You and appreciate all that You have done for me. I don't think that I have struggled with jealousy. I have felt the effects of jealousy targeted against me and I choose to forgive those who have loosed bitter resentment against me. I ask that You heal me of the effects of this target, and I cancel the assignments of jealousy that have been loosed against me.

Although I cannot specifically remember a time, I am thinking because I am a human being and we all deal with disappointments that I have likely felt pangs of envy or jealousy in my life. I repent for any way that I have given into these spirits and ask that You show me anything specific of which I may not be aware.

I am not aware of any time where I have coveted or struggled with lust. I ask You to help me stay on guard to remain free of lust or any sexual sin.

(If you have not personally dealt with issues of jealousy, covetousness, or lust but have seen this in your family, go ahead and pray the generational prayers listed above to cleanse your bloodline.)

Father, I ask that You help me to walk in peace and humility. I ask that You help me to stay in your perfect timing and forgive me for those times when I have been slow to obey or have rushed Your timing because I was impatient. In the name of Jesus, I pray. Amen.

Alternate Prayer B

Lord, this does not seem right to me. I have struggled so much and have lost so much in my life. It often feels as though my bucket is full of holes or that the bucket You gave me is much smaller than those around me. I see others prosper while I waste away. It hurts. It does not seem right. Why do others have things so much better and easier than me? Why do others seem to be much more easily accepted than me? Why is my health poor when those around me seem so healthy? I have tried to do what is right, but I suffer.

Lord, I don't feel jealous. I don't feel resentful. I feel sad and disappointed. It feels like You are expecting me to say all of this is my fault. That does not seem fair. I do not think that I am controlling. Honestly, if I don't do it, no one else will. Why doesn't anyone help me?

Lord, I often feel like others are trying to control me and
it is all I can do to stand up for myself. If I do not fight,
things will never work out for me.
I will always have to give in.

Optional Alternate Prayer

Lord, I cannot begin to speak up for myself. The people around me are so strong and capable that I feel small and weak around them. I cannot speak up because they drown out my voice. I am afraid of what would happen if I disagreed with them. I would lose my relationships and have no one to love me or to be my friend. I must be quiet to keep the peace.

This is really hard for me to pray but I am asking You to help me to see things from Your perspective because my point of view seems to be killing me if what I have read in this book is true. Holy Spirit, I give You permission to open my eyes to see and my ears to hear what the Lord is speaking to me. Help me come into agreement with You so I can be free of this torment. In the name of Jesus, I pray. Amen.

Walking It Out

- Look for ways to express generosity.

- Be faithful to tithe. Although we haven't discussed this principle, it is a vital aspect of walking with God in faithfulness. I promise, you will reap exponentially more than you sow. God said so. "Honor the Lord with your wealth, with the first fruits of all your crops; then your barns will be filled to overflowing, and your vats will brim over with new wine" (Proverbs 3:9–10).

- Pay attention to how you feel when a friend or coworker receives praise. Do you feel slighted? Do you feel that they got something that you deserved and they did not? Do you resent the accolades that they received?

- If you notice that you are unable to celebrate the success of another, ask the Holy Spirit to help you understand why and to reveal the lie under which you are living. Break agreements with the lie through prayer and ask the Holy Spirit to replace it with truth. For example, if you are feeling resentful about a coworker's promotion and the Holy Spirit reveals to you that you believe that evil always triumphs and that good guys finish last, you can pray something like this: "Lord, I break agreements with the lie that those who are unrighteous have an unfair advantage and that the good guys never get honored or promoted. I crucify this lie in Christ and resurrect the truth that God honors those who walk with him. Forgive me for believing a lie and for resenting my co-worker's promotion. I ask that You bless them in their new position and bless me in the place that You have called me to walk."

- Ask the Holy Spirit to reveal to you anytime that you are trying control situations. When you see you are trying to control, relinquish control back to God in prayer. Ask him to help you walk in godly submission.

- If you have been a doormat, ask the Holy Spirit to teach you how to be assertive. Break agreements with the lie that people who are assertive are mean, rude, and only care about themselves.

- Ask the Holy Spirit to restore your ability to hear the voice of God. If you think that you have never been able to hear His voice, pray this anyway. You probably don't remember being able to hear Him as a very young child. I believe children have an innate sense of hearing God.

- Practice hearing the voice of God. Do not ask yes or no questions but seek Him on the issues you are facing in your life. A great place to start is to ask Him what He thinks about you. Be sure to submit what you heard to someone else to confirm if the response sounded like God or like you.

- Be quick to repent and slow to justify your sinful reactions to the success or possessions of others.

- Glorify God! Make it a daily habit to offer him a sacrifice of praise. This does not have to be a marathon that takes hours. A minute or two here and there goes a long way.

Additional Resources

If you feel that you need to explore this topic more deeply, the following resources may prove to be helpful in your endeavor.

Jealousy the Sin that Nobody Talks About: How to Overcome Envy and Live a Life of Freedom by R.T. Kendall.

Healing the Orphan Spirit by Leif Hetland.

The Supernatural Ways of Royalty: Discovering Your Rights and Privileges of Being a Son or Daughter of God by Bill Johnson and Kris Vallotton..

Lead Like Jesus Revisited: Lessons from the Greatest Leadership Role Model of All Time by Ken Blanchard, Phil Hodges, and Phyllis Hendry. (This is a great book about servant leadership which it the polar opposite of controlling spirits.)

The Talk: God's Perspective on Sex: https://www.youtube.com/watch?v=B1xADmSCHAQ&t=148s

I always knew that he would
take me with him if he ever left.
But he did not.
As I clung to his pantleg begging to go,
he shook me loose and walked out the door.
I cried.
I screamed.
I broke into a thousand tiny pieces,
shattered by the knowledge that there really was
no one I could depend upon.
He did return.
But I had already learned in my heart that he could leave.
I decided to never rely on another person again.

CHAPTER SEVEN

Sloth—Trudging Through the Mire of Acedia

"…nor the plague that destroys at midday."
Psalm 91:6 NIV

After an argument, my father had decided to leave my mother that day. I was heartbroken to be left behind. During my early childhood, my parents argued a lot and while I had suspected the day would come when he would leave, it never occurred to me that he would not take me with him. As I stood on the porch and watched him drive away, the fractured pieces of my heart were forming a barrier against the pain. I decided to never depend upon another person again. I did not dream of growing up and having a family of my own. I dreamed of being fiercely independent and protected from being hurt again.

My father returned home and never again did he leave. He and my mother were married for 47 years before he died. Despite their ups and downs, they chose love and were happily married for many of those years. However, it took decades before the Lord unmasked the wound inside my soul and my heart began to recover. Sometimes things happen like that. Sometimes things can hurt so badly in a moment that we begin to live with false protections that are meant to free us from pain. They are entrapments that bring death to our souls. The sloth is much more than a weird animal that makes us laugh. It is a deadly attachment that causes us to trudge through life as if we are walking in quicksand.

What is Acedia?

The closest word we have in our modern vernacular to describe acedia is the word apathy. Apathy is the inability to experience joy or the inability to care about things that one would normally care about. While this sounds an awful lot like depression, there is a significant difference between acedia/apathy and depression. In her book, *Acedia and Me,* Kathleen Norris makes this distinction between the maladies:

> *Having experienced both conditions, I think it likely that much of the restless boredom, frantic escapism, commitment phobia, and enervating despair that plagues us today is the ancient demon of acedia in modern dress. The boundaries between depression and acedia are notoriously fluid; at the risk of oversimplifying, I would suggest that while depression is an illness treatable by counseling and medication, acedia is a vice that is best countered by spiritual practice and the discipline of prayer.*[215]

Notice the references to boredom, escapism, inability to make a commitment and to the feeling of being so drained of energy as to cause despair. This thing will try to suck the joy right out of us and

215   Kathleen Norris, *Acedia & Me: A Marriage, Monks, and a Writer's Life* (New York: Riverhead Books, 2008), 2, Kindle.

block us from embracing life. It is the manifestation of boredom with life itself.

This condition has been called a number of things: acedia, apathy, sloth and the noon day demon. These terms describe a malaise that can be difficult to pinpoint. When not being mistakenly identified as depression, it is commonly viewed as laziness. According to R. J. Snell, "it is a mistake to think that sloth is laziness."[216] As a matter of fact, one suffering with acedia may exhibit a frenzy of activities – none of which accomplish a durn thing. Acedia kills fruitfulness.

Charles Nault describes acedia as "a profound withdrawal into self."[217] In this condition we will find it difficult to experience or project Christ-like love. According to Nault, our actions will be motivated by the "fear of 'losing' something."[218] More than being afraid of losing love, this malady fears losing freedom most of all. It is the bondage that occurs when we love ourselves more than the purposes of God. Sloth is the result of demanding freedom from God and his plans for our lives.

For the purposes of this chapter, we will explore the spiritual roots of acedia and how to overcome it, agreeing with Kathleen Norris' suggestion that depression is another entity that is more physical in nature than spiritual. We will see how this thing manifests itself in our lives and how to be set free from its chokehold.

Manifestations of Acedia

Let's look at some examples of how this can manifest in our lives to better understand what it is and how it can affect us. A person struggling with this may experience:

---

216   R.J. Snell, *Acedia and Its Discontents: Metaphysical Boredom in an Empire of Desire* (Kettering, OH: Angelico Press, 2015), 10, Kindle.
217   Snell, *Acedia*, 10. Kindle.
218   Snell, *Acedia*, 10, Kindle.

- Difficulty in submitting to authority born from an intense desire to be free.

- Feelings of finding daily activities pointless. For example, why bother making the bed when you're just going to mess it up again anyway.

- Feelings of drudgery concerning present commitments even though the thought of them in the future tense may have seemed pleasant. A person may feel excited about attending their best friend's wedding only to have no desire to go when the date arrives.

- Hesitancy to make commitments.

- Feelings of chronic boredom. Things that once seemed pleasurable may begin to feel laborious.

- Loss of joy.

- A yearning for freedom from the daily grind.

- A driving need to accomplish tasks out of fear of losing something such as love or reputation rather than for the joy of doing them.

- A constant need to escape daily life. May spend many hours each day playing games, staring at television, or reading books. While these activities may have initially brought some form of pleasure through escapism, the feelings of comfort will continually decrease. The activity will no longer bring pleasure but the need to persist in it will continue and lead to greater feelings of drudgery.

- Self-centeredness.

- Gluttony. The inability to be satisfied births insatiable desires within our bodies and souls.

- Inability to be fruitful.

- Perpetual busyness.

- Inability to truly give ourselves in relationships.

- Feelings of inability to love others and God well.

Why Am I Here?

"Woe to him who strives with him who formed him,
a pot among earthen pots! Does the clay say to him who forms it,
'What are you making?' or 'Your work has no handles?'"
Isaiah 45:9

While my troubles with apathy may have begun on the front porch the day my father left, they were certainly acerbated by my response to the Christian's purpose of life. I was very excited to go to a private school in fourth grade. Part of my anticipation was that I would get to learn about God because the school was associated with a church. With much anticipation, I received my copy of *The Westminster Shorter Catechism*. It was very small and rectangular. I can still see the glossy white pages. Each unblemished page had questions with the appropriate answer written upon them.

I was looking forward to the assigned task of memorizing certain questions and corresponding answers until I read the first one.

Q. 1. What is the chief end of man?

A. Man's chief end is to glorify God, and to enjoy him forever.[219]

I read it again, and again. It could not be. I was sure that I must have misunderstood the answer. I wanted to know why I was born. I wanted to understand what life was all about. I wanted to know that I had a purpose and what it might be. But this was not the answer I expected.

My soul was full of pain. Was this the truth? All of the pain and hurt that I had endured was to make God look good? I was supposed to suffer and feel insignificant and small so that He could appear big and glorious? I was supposed to say that it did not matter what happened to me because God was good? Nope. That was not sufficient. I set aside the book and never again bothered with the assignments to memorize the contents. Deep down, I wondered if I was missing something but in my limited life experience, I could not imagine what it would be.

I almost threw the book in the trash, but decided to hold onto it to see if it made more sense later in life. Several years passed and I ran across the tiny booklet tucked between others on my shelf and decided to review the answer to the question. Hoping the answer would change, I opened the first page. The print hadn't changed, nor to me had the meaning. This time I threw the book away.

I did not know that I was opening the door to a life full of sloth, acedia, apathy, despair or whatever name it may be called. I was closing the door to choose life because life appeared to be devoid of joy. I did not want to be enslaved to a god who was so egotistical as I imagined the God of Abraham to be and I did not want to be burdened by the yoke of drudgery that manifested through ordinary life. I had

219   Assembly at Edinburg, "Westminster Shorter Catechism." Assembly at EDINBURGH, July 28, 1648. Sess. 19. https://prts.edu/wp-content/uploads/2013/09/Shorter_Catechism.pdf. accessed April 25, 2023.

this whole thing backward and yearned for freedom from the life I was given. I was making an agreement with sloth.

In response to what he calls sloth's terrible covenant, R. J. Snell writes, "as we become like him, rejecting the thickness of the created order, our freedom becomes unbearable light and we bleach out the dignity of the real in a fit of violence; we embrace a culture of death."[220] This culture of death teaches us to abhor the very things in life that will bring us joy; work and relationships with God and with others.

The Paradise of Work

In the beginning there was God. Before the beginning, there was God. My mistake was in viewing God as a being that was just smarter and more powerful than me. While He certainly is those things, He is so very much more. Snell puts it like this, "God is not the first beings among beings but transcendent, we do not bump into each other for glory or worth or freedom."[221] He is saying that God surpasses our ordinary state and is extraordinarily beyond our human experience. We are not in a power struggle with God because we are not even on the same playing field.

Therefore, God is not intimidated nor challenged by the abilities he places within man. Let me repeat one of my favorite verses, "As a father has compassion on his children, so the Lord has compassion on those who fear Him; for He knows how we are formed, He remembers that we are dust" (Psalm 103:13-14). He delights in us when we are submitted to his truth.[222] He designed us to be creative in our work to maintain and care for the world that he spoke into

---

220   Snell, *Acedia*, 5, Kindle.
221   Snell, *Acedia*, 21, Kindle.
222   "For the Lord takes delight in his people; he crowns the humble with victory" (Psalms 149:4).

existence, while at the same time building upon this incredible earth as we co-labor with him.[223]

After creating the universe, "The Lord God took the man and put him in the Garden of Eden to work it and take care of it" (Genesis 2:15). Leon Kass observes that "the earth's fruitfulness, we learn from the start, needs both the rain of heaven and the working of man… even before we meet him, man is defined by his work…"[224] In his estimation, Kass views man as a servant rather than a ruler.

God created the earth and observed that there was no one to "work the ground" (Genesis 2:5). The Hebraic word translated as *work* is 'avad which "means 'to work' but also 'to serve.'"[225] This is the very same word used in verse 15 when God puts man in the Garden to work and take care of the land. Scripture reveals that God gave man dominion to rule.[226] But we can see through the dual meaning of 'avad, that this is not a tyrannical rulership. It is a type of rule that denotes the same compassion and care God has for us. This concept of governing with a servant's heart is further reflected in the teaching of Jesus to his disciples.

> *"So Jesus called them together and said, "You know that the rulers in this world lord it over their people, and officials flaunt their authority over those under them. But among you it will be different. Whoever wants to be a leader among you must be your*

---

223   "He has filled them with skill to do all kinds of work as engravers, designers, embroiderers in blue, purple and scarlet yarn and fine linen, and weavers—all of them skilled workers and designers" (Exodus 35:35). This is an example of God gifting man with creativity.
224   Kass, Genesis, 58.
225   Kass, *Genesis*, 58.
226   "Then God said, "Let us make mankind in our image, in our like-ness, so that they may rule over the fish in the sea and the birds in the sky, over the livestock and all the wild animals, and over all the creatures that move along the ground" (Genesis 1:26).

servant, and whoever wants to be first among you must be the slave of everyone else. For even the Son of Man came not to be served but to serve others and to give his life as a ransom for many." Mark 10:42-45.

When we embrace the servant heart of Christ and seek to honor the Lord through our work, there is peace and rest in it. Snell remarks that "through good work both we and the world are perfected, made suitable adornments for God's own temple."[227] This view requires that we embrace the world as good. Paul, quoting King David, exhorted the church at Corinth to embrace the truth that "The earth is the Lord's, and everything in it" (1 Corinthians 10:26 and Psalm 24:1).

If the earth is God's and God declared it to be good, then it is indeed good. As we embrace the truth that the world is good, we begin to walk in life. Acedia hopes to ensnare us in the lie that the world is not worth our time nor our energy. It desires to focus our attentions upon evil and to convince us that our purpose is simply not worth pursuing.[228] Pardon my language, but sloth exclaims, "Life's a bitch, then you die."[229]

It also tries to make us believe that we are the center of our own universe and that our own needs and desires should be the primary focus of our being. When we grab hold of the idea that we are sovereign over our lives, we begin to pursue empty pleasures that never satisfy. We see ourselves as autonomous. With the freedom to govern our own affairs unencumbered by Christian values, we eventually become lethargic and bored at the futility of it all. We reject the

---

227   Snell, *Acedia*, 95.
228   Snell, *Acedia*, 95. Snell states that "the slothful...have a repugnance (sadness) at their own purpose."
229   A religious spirit would be offended by this statement. Aren't we glad we dumped that bugger bear in an earlier chapter?

dignity of others chasing our own exaltation. When we choose, with God's help, to love the world and to care for others, we are agreeing to dump the chains of apathy and pick up the yoke of Christ. Jesus exhorts us to "Take my yoke upon you and learn from me, for I am gentle and humble in heart, and you will find rest for your souls. For my yoke is easy and my burden is light" (Matthew 11:29-30).

The Paradise of Companionship

"Then I was constantly at his side. I was filled with delight day after day, rejoicing always in his presence, rejoicing in his whole world and delighting in mankind."
Proverbs 8:30-31.

We have noted that God looked upon His creation and declared it good. But as He looked upon Adam's aloneness, he declared that it was not good.[230] Gordon Wenham notes that "The God of Genesis is totally concerned with man's welfare. Man is to be more than a tiller of the ground, his need is for companionship, a lack which the creator is anxious to fill."[231] While Adam slept, God fashioned woman from his side.

Notice Adam's response, "This one at last is bone of my bones and flesh of my flesh; this one will be called 'woman,' for she was taken out of man" (Genesis 2:23, NEV). While Adam had been busy naming the animals, it was noted that "no suitable helper was found" (Genesis 1:20). Yet, when he is presented with Eve, he exclaims, "At last!" It seems to portray a picture of man noticing that

---

230   "The Lord God said, "It is not good for the man to be alone. I will make a helper suitable for him" (Genesis 2:18).
231   Gordon John Wenham, *Genesis 1-15, Volume 1*. Word Biblical Commentary (Grand Rapids, Michigan: Zondervan Academic, 2014), 53.

an extraordinary thing had occurred. After viewing countless creatures, he finally finds someone like himself. Rather than looking at her with suspicion or contempt, he accepts her and rejoices over their relationship. Like the Father, he sees that she is good and accepts the gift of intimacy and vulnerability.

Adam also said that she was bone of his bones and flesh of his flesh. We can find the significance in this through the exploration of what these words often depict in the Bible. Flesh often represents weakness while bones reflect strength. Comparing this to David's covenant with Israel in 2 Samuel 5:1, Victor P. Hamilton reflects that:

> *Taken this way, the man's this one, this time, is bone of my bones and flesh of my flesh becomes a covenantal statement of his commitment to her. Thus it would serve as the biblical counterpart to the modern marriage ceremony, "in weakness [i.e., flesh] and in strength [i.e., bone]." Circumstances will not alter the loyalty and commitment of the one to the other. So understood, the verse does not attribute strength to the man and weakness to the woman, as if he is the embodiment of bone and she is the embodiment of flesh. Both the man and the woman share the entire spectrum of human characteristics, from strong to weak.[232]*

Man had done a very good thing. Adam and Eve embraced each other and the world around them as good. Snell expounds, "The instruction of Genesis helps us understand that we are responsible to love all that is good…our self is perfected by activity, even if we need

---

232   Hamilton, Victor P. Hamilton, *The Book of Genesis, Chapters 1-17: New International Commentary on the Old Testament* (Grand Rapids, MI: Wm. B. Eerdmans Publishing), 180, Kindle.

to come to learn this through our work."[233] Just as Adam and Eve accepted their purpose and accepted relationship with one another with joy and commitment, we, too, need to come into agreement with God's purpose for our lives. We need to love the Lord our God and to love one another as we love ourselves. Sloth hates that.

The Paradise of Intimacy with God

"How priceless is your unfailing love, O God!
People take refuge in the shadow of your wings."
Psalm 36:7

In the Garden, man had purpose and experienced fellowship with God. It is such a beautiful picture to imagine God bringing the animals to Adam to name. We can almost see the gleam in God's eye as Adam pronounced a name upon each creature. Likewise, Adam's eyes must have shown with joy over God's acceptance of his choice. Did Adam and God laugh at the silliness of the monkeys? Did Adam look at God with awe and appreciation of the majesty of the lion or the beauty of the elephant? Did they stand together in appreciation of the goodness that God had designed?

When man fellowshipped with God, he came into the presence of his Creator who had declared not only that he was good but was very good. He was able to bask in God's unfailing love and take refuge in the shelter of his wings. He had purpose and had no experience of shame: until he decided that he wanted reason apart from God and craved a wisdom he was not equipped to handle. They thought they would experience freedom. So they ate and with their

---

233   Snell, *Acedia*, 34.

new perspectives, their eyes were opened to shame. They were liberated into bondage.

The Cost of Freedom

When I was about sixteen years old, I took up an interest in writing poetry. Pouring my heart onto the pages through my pen, these words appeared on the paper, "perhaps I have become enslaved by my quest for freedom." I had no idea how true those words were.

Sloth demands complete independence even from God and the plans he has for our lives. Charles Taylor observes that "The ethic for freedom and order has arisen in a culture which puts at its centre a buffered self."[234] He describes a buffered self as one who believes he has attained a semblance of power to create some type of order within himself and the world in which he exists. He says that "beyond power and reason…there is a sense of invulnerability."[235] Ah, there's that fig leaf, another attempt to hide. It reminds me of hiding under the covers as a child. If I cannot see you, then surely you cannot see me. But we are seen. Not only are our attempts to hide ineffective; they are costly.

When we seek to disrobe ourselves from God's covering, preferring instead the fig leaves of our choosing, we are removing ourselves from the divine order of things. Rather than being invulnerable, we become more vulnerable to the effects of sin. As a result, we experience a "sense of malaise, emptiness, a need for meaning."[236] We buy our ticket to this illusion of freedom at a very high price, "the loss of anything worth dying for."[237] This idea depicts a loss of passion

---

234   Charles Taylor, *A Secular Age*. Gifford Lectures, 1999. (Cambridge, MA: Harvard University Press, 2007), 300.
235   Taylor, *Secular Age*, 300.
236   Taylor, *Secular Age*, 302.
237   Taylor, *The Ethics of Authenticity* (Cambridge MA: Harvard University Press, 1991), 12, Scribd.

which diminishes those things in our lives that are worth living for. In our demand for autonomy, the freedom we seek leads us into an apathetic bondage. The inability to truly care about life and others robs us of not only of joy, but the ability to embrace life.

When we put ourselves at the center of the universe, it is only a matter of time "that the dignity of others must be rejected, for everyone else threatens our unchecked sovereignty."[238] When someone dares require of us more than we are willing to give or disagrees with our point of view, we become angry or enraged. Their defiance of our sovereign rule is considered blasphemous to our being and hatred grows. In contemplating the effects of acedia, Evagrius of Ponticus, a fourth century monk wrote, "Moreover, the demon sends him hatred against the place, against life itself, and against the work of his hands..."[239]

Ultimate Price of Freedom

It is written, "Then the man and his wife heard the sound of the Lord God as he was walking in the garden in the cool of the day..." (Genesis 3:8a). This sounds nice. Pictures of a lush, green garden colored by the setting of the sun fill our minds with peace. But the scene is not peaceful at all. Man does not experience peace at the sound of God's footsteps because man's response was to hide "from the Lord God among the trees of the garden" (Genesis 3:8b).

An early church father, Chrysostom, finds it appalling that we would assign feet to God and assume that He actually strolls.[240] To him, the idea seems to negate the omnipresence of God. Perhaps it is as another father of the faith, Ephrem the Syrian, suggests that "God

238   Snell, *Acedia*, 13.
239   Snell, *Acedia*, 10.
240   Andrew Louth, ed., *Genesis 1-11* (Westmont IL: InterVarsity Press, 2001) 222. ProQuest Ebook Central, accessed April 19, 2023.

endowed his silent footsteps with sound so that Adam and Eve might be prepared, at that sound, to make supplication before Him who made that sound."[241]

Suddenly, in their desire for autonomy, to be god-like, the presence of God became undesirable to them. While they covered only their private parts from each other, they hid their entire selves from God in shame. Shame speaks. Kass explains that it "expresses pain over the gap between our wished-for estimable or idealized self-image and the now discovered fact of our lowliness or baseness."[242]

It is reminiscent of a child who always looks forward to their parents coming home. When I would arrive to pick up my daughter after a long day's work, she would run full force and jump into my arms. This is something that my puppies still do. They are delighted to see me. Unless, of course, they are in trouble. Then they, like our children, hide hoping to avoid the consequences of their misdeeds. Adam and Eve hid.

Jonah

When talking about the rejection of one's purpose and the hatred of life itself, Jonah comes to mind. He was sent to bring the gospel to the Ninevites. The problem was that he hated them. He certainly had some significant reasons for his opinion. The prophet Nahum prophesied against the people and his description of the city was not good. "Woe to the city of blood, full of lies, full of plunder, never without victims!" (Nahum 3:1). Sounds like a gruesome place, doesn't it? God was sending one of his prophets to a significant enemy of Israel. Jonah was not happy to have been chosen. "He simply wanted no

---

241   Louth, *Genesis*, 222.
242   Kass, *Genesis*, 91.

part of something so horrible as mercy shown to a brutal, oppressing, enemy nation."[243]

Instead of going to Nineveh, Jonah boards the first boat in the opposite direction. He did not want to give his enemies a chance to repent so he "ran away from the Lord and headed for Tarshish" (Jonah 1:3). Jonah did not merely stay home and disobey the Lord. He set sail to another place. Douglas Stuart suggests that "Jonah's attempt to flee is not entirely illogical, no matter how ultimately unsuccessful it may have been."[244] Jonah was removing himself from the place where he believed that God spoke. By leaving Israel, he was hoping to be spared hearing any more directives from the God of Israel.

When we seek to flee from the shelter of the Almighty, deciding instead to do our own thing, we become susceptible to the storms of this world. Jonah was no exception. He rejected his purpose and pursued the open sea away from his Creator. Sure enough, a violent storm arose and Jonah was thrown overboard and into chaos.

Going Against the Designed Order of Things

Jonah defied God's call and found himself in a terrible fix. Scripture teaches that there are several laws that govern our lives. They are like gravity—what goes up must come down. If you throw an apple up into the air and it falls and hits you on the head, the apple is not getting even with you. It is merely subject to the laws of gravity. There are certain spiritual laws that work much the same way.

Sometimes, like with Jonah, God will send storms to bring you back to life. We will see this type of God's grace upon Jonah shortly. Before we explore that, let's look at the spiritual laws that are like

---

243   Douglas Stuart, *Hosea-Jonah, Volume 31*. Word Biblical Commentary (Grand Rapids, MI: Zondervan Academic, 2017), 453.

244   Stuart, *Hosea-Jonah*, 450.

gravity where there is an expected outcome for certain actions or inactions.

- "Honor your father and your mother, as the Lord your God has commanded you, so that you may live long and that it may go well with you in the land the Lord your God is giving you" (Deuteronomy 5:16). Conversely, those areas in our lives which we dishonor our parents will not go well. John and Paula Sandford taught that this "goes far to explain the cause of most marital problems, child-rearing dilemmas, and moral and immoral inclinations."[245] Not all parents are the best role models. While we may not always be able to respect the actions of a parent, we are called to honor their position as our parents. This can require Holy Spirit help especially in cases of abuse or neglect.

- "Do not judge, or you too will be judged. For in the same way you judge others, you will be judged, and with the measure you use, it will be measured to you." Matthew 7:1-2. No kidding, just as soon as we look at our neighbor and decide they are an arrogant jerk of epic proportions, someone is going to look at us and decide that we are a great big jackleg full of pride.

- "For if you forgive other people when they sin against you, your heavenly Father will also forgive you. But if you do not forgive others their sins, your Father will not forgive your sins" (Matthew 6:14-15). We have spoken about forgiveness previously, but a reminder never hurts, does it? If there is a struggle to forgive someone in our lives, we must ask God to

---

245   John Loren and Paula Sandford, *Transforming the Inner Man* (Lake Mary, FL: Charisma House, 2007), 88-89.

help us to be willing and to help us be able. Often in prayer, I give God permission to change my heart.

- "Do not be deceived: God cannot be mocked. A man reaps what he sows" (Galatians 6:7). We cannot plant seeds of unforgiveness, bitterness, disobedience and the like and expect to live in a garden of compassion, love, and unity. It does not make sense. It we are reaping ugly, then we need to check our hearts.

What Sloth Delivers

It appears that Adam and Eve walked in unity until they went against God and determined to be free from relying upon Him for wisdom. They ate from the forbidden tree and then they began the art of hiding. Not only did they hide, but they also learned the art of blaming. Eve blamed the serpent. Adam blamed Eve and in a sense blamed God. When God asked Adam if he had partaken from the forbidden tree, Adam replied, "The woman you put here with me—she gave me some fruit from the tree, and I ate it" (Genesis 3:12). Did you catch that? He reminds God that it was God's idea to bring the woman into the Garden.

One can almost envision a sloth hanging from that durn tree tempting man with independence from God, saying with a wink that God couldn't have really meant what He said. We can see that old sloth wagging tickets at the seaport saying with an understanding tone, "Of course, you can't do what God has asked you to do. Why, that's just impossible."

Kass teaches that man learned that "his choice for humanization...or autonomy really means at the same time also estrangement from this world, self-division, division of labor, toil, fearful knowledge of death, and the institution of inequality in, rule and subservience."[246] Dang, this is not good stuff. Sloth promises freedom but it delivers death. Let's look at what its deadly strongholds look like.

Boredom and Dissatisfaction

"A sluggard's appetite is never filled,
but the desires of the diligent are fully satisfied."
Proverbs 13:4

When we partake of sloth's temptations of false freedom, we experience an overarching sense of boredom. Boredom is the inability to occupy our minds and feel settled within our souls. We find ourselves restless and unable to engage with life. We simply do not know what it is that we are supposed to do. This happens when we fail to embrace God's purpose for our lives. Instead, we binge eat and try to escape into fantasy worlds of television, books, sex, shopping, drugs or the internet.[247] Perhaps sloth does not affect any one part of our bodies as much as our thumbs as we lifelessly scroll through social media hoping to find enjoyment through other people's lives. But, despite all our efforts, nothing satisfies the longing in our souls.

---

246   Kass, *Genesis*, 95.
247   We did not specifically discuss gluttony in this chapter for the sake of time. But it can be a symptom of sloth. "A sluggard buries his hand in the dish; he will not even bring it back to his mouth!" (Proverbs 19:24). Mindless eating and never feeling satisfied can be a sure sign of the perpetual boredom of sloth.

Blocked and Ineffective

> "The way of the sluggard is blocked with thorns,
> but the path of the upright is a highway."
> Proverbs 15:9

Remember we discussed earlier that sloth does not always manifest as doing nothing. Sometimes it reveals itself in perpetual busyness that accomplishes very little if anything at all. When we have gone against God's divine order, our paths become littered with thorns. Life will feel like an uphill battle. Whether in relationships or work, we will feel blocked at every turn. Instead, when we come into God's sheltering embrace, he promises that "he will command his angels concerning you to guard you in all your ways; they will lift you up in their hands, so that you will not strike your foot against a stone" (Psalm 91:11-12).

Irreverence and Lack of Wisdom

> "Timothy, guard what has been entrusted to your care.
> Turn away from godless chatter and the opposing ideas of what is falsely
> called knowledge, which some have professed and in so doing
> have departed from the faith."
> 1 Timothy 6:20-21

When we choose to turn our backs on God and go our own ways, we will begin to embrace "godless chatter" and find ourselves speaking against God and His truths. I believe that is called blasphemy. We fail to embrace the wisdom of God and instead choose the worldly wisdom. Scripture tells us the end result of this path, "There is a way that appears to be right, but in the end it leads to death" (Proverbs 14:12).

Excuses, Excuses

> A sluggard says, "There's a lion in the road,
> a fierce lion roaming the streets!"
> Proverbs 26:13

Sloth will offer all sorts of excuses to not do what God has called us to do. What lion is laying in your road? Do you find that you ignore the yearnings God has placed in your heart for some really good reasons? Perhaps you think things like, "I am too shy" or "I do not have enough money" or "I have too much on my plate already; I am just too busy."[248] All of these are excuses, imaginary lions in the road used to avoid embracing our purposes—the very life God has ordained for us. I never felt wise enough, or healed enough to do what God was calling me to do. Finally, years had passed and I realized that I would probably be nearly a hundred before I was grown up enough to answer God's call. What I needed was the maturity to believe that "Lord, you establish peace for us; all that we have accomplished you have done for us" (Isaiah 26:12). God accomplishes for us all that he

---

248   You may have noticed that when Kass mentioned autonomy, he said that one of things that came along with it was inequality. Men and women were both created in God's image. Woman came from man but man is birthed through the woman. We need each other. Likewise, scripture teaches that "There is neither Jew nor Gentile, neither slave nor free, nor is there male and female, for you are all one in Christ Jesus" (Galatians 3:28). When we embrace inequality, whether it is based upon gender, race or skin color…it is embracing a structure of death. We agree with sloth when we use any of these issues to avoid our destiny. I cannot do that because I am the wrong color or I am a woman or I am an American—these are all excuses. We are equal before God. No more excuses.

wills us to do. When we say yes to Him, He does the rest. We just need to keep saying, "Yes, Lord!"

Failure to Take Responsibility

> "Godly sorrow brings repentance that leads to salvation
> and leaves no regret, but worldly sorrow brings death."
> 2 Corinthians 7:10

We make mistakes. We sin. There is a sorrow that all too often stops short of bringing life back to the areas in which we have partnered with death. This is worldly sorrow that is mostly concerned with hating the consequences of our sin. We are sorry we got caught and we are sorry for what we have lost as a result of our actions but that is about as far as our sorrow extends. It does not grieve for the offense against God. Godly sorrow means that we change. It means that we submit the area of our lives to God which had previously rebelled against him.

You may recall that Adam and Eve had a bit of difficulty with this. Their fingers were pointing in all manner of directions trying to excuse what they had done. With God's help they were able to admit their wrong and receive his covering. We must take responsibility for our actions like the prodigal son. He came to his father and exclaimed, "Father, I have sinned against heaven and against you…" (Luke 15:21). Lord, give us the wisdom and the humility to acknowledge our sin before you. Give us repentant hearts so that we can be free to be yoked with Christ and live the life you have called us to live!

A Whale of Grace: Becoming Free

Last place we left Jonah, he was fleeing from God. This flight left him drowning in a stormy sea. God, in His mercy, sent a big fish to swallow Jonah. The fish was not punishment. It was provision. It was a lifeboat. A very strange one, but it got the job done. Although he was running from God, God did not run from him. Stuart does not think Jonah believed that his attempt to escape would prevent God's message from reaching Nineveh rather he writes that Jonah "thinks he has a chance to avoid a restatement of the divine call by fleeing."[249] Perhaps it was as Stuart suspects that Jonah felt if he ran from God that God would supply someone else to do the job and he could live peacefully in a land where God's call would no longer reach his ears. Do we likewise sit on the sidelines assuming that if we ignore God's prompting someone else will step up to the plate?

Instead of living peacefully in a cocoon of obscurity, Jonah is floundering in a sea of rebellion and eventually finds himself inside the belly of God's grace. The big fish, while it must have been quite unpleasant, provided safety from drowning. It was God's mercy to give Jonah time to think things out and decide to embrace God's call. Sitting in the muck and mire of life apart from God, Jonah cries out:

> *"When my life was ebbing away, I remembered you, Lord, and my prayer rose to you, to your holy temple. Those who cling to worthless idols turn away from God's love for them. But I, with shouts of grateful praise, will sacrifice to you. What I have vowed I will make good. I will say, 'Salvation comes from the Lord.'" Jonah 2:7-9*

---

249   Stuart, *Jonah*, 452.

Stuart translates part of this verse as "How foolish are those who seek help in life via the הבלי שׁוא, the empty nothings!" Like Jonah, we can recognize the foolishness of seeking empty nothing and denying the purposes of God upon our lives and call out to him in our distress. Then we will be vomited from the belly of our captivity onto the calm and peaceful shore of God's grace.

Needing to be Regurgitated

Before I received emancipation from the death I had embraced, I was wallowing in the slothful mire of boredom. I had ceased to care. To be sure, I had moments when I embraced life and came pretty darn close to thriving. For the most part, I considered this part of the ebbs and flows that are natural to life. We are not always going to be flying high nor are we always destined for debilitating lows.

Eventually I found myself in an incapacitating low from which I could not seem to escape. God had broken my heart. I had been living my life and honoring the Lord to the best of my abilities. Unfortunately, without realizing it, I had formed an expectation in my mind. Perhaps I had read too many fairytales, but it is as if I expected to finally cross a bridge into my happily ever after. I did not realize I had embraced an expectation that if I truly loved the Lord and received enough inner healing I would never again experience disappointment. I had no idea that I had embraced a lie that guaranteed all rainbows and roses if I followed God with all of my heart.

Eventually the events of my life came together to form the perfect storm. I had weathered many hardships as a single parent. I had overcome many of the painful wounds of my past and I had married an amazing man, for whom I am grateful to have by my side. I was moving towards that anticipated paradise. Or so I thought.

After growing under the leadership of a compassionate and wise man of God, my beloved pastor retired and an ungodly man took his place. He seemed to make a point of hurting me. We eventually moved to another town but were unable to find a church home. For the first time in many years, I was without solid spiritual advisors. And that's when it happened: God broke my heart.

It felt as if everything I had worked for in the Lord went up in smoke. There were some things that happened in my family that devastated me. My happily ever after in the Lord turned into broken heartedness. While I had done my part, it did not seem that God had honored His part of the bargain. I could not understand how things had gone so very wrong.

In this disillusionment with my faith, I began slowly to edge God out of my thoughts. Where He was once the central focus of my mind, He was rapidly being replaced with absolutely nothing. I quit meditating upon His majesty, my prayers ceased and my life continued to spiral into a pit of despair. Life did not seem like a worthwhile endeavor. And faith? Well, it began to appear silly to me. Honestly, I was almost embarrassed about what I once believed about God.

One day, the word apathy popped into my mind. Out the blue, bang! That was it! Apathy was the word that best seemed to described my problem. While I had turned my back on God, He had not turned His back on me. He mounted a rescue mission to deliver me from my own, dare I say it, sluggard stupidity. I had unreasonable expectations and like Ahab, I had embraced a terrible pout when things did not go my way. God's plan to restore my soul was a gradual one: it did not happen overnight.

First, He planted a tiny seed of hope in my heart through a book I read by Bill Johnson called *Dreaming with God*. Next, while I was dusting my furniture one afternoon, God interjected himself into my thoughts. The God that I no longer was convinced was real, spoke a question into my mind, "Where is your Bible?" I stopped what I was doing and pondered the question. I did not know where it was nor when I'd seen it last. I sensed another question coming that I did not want Him to ask because he knew I did not know the answer to that question either. I had no idea when I had last offered any kind of prayer to my Savior, to the One who loved me.

Then, something that had happened between God and me many years earlier popped into my mind. He reminded me of a time shortly after I was saved when I was contemplating the great men and women of the Bible. It hit me like a ton of bricks how each of these amazing men and women of God had all failed in the faith in some way. David cheated with Bathsheba, Peter denied Christ, Miriam tried to take her brother's place and Sarai even laughed at God's promises. Anguish overwhelmed my soul and I began to cry out to the Lord pleading with Him to never let me turn my back on Him. I felt the Holy Spirit prompting me to pray, "Even if I think that I hate You, see my heart that wants to serve You forever and come and rescue me."

Well, dang. I had forgotten that. I thought about what the Lord had brought back to my mind and I only had one thing to say. "Well, I guess we had a deal, didn't we? This is on you then, isn't it?" And I went back to work. My heart was cold. Sloth had deeply afflicted my heart because I did not care to embrace my relationship with Jesus much less my God-given purpose any longer. I just could not care that I did not care.

Years later, the Lord showed me his response to my ugly that day. He said, "Yes, we have a deal, Bethie girl, and I am coming to get you!" Wow! That's the kind of God we serve. He is that good and that compassionate. He never quit loving me just because I thought I no longer loved Him. Our God is amazing. He really is.

Eventually, I was drawn to a conference led by Randy Clark called Voice of the Apostles—this is the conference I mentioned earlier. It came as a surprise to me that I wanted to go because I had not sought the Lord in a long time at this point in my life. At the last minute, I got frustrated trying to plan the trip and decided not to go. My husband, knowing that I needed to do something to break out of this terrible rut, convinced me to make the trip anyway. He even made the arrangements for me.

I had hoped to get there and get delivered of apathy right off the bat. It did not work out like that. I went forward for prayer at every opportunity. I even told them that I needed deliverance from apathy. But no one prayed for my freedom. I now know that is not typical for this event. The prayer partners were well equipped to pray for such things but it was not happening for me. I kept trying over and over again. When I was about to give up and return home, I finally got free. It took a while for me to see the irony in what God was doing. He was rebirthing hope and Godly desire into my spirit. He was causing me to get off the sofa of apathy and work for my freedom in Christ. I am eternally grateful for his compassion to me.

Now, you might be thinking that you and God have never made such a deal. But, my friend, you have just the same deal with Him that I have. It is written, "The one who calls you is faithful, and He will do it" (1 Thessalonians 5:24). What will He do? He will uphold us with his righteous right hand, He will never leave nor forsake us, and He will give us rest. We love Him because He first loved us.[250] He draws us to Him in his love and compassion. He will deliver us into the man or woman He has created us to be.

There are some practical steps that we can take to be regurgitated into our purpose and live a life of rest and joy in the Lord. Let's take a look.

Choosing God

> "But seek first his kingdom and his righteousness,
> and all these things will be given to you as well."
> Matthew 6:33

The first thing, the main thing, is to choose God. It is to not only seek God for a pretty cool place to go when you die, but to make Him Lord of your life in the here and now. I thought I had made him Lord of my life. When I realized how often I said "no" to the Lord, I was surprised. I thought I was a pretty obedient daughter of the King. It was only when I prayed that He would turn all of my "noes" to him into "yeses," that my eyes were opened to the vast number of times that I had either pretended I'd heard Him incorrectly or just plain ignored the request. When I decided to say yes to God, my life became a life of productivity and joy. Sometimes, I am still amazed at the life I get to lead. It only happened when I put God first.

---

250   "because God has said, 'Never will I leave you; never will I forsake you'" (Hebrews 13:5 and Deuteronomy 31:6). "So do not fear, for I am with you; do not be dismayed, for I am your God. I will strengthen you and help you; I will uphold you with my righteous right hand" (Isaiah 41:10). "Come to me, all you who are weary and burdened, and I will give you rest" (Matthew 11:28). "We love because he first loved us" (I John 4:19).

Rest

> "Come to Me, all you who are weary and burdened,
> and I will give you rest."
> Matthew 11:28

Resting in the Lord requires trust. We cannot begin to trust someone that we do not know. Spending time in scripture and prayer will help develop intimacy with God. This may have been difficult for us in the past, but when we break agreements with sloth it will get easier. It is like any other form of exercise. The more we do it, the easier it gets.

After a battle with an illness, I found myself in less than stellar physical condition. I would get winded by walking down my driveway to the mailbox. This weakened condition left me feeling overwhelmed at the thought of exercise. Although it seemed like an insurmountable task to try to get back into shape, I eventually began taking leisurely strolls around my neighborhood. It was hard, but in no time, I was getting much stronger. It was surprising how quickly my strength returned.

We often avoid unpleasant circumstances or tasks. Let's face it, spending time with the Lord when sloth has had its claws in us is miserable. But the prayers at the end of this chapter will help you break free if you are sincere in your request before the Lord. Start spending time with the Lord and do not feel that it must be a marathon. Take those baby steps of reading scripture for five to ten minutes and ask the Holy Spirit to be with you as you read and contemplate the meaning. Start with passages that you enjoy.

Find fun ways to talk to God. There is no need for formal language. Sometimes I talk to God by making silly rap songs. Sometimes I talk to God by sharing with him how I am feeling, even when my feelings are ugly. He can take it. We can be honest with Him. Being in relationship with our Creator is the number one key to life, especially a life free of sloth.

Worship

> "And when they heard that the Lord was concerned about them
> and had seen their misery, they bowed down and worshiped."
> Exodus 4:31

Take time each day to offer a bit of praise and worship to God. It can be by taking one minute to share with him the things for which we are grateful. It is great to take a break from popular music and turn on some praise and worship music that is in a style that we like. Today's worship comes in all types of genres. We can always find a style that suits us.

The Holy Spirit is happy to help us be creative, all we have to do is ask. With his help, we can think of all kinds of fun ways to worship God. We can dance, we can sing, we can speak, we can write, we can paint or draw…there are countless ways. Even donating to the poor or offering a word of encouragement to a stranger counts as worship to the Lord when we are doing it to glorify Him.

Choose Relationship

> "A new command I give you: Love one another.
> As I have loved you, so you must love one another."
> John 13:34

Just as we must allow ourselves to develop a relationship with God, we need to embrace relationships with others. God said that it was not good for man to be alone. He also said that the second greatest commandment is to love others. We cannot claim to be God's child and hate others.[251] We have created many euphemisms to avoid admitting that we hate. We say things like, "I really don't like" when what we really mean is that we hate. We must ask the Holy Spirit to help us love others because it is written that "Whoever does not love does not know God, because God is love" (1 John 4:8).

Let's take a final look at Jonah. He did not want his enemies to taste the goodness of God. Although he repented of running from God's plan for him and he had personally tasted God's compassion for him, he had not allowed it to transform his heart for others. Jonah's anger at God's compassion towards his enemies led him to a very dark place. He said, "Now, Lord, take away my life, for it is better for me to die than to live" (Jonah 4:3).

When we plant the seeds of hatred towards mankind in our souls, we reap death; even when the feelings are directed towards those who have hurt us. When we fail to value the lives and dignity of others, our own lives become pitiable, boring, and fruitless. We must ask the Holy Spirit to give us the courage to admit that the feelings of negativity we have against our brothers and sisters may honestly be hatred.

Concern For the Earth

Finally, it is imperative that we see the world as good and care about what happens to this amazing planet upon which we live. As Christians we are too often unconcerned with the earth because we believe that it will be destroyed. There are differing views about the sequence of end time events. There are, however, three basic creeds

---

251   "Anyone who claims to be in the light but hates a brother or sister is still in the darkness" (I John 2:9).

that Christianity has accepted regarding these events: Jesus will return to earth, He will establish God's rule and reign upon the earth—a rule and reign which has been and is currently being manifested within the earth—and a new heaven and earth will be established by God that will last forever.[252]

God is in the business of redemption, not destruction. His plan has always been to redeem rather than destroy. While we understand this for mankind, we often fail to apply this reality to the earth that he created and declared good. N. T. Wright writes that we are not to be like suicide bombers who are happy to leave this world to escape into some glorious otherworld, rather, "people who believe in the resurrection, in God making a whole new world in which everything will be set right at last, are unstoppably motivated to work for that new world in the present."[253]

Imagine that! When we grasp that God's refining fire will purify the earth and leave behind a new heaven and a new earth upon which we will live forever with Him in our glorified bodies, we will be filled with an unshakeable hope. God created the earth and gave mankind the responsibility to care for it. In accepting the task to care about the earth, we are embracing hope. Sloth hates that too.

Deciding to Care

Snell reports that many in the "contemporary West are deeply infected with the vice of sloth [and, he continues to report,] We have made a terrible covenant with sloth—we give it our deepest hopes and longings, and in return, sloth promises each of us our own

---

252   Roger E Olson, *The Mosaic of Christian Belief: Twenty Centuries of Unity and Diversity*, 2nd ed. (Downers Grove, IL: InterVarsity Press, 2016), 366.
253   N.T.Wright, *Surprised by Hope: Rethinking Heaven, the Resurrection, and the Mission of the Church,* 1st ed. (New York: HarperOne, 2008), 214, Kindle.

Empire of Desire."[254] We have seen how our Empires of Desire lead to destruction and death. We are, however, God's children and we have been given an incredible hope. We can turn from the love of self which leads to hatred and embrace the love of God. Let our hearts cry out, "May your unfailing love be with us, Lord, even as we put our hope in you" (Psalm 33:22).

Let us embrace Paul's exhortation to Timothy and no longer "fix [our] hope on the uncertainty of riches, but on God, who richly supplies us with all things to enjoy" (1 Timothy 6:17). It is time to set aside drudgery and let our hearts be filled with God's joy as we follow Him in the obedience of faith. Or, as Kass so beautifully puts it, "The upright animal, his gaze uplifted and his heart filled with wonder and awe, begins to suspect that he may in fact stand tallest when he freely bows his head."[255]

Let's bow our heads and go to the Lord in prayer so that we can stand. Let us give God our all so that He can give us his.

Preparing to Pray

Holy Spirit, I ask that you help me see any way in which I have come into agreement with sloth. Please show me the ways in which I have rejected my life, my call, and my relationship with you and with others. I do not want to stay stuck in the miry clay anymore. I do not want to believe lies that my life is not important or that my life is more important than God's plans or the lives of others. I do not want to feel stuck, lethargic, or bored with my life any longer. I want to be free to experience joy in this adventure called life.

Help me renounce the lies that I have believed and receive the truth that I am a child of God and Your yoke is easy.

---

254   Snell, *Acedia*, 1, Kindle.
255   Kass, *Genesis*, 53.

The prayer on the next page is formatted a little differently than the others. We have seen that acedia or sloth can manifest in a number of different ways. Maybe some of the ways resonated with you while others did not. Prayerfully look at the things listed in the prayer and make note of anything the Holy Spirit highlights to you. Those are the things that you should say out loud in your prayer. Feel free to leave out the things that do not resonate with you. Remember, the more specific you are in your prayers, the better.

Prayer to Break Agreements with Sloth

Father, I come before You with a humble heart and ask that You set me free from the bonds of sloth. Lord, I am sorry for the ways that I have rejected You and tried to run away from You and the plans and purposes that you have for my life. I am sorry for thinking that my time was my time instead of remembering that it is Your breath in my lungs. My life comes from You and my time belongs to You. I am Yours. Today, I commit my life to You. I commit my time, my purpose, my plans, my hopes and my dreams to You. I commit my family, my work, my ministry, and my recreation to You. I ask You to be in all things in my life.

I am sorry for every time that I have been upset with you because things in my life did not work out the way I had hoped or expected. I break all agreements with the lie that has tried to convince me that those who hope for the best will always be disappointed.

I am sorry that I have looked upon the world, others, and myself with disdain.

Lord, I am sorry that I have chosen to fantasize about a future that does not exist while hating the present reality of my life. I ask that You show me the difference between dreaming big with You and fantasizing with the enemy of sloth. I come before You now and repent of:

- Judging you incorrectly and any way that I have misconstrued your intentions toward me and toward mankind.

- Thinking that You are not a loving and compassionate Father.

- Fleeing from You instead of running to You.

- Repent for trying to lord my authority over others instead of being a servant leader like Jesus.

- Dishonoring my parents.

- Refusing to be vulnerable.

- Judging others without compassion.

- Holding onto bitterness instead of choosing forgiveness.

- Judging the world as evil and not worth my time or effort. Thinking that the world should be destroyed rather than redeemed.

- Rejecting the work that You have given me to do.

- Pursuing empty pleasures instead of loving my family, friends, and the work You have set before me.

- Failing to enjoy life through experiencing pure pleasures that You have gifted to me.

- Thinking that my desires were more important than Your plans or the needs of others.

- Believing that whatever You would ask me to do would be something that would make me miserable.

In the mighty name of Jesus, I choose now to break all agreements with sloth that I have made whether those agreements were made intentionally or unintentionally. I break agreements with every lie that I have embraced whether knowingly or unknowingly that life is too difficult and is full of drudgery. I break agreements with the lie that I can do life better without You and the lie that I do not need other people. I renounce the idol of independence from God, I renounce sloth and all the attachments that come with it.

Holy Spirit, I choose to forgive each and every one of my ancestors for any agreements they made with sloth and I come into agreement with every legitimate claim the enemy has against me and my bloodline regarding sloth and all of its attachments. I ask that You cleanse me and my bloodline from sloth. Wash me and my bloodline with the blood of Jesus and fill me and my descendants with the truth of God. I ask that you restore any and all generational blessings to me, my family, and my descendants that have been stop-gapped by this generational sin.

I embrace the truth that the yoke of Christ is easy and light and that God always has my best interests at heart. I declare that the world is good, that God is good, and that mankind is created in His image and therefore worthy to be treated with dignity and compassion.

I embrace the truth that Your grace is sufficient for me and You are the Light of the World. I proclaim that I can trust You, therefore I can be vulnerable and withstand the storms of life with joy in my heart. I choose to trust in the Lord with all of my heart and to no longer lean on my own understanding. I choose to submit to You, my Lord and King and trust You to make my paths straight. I ask that You, Lord, make this possible by the resurrection power of Jesus Christ through the Holy Spirit.

Holy Spirit, please come fill me now with the joy of the Lord, fill me with Godly purpose, and fill me with the desire to pursue that purpose. I choose to embrace the plans and purposes that You have for my life. I bow before You and receive Your yoke upon my body, soul and spirit. I ask that you take all of my nos to You and turn them into yeses. I give You permission to change my heart to bring me into kingdom alignment with my Father who created me and loves me. In the name of Jesus, I pray. Amen.

Alternate Prayer A

Lord, I thank You for this teaching, but this has not seemed to be an issue in my life. If I have missed something, I ask You to reveal to me any way that I may have partnered with sloth and do not know it. I have, however, noticed others in my family who seem to be plagued by this noon-day devil. So, I come to you in forgiveness for all of my ancestors for each and every way they partnered with sloth and released this into my bloodline. I forgive my ancestors for any way that they rejected your plan and purpose for their lives and pursued life without You in the center of it. I ask that You cleanse me and my bloodline of this terrible sloth and fill me and my descendants with humble submission to you. In the name of Jesus, I pray. Amen.

Alternate Prayer B

Lord, I want to believe that by choosing Your path for me that I will be free from the drudgery that fills my soul. I am simply too tired and too discouraged to think that it is possible. I do not think that I could fulfill Your plan for my life so it is better not to try. Honestly, I am not even sure that You have a plan for me. If You do, it would probably be something that I would not enjoy.

But I am tired of running and I am tired of this overwhelming nothingness. Is there really something You will do to help me? If You are a loving and compassionate God, and You won't make me do things that I hate, then I ask You to change my heart and help me come into agreement with You. In the name of Jesus, I pray. Amen.

Lord, I pray that you fill this soul with the light of Your love. Help them see that you did not create them as someone less desirable than others and that they are not perpetually cursed to live in the pain of drudgery. Lord, I pray that You set them free from all bonds of acedia and deliver them into the joy of living their lives. In Jesus' name, I pray. Amen.

Walking It Out

Breaking the bad habits that come along with sloth is imperative to living a beautiful life. Here are some of the ways that you can embrace life and cut the ties with this destructive force.

- Avoid chronic busyness by scheduling time to rest with God. Make a point of setting aside time to spend with God. It is never time wasted. Actually, people report finding themselves much more productive after taking a moment to rest in the Lord's presence.

- Spend time in the Word. Ask the Holy Spirit to read with you, grab a pen and paper, and journal what the Lord highlights to you as well.

- Maintain a healthy diet to properly fuel your body goes a long way to feeling more vibrant. Avoid chasing those carbs and sugar highs!

- Avoid drinking alcohol more than 3 times per week.

- Exercise. Don't shoot the messenger here! A little bit of movement goes a long way. Take time to get up from the computer or your desk and move your body. Stretching feels amazing. Five minutes here and five minutes there can be helpful.

- Listen to your self-talk and embrace your purpose. Chances are that a habit to ignore the leadings of the Lord has been formed. Ask the Holy Spirit to give you ears to not only hear His leading but to hear your response. Remind yourself that you have chosen to no longer give into excuses but that you are choosing to follow God's call.

- Embrace the responsibilities that God has placed within your life. Ask the Holy Spirit to help you find joy in the small things and in things that may have once seemed tedious.

- Praise and Worship. Honoring God with your mind, your mouth and your body brings peace and joy. Take time to offer a sacrifice of praise.

- Notice nature. God's creation is absolutely amazing. Being restored to a mind of awe and wonder is exhilarating. Look at the beauty around you. Birds, flowers, sunsets...there are so many incredible things to see and admire.

- Find opportunities to do things for others. This can range from helping someone reach something on the top shelf at the store to taking a meal to a sick friend. Sometimes just offering a smile to a stranger can be a blessing, both to you and the stranger.

- Be generous. Sloth says mine, mine, mine. It wants us to hold onto what we have.   In God's economy, the more we give of what we have been given, the more we get. Feel free to let go and share what you have been given.

- Honor God with your tithes. The Lord loves a cheerful giver. Remember that we have already learned that the earth is God's along with everything in it. When we tithe, we are giving back to the Lord what He has shared with us in appreciation of his generosity. We have also learned that we reap what we sow. It only makes sense that we would want to sow generosity and generous giving.

- Choose to love. We all need a bit of help with this one and God is faithful to help us love others when we ask Him to help us. Love is a choice.

- Practice honoring and respecting others.

- Enjoy pure and lovely pleasures. God has given us many things to enjoy. Ask the Holy Spirit to direct you to pleasures that will bring you joy and take time to rest in them.

Additional Resources

Acedia and Its Discontents: Metaphysical Boredom in an Empire of Desire by R. J. Snell.

Healing for Damaged Emotions: Recovering from the Memories that Cause Our Pain by David A Seamands.

As I bent to pluck the flowers from the vase in the ground,
I wondered why I was seeing the sky.
I hit the ground hard—flat on my back.
Burning pain coursed through my body.
I had been shot.
Who would shoot me? And why?
Ah, I saw the hornets and realized I had only been stung.
I thought I would be fine only to discover I could not move.
My breathing had become labored.
As I lay there, gasping for breath amongst the tombstones of
my ancestors,
I remembered.
And I began to laugh.

CHAPTER EIGHT

Conclusion—Dying to Live

As I lay there surrounded by the tombstones of my ancestors, a thought formed in my mind. I recalled the scripture, "They will pick up snakes with their hands; and when they drink deadly poison, it will not hurt them at all; they will place their hands on sick people, and they will get well" (Mark 16:18). I smiled and with barely a whisper I spoke this verse out loud, adding the line, "so no buzzy thing can harm me either."

Then I remembered something of monumental importance—my name is written in the Lamb's Book of Life. I belong to Jesus. Again, I stated this truth out loud, adding another important detail. I said, "If you want a piece of me, then go ask God. I don't think that is going to go very well for you but go for it. I do not give you permission to take my life any longer!"

Another thought formed in my mind, and then I really began to laugh. Before I left my home that morning, I had taken an antihistamine. I never take those things because they make me sleepy. But as I was taking my daily multivitamin, a thought kept coming to my mind that I needed to take *my antihistamine*. This was weird. Why was I thinking about *my* antihistamine? I don't routinely take them and the only reason I had them is because my hairdresser had given them to me a few days earlier when she noticed I wasn't my usual self. I had mentioned I thought the pollen was dragging me down a bit so she went to the store and purchased a box of antihistamines for me. It was an unusual thing for a hairdresser to do. Yet, despite her concern, I had not taken them but had left them out on my kitchen counter.

The thought persisted in my mind and I eventually swallowed a tablet, wondering if the Holy Spirit was encouraging me to take it. As I lay there on the ground, I realized that I was doubly protected from this vicious attack. I was sprawled upon the graves thinking about these truths and began to offer praise to God in my mind because making audible sounds was no longer possible. I had perfect peace as I was sprawled upon the earth, giving thanks to my Savior. My breathing began to return to normal and within two hours, it was not evident that I had been stung at all.

The next morning, I began to have doubts about my miraculous recovery, thinking that I probably was not allergic and was merely hyperventilating from the shock of the event. I did not want to share a "miracle story" that was not a miracle at all. I absolutely believe in divine healing and have seen it first-hand. I know that God is ready, willing, and able to heal. I also know that He does not need us to embellish or exaggerate what He is doing. I was reluctant to share what had happened until I knew that it was, in fact, a supernatural event. I did not want to diminish God's miraculous hand by attributing something to Him that was merely a natural occurrence. Maybe, I reasoned, hornet stings hurt like the dickens, but if you are not allergic, there is no real harm.

God wanted me to understand what had happened and within minutes of thinking it was possible that I was not allergic and maybe it was not divine intervention after all, my breathing became labored.

I remained short of breath for two weeks! It happened that I had a doctor's appointment several days later and she added a test for bee allergies to my bloodwork. The results came back that I am indeed allergic to not only hornets but all types of wasps. The battle was real. Through Christ, I defeated the death assignment on my life.

You may recall that I had been delivered of this durn spirit of death at a conference only to have it return. This time when it tried to return, I knew how to hold onto my healing and freedom. I want you to know this too. Let's get down to business.

Repeat Offenders

"When an impure spirit comes out of a person, it goes through arid places seeking rest and does not find it. Then it says, 'I will return to the house I left.' When it arrives, it finds the house swept clean and put in order. Then it goes and takes seven other spirits more wicked than itself, and they go in and live there. And the final condition of that person is worse than the first."
Luke 11:24–26

While I was writing my testimony of being delivered from hornet stings for this book, I noticed I was feeling rather poorly. I did not think much of it and decided to stop for the day to get some rest before going to a friend's house for the evening. During my visit, my leg began to itch. Much to my surprise, I discovered a tick on the back of my knee.

I reacted in fear. I have battled Lyme disease and am sensitive to insect bites. I was immediately filled with dread and concern for my health. I reached out to my faithful intercessors and shared my need for prayer. The next morning, the Lord pointed out to me that I had just finished writing a testimony of faith when I discovered the tick. I had to chuckle that I had missed the connection. Just like that, I failed to remember my own testimony of victory and accepted the attack against me.[256] One by one my intercessor friends began to very politely send messages indicating that they were sensing fear. I repented. It is a poignant reminder of how we need to have our Shepherd's oil poured upon our heads continuously to keep our minds free of parasitic thoughts, fears, and insecurities.

In the passage above, Jesus was answering an accusation against him by the Pharisees. They were saying that he drove out demons through the power of Beelzebul. Keener explains that Jesus was telling the religious leaders that he drove out demons by the finger of God but they invited them back in and in "greater numbers."[257] We must not invite in what God has driven out. We must be filled with the Holy Spirit and keep our eyes focused on our Savior.

We are in a war. Wars are made up of battles. Notice that the word is used in the plural sense. There are battles. Our opponents are not stupid and they are not particularly creative. They figure that if it worked before, why not try it again? The point is that we can be delivered of a thing and that thing will try to return. We must be wise and refuse to allow it to regain a stronghold in our lives. If we had found and removed an intruder from our homes, we would not let the intruder return simply because it rang our doorbell.

Imagine hearing the bell ring and seeing the intruder standing on the other side of the door. We would not say, "Oh my, he is back!" and open the door to let him in. No! We would shout and tell him to leave. We would call the authorities. We would not think that just because he rang the doorbell he had a right to return and plunder our homes. So why do we do this in the spirit?

---

256   Not every insect bite or accident is a spiritual attack. Some things happen that are purely natural occurrences. We must ask the Holy Spirit for discernment in this area. While we do not want to ignore the possibility of spiritual attacks, we do not want to become so demon focused that we lose sight of the Lord.

257   Keener, *IVP New Testament*, 210.

We must learn to apply these same principles in the spiritual realm. When death and his cohorts come calling, we must say no and call the authorities. This means we rebuke it and call upon the name of the Lord. It is understandable that we can forget for a moment, just like I forgot. Sometimes it is because it is so familiar that we are inclined to accept it. Sometimes, it is because we are worn down. Throughout this book, you have learned prayers to overcome giants. I encourage you to use them to help you say 'no' to the repeat offenders trying to trick their way back into your world.

Thousands Falling at Your Side

"A thousand may fall at your side,
ten thousand at your right hand, but it will not come near you."
Psalm 91:7

This is a powerful scripture about the protection of God. As a matter of fact, the entire Psalm covers every evil both natural and supernatural that can come upon man and covers him at every moment of the day and night. One of the things that we should note about this particular passage is the vast numbers that it mentions. This is a war and in the battles we will experience thousands falling at our sides when we stay in the shelter of God through the obedience of faith. Obedience of faith means that we trust God and our actions reflect that trust. If I trust God to never let me drown but refuse to go into the water…is that faith?

The fact is the sheer number of attacks can be overwhelming. That is why we must keep our eyes focused on the Lord. During the writing of this book, it certainly felt like thousands coming against me at times. I believe that is why I reacted in fear over the tick bite.

I had become tired. I did not, however, remain there. The Lord through the Holy Spirit and my intercessor friends showed me what was happening. I rebuked the attack and I began to praise the Lord. Once my focus shifted away from the possibilities of what could go wrong in my body because of this bite and returned to the power and love of my Father, I began to feel better. As a matter of fact, I experienced joy deep down in my soul.

We cannot let ourselves get overwhelmed at the number of things that come against us or the evil that we see in the world. God's word says that he will protect us and that we can seek shelter under his wings. When we see that we have fallen into the same old trap, here is what we must do.

Acknowledge the Lapse

If we have embraced a lie or a sin of which we have previously been delivered, then we must acknowledge it before the Lord. For example, if we have broken agreements with jealousy but find ourselves in a situation in which we reacted with jealousy, we admit it.

Repent

Then we repent. The repeat action or thought does not mean we are ensnared again and are seven times worse than before. It means that we developed some bad habits in the enemy's camp and are learning how to break them. Be honest with yourself in recognizing bad habits and be gracious to forgive yourself while you are learning to walk out your newfound freedom.

Confess Freedom

Sometimes we can be filled with thoughts of things we have done in the past. If we have already repented of the thing that is coming into our minds, then we say so. It is beneficial to say it out loud. The confession can sound like this: "Yes, I lied to my parents about the car wreck. I have confessed my lie and received God's forgiveness. I have forgiven myself and this sin no longer has a hold on me. I am forgiven and free."

Sometimes, I have been reminded of things that I have done for which I have not specifically repented. Throughout this book, there have been some generalized prayers of repentance. The Holy Spirit may continue to remind you of some specific instances that He wants you to release. The enemy may want to remind you of some things as well. If the reminder comes with conviction, it is God. If it comes with feelings of shame and guilt, it is not God.

If I have prayed to break agreement with the general sin of jealousy and am reminded of a time when I was jealous that I have not specifically repented of previously, I will repent no matter who is doing the reminding. How I repent may look a little different depending on whether the reminder came from the Holy Spirit or an evil spirit.

If the enemy is trying to entangle us in shame and guilt over the past, we must not agree with the shame or the guilt, but we should agree with the fact that we committed the sin. Before I was delivered of a religious spirit, I would be bombarded with shame over things I had done in my past. After I broke agreements with this religious spirit, I began to celebrate the enemy's reminders of past sins so I could repent. I would not submit to the torment, but rather would agree with the accusation and confess it to the Lord in repentance. The enemy meant it for harm, but it was used for my good. It quit being fun for the enemy because instead of being tormented, I was being set free. Remember: if you have already repented, then say so. If the reminders continue to come, ask the Holy Spirit if there is something that needs to be addressed for you to be free.

New Giants in the Land

Sometimes the giants we face are not the same ones we have already battled but are new players that look similar. When David faced Goliath, Goliath was not the first giant the Israelites had encountered. Their fathers before them were no strangers to these tall beings. Coming out of the wilderness in pursuit of the Promised Land, God led Moses through the land of Heshbon. Moses sent a message to their king, Sihon, requesting peaceful passage, but the king refused. Christopher Wright explains that Sihon was a "king of an Amorite people."[258] Therefore, this would be considered the Israelite's first battle for the land God had promised to them. The Amorites were considered a race of giants, so this guy and his army would have stood very tall.

After they defeated Sihon and his sons, they went up the road to Bashan where they encountered its king, a man named Og. Now here is what scripture reports about this king: "Og king of Bashan was the last of the Rephaites. His bed was decorated with iron and was more than nine cubits long and four cubits wide" (Deuteronomy 3:10). This means his bed was fourteen feet long and about 6 feet wide–talk about tall. This guy was huge.

What we are discovering is that the Israelites had just defeated one giant and his army only to encounter another. We would think it would have been rather ridiculous if they would have taken a look at Og and decided that their defeat of Sihon must not have been successful after all because now there was another great big giant standing right in front of them. With a mentality like that, they would have turned around and headed straight back into wilderness wanderings.

---

258   Christopher J.H. Wright, *New International Biblical Commentary: Deuteronomy* (Peabody MA: Hendrickson Publishers, 1996), 38-39.

But this is exactly what we do when we find victory in the Lord only to accept the very thing we have overcome back into our lives. Sometimes it is the same thing trying to regain access but other times, like this, it is a new giant that is rather similar to what we have faced before. One day it is a band of hornets and the next it can be a nasty tick. Both are giants injecting poison into the body, but they are not the same.

For me, the hornets were death trying to regain access to my life. The tick? Well, to tell you the truth, I had allowed myself to become re-aligned with offense. I gave that durn giant access to my life and will have to take a round of not one but two antibiotics for thirty days for my troubles. I will overcome. I have the victory. Unfortunately, I took the long route to victory instead of slapping a quick and decisive blow against the attack. I should have responded in faith rather than fear. My bad.

Dying to Live

Throughout this book, we have slain some giants in our lands to become free to live the life God designed for us. We have faced some tall issues to be delivered into our purposes so that we can do more than survive—we can begin to thrive. This is good stuff. We have been learning to die to ourselves and to live for Christ.

> *Or don't you know that all of us who were baptized into Christ Jesus were baptized into his death? We were therefore buried with him through baptism into death in order that, just as Christ was raised from the dead through the glory of the Father, we too may live a new life.*
>
> *For if we have been united with him in a death like his, we will certainly also be united with him in a resurrection like his. For*

we know that our old self was crucified with him so that the body ruled by sin might be done away with, that we should no longer be slaves to sin— because anyone who has died has been set free from sin.

Now if we died with Christ, we believe that we will also live with him. For we know that since Christ was raised from the dead, he cannot die again; death no longer has mastery over him. The death he died, he died to sin once for all; but the life he lives, he lives to God. (Romans 6:3-10)

Keener explores these passages and teaches that "those who are in Christ (in whom Adamic sin and death died) should no longer identify themselves with the toxic legacy of fallen humanity, but rather with their eternal identity secured by Christ."[259] When we share in the death of Jesus, we share in his resurrection. We become free of the law of sin and death and alive to our identities which are "defined by [our] union[s] and future[s] with Christ."[260]

We are free to choose. Are we going to live as slaves to Christ which brings life or the passions within ourselves that bring death? Are we going to embrace a future that has an incredible hope in which we will not be disappointed? Or are we going to continue to trust in horses and chariots that will cause us to shrink back in fear?[261]

---

259   Craig S. Keener, *Romans: A New Covenant Commentary.* 1st ed. (The Lutterworth Press, 2009) 87, Kindle.

260   Keener, *Romans*, 89.

261   This is a reference to the woe that was spoken upon those who chose to trust in Egypt's (worldly) protection rather than God. "Woe to those who go down to Egypt for help, who rely on horses, who trust in the multitude of their chariots and in the great strength of their horsemen, but do not look to the Holy One of Israel, or seek help from the Lord" (Isaiah 31:1).

Abiding, Bearing, and Love

If you have read this far in the book, you have been on an incredible journey. Whether it has been a tiny first step or a giant leap, something amazing has happened in your soul. It may be the loosening of chains or you may be in a place where the chains were destroyed. Either way, it is good. I celebrate your healing and rejoice in your journey. Let us explore the point of the process.

Often we approach inner healing as if the goal is to make us less despicable people. We are hoping that God will clean us up so that we will be more likeable. That's not the point. God's desire for us is a return to the deep intimacy we once had with Him before everything went to hell in a handbasket. Let's look at the words of Jesus to understand God's desire for us.

The Vine

"I am the true vine, and my Father is the gardener."
John 15:1

It is interesting that Jesus compared himself to a vine. The culture into which Jesus was born was steeped in the cultivation of the land. Given their soil and climate, they specialized in crops that were drought-resistant. The most commonly produced crops were fig and olive trees along with the grapevine.[262] Jesus spoke in the language of the times using common illustrations to teach his point. This lesson was no exception. He was using their heritage of land cultivation to show them his Father's heart. He could have, however, used the olive

---

262   Colin G. Kruse. *John: An Introduction and Commentary*. Vol. Revised edition. Tyndale New Testament Commentaries. (Downers Grove, Illinois: IVP Academic, 2017), 171.

tree as an example. Was there a specific reason he used the grapevine instead?

I believe so. See, a tree has a definite trunk. The branches are clearly the branches and are easily discerned from the trunk from which they sprout. Not so with a vine. The branches twist as they grow and can become nearly indistinguishable from the trunk. I believe that the Lord was painting a picture of how our lives in him should look. Jesus perfectly mirrored the Father, and calls us to do the same. Our Lord desires us to be so intertwined with Him that it may be difficult for the world to see where we end and He begins.

Producing Fruit

He cuts off every branch in me that bears no fruit, while every branch that does bear fruit He prunes so that it will be even more fruitful. You are already clean because of the word I have spoken to you. Remain in Me, as I also remain in You. No branch can bear fruit by itself; it must remain in the vine. Neither can you bear fruit unless you remain in me…
This is to my Father's glory, that you bear much fruit,
showing yourselves to be My disciples.
John 15:2-4,8.

The purpose of this journey is for us to abide in Christ. As we abide in Him, we are pruned. We have submitted to his pruning process throughout this book. When we partner with death, we are separating ourselves from the True Vine. We are separating ourselves and hiding from God. As we have broken these partnerships, we have allowed ourselves to be pruned so that we may bear much fruit to bring honor and glory to God.

Pruning allows us to become more intimately entwined with Jesus. This is not about punishment or becoming more lovable. This passage about abiding and being pruned happens to be sandwiched between passages about love!

Being in Love

> "As the Father has loved me, so have I loved you.
> Now remain in My love."
> John 15:9

Jesus follows his teaching on pruning, God's corrective love, with the exhortation to remain in His love. That is why Jesus came because the Father has loved us before we ever dreamed of loving him. Jesus came to reconcile us to love. Our acceptance of his love is reflected in obedience. We are pruned and given commands to follow because he loves us and desires for us to live an abundant life in fellowship with him and with each other.

We cannot experience this when we are disobedient and in partnership with death and its cohorts. By calling us to abide in the vine, Jesus admonishes us to come into agreement with His love and to lose ourselves in Him. He knows the cost of failing to abide. He understands that He is the source of life, and when we remove ourselves, our hearts wither and die. We must remain in selfless Love to live. Abiding in selfishness is "the fruitlessness of a life dried up by lovelessness and self-assertion; and such a life ends in despair…"[263] Pride, jealousy, offense…these things are incompatible with love. So is fear.

---

263   Ernst Haenchen, Robert W Funk and Ulrich Busse, *John 2: A Commentary on the Gospel of John, Chapter 7-21* (Augsburg Fortress Publishers, 1988), 132.

No Fear

We often think that faith is the opposite of fear. It is love that is fear's opposite. Perfect love casts out fear.[264] That is why there is not a chapter on it in this book. Fear will find that it no longer has a hook upon which to hang its hat when we break these unholy death agreements and walk in the truth of the Father's love. We step out of life's violent storms and into the shelter of the Almighty. We are covered in his feathers.

We can be at peace and rest because the promises of Psalm 91 cover everything that can come against us at any hour of the day or night. To stay in his covering means that we walk in obedience to Love, no longer agreeing with the lies of death and its minions. Jesus taught that we are empowered to obey Him when we love Him.[265] By receiving His love and loving Him in return, we are free to live. We are free to share love and multiply it through making disciples who make disciples.

Fishing in the Vine

Do you remember when I became upset thinking that life was about bringing glory to God? The idea that the purpose of my life was to make God look good was offensive. I did not know God yet, so this seemed egotistical to me on His part. God did not need me to make Him look good. He does, however, call us to glorify Him. It turns out, I was the one with the ego problem.

As I began to know God and be healed under the power of his relentless love, I began to see things differently. Loving Him caused

---

264   "There is no fear in love. But perfect love drives out fear, because fear has to do with punishment. The one who fears is not made perfect in love" (I John 4:18).

265   "Jesus replied, 'Anyone who loves me will obey my teaching'" (John 14:23a).

me to desire to glorify Him. It caused me to want to honor him. It created a deep yearning in my heart to know Him more and to introduce Him to others. I began to want to serve Him more than anything else. Yes, I still had to work out my salvation with fear and trembling as many of the stories have proven.[266] Like Peter, my journey has had its share of ups and downs. Despite my frailties, God always found a way to let me partner with him in kingdom business. Isn't it amazing that He uses us to accomplish something as monumentally important as his plans? In reality, all we do for Jesus is really for us.

Fruitless to Fruitful

Peter, his business partners, James and John, the sons of Zebedee, along with their crew, had been out all night fishing. They caught nothing. Imagine working hard all night to find out that it produced zero, zilch, nada. That means there was no money to pay the bills nor to buy food to eat. And yet, they still had to clean their nets to prepare for another night's work before they could go home and get some rest.

In the midst of this, Jesus gets into one of Peter's boats and asks him for a favor. He asked him to set out a little bit from the shore. We can all imagine that this was a bad mood moment for Peter. He was tired and most likely irritable. Surely his muscles ached from a hard night's work. Yet Jesus hops into his boat and says, "Let's go."

What was Peter to do? Kenneth E. Bailey offers additional insight into this passage. He explains that "returning favors is an integral part of many societies in general and Middle Eastern culture in

---

266   "Therefore, my dear friends, as you have always obeyed—not only in my presence, but now much more in my absence—continue to work out your salvation with fear and trembling, for it is God who works in you to will and to act in order to fulfill his good purpose" (Philippians 2:12-13).

particular."[267] In the previous chapter of John, we learn that Jesus had just healed Peter's mother-in-law.[268] Essentially, Peter owed Jesus a favor. He could not say no.

In the boat they go, and Jesus begins to preach to the crowd upon the shore. Now, let's think about this for a moment. We cannot get in a boat, row out a little way from the shore and expect to simply stay in one place. The currents and the winds will cause us to drift. Bailey puts it like this, "Jesus genuinely needs Peter to control that drift if the boat is to be effective as a pulpit."[269] Jesus is teaching the people, and all the while, Peter is rowing his heart out.

Let's think on this a minute, too. Did Jesus really need Peter? After all, we later learn that Jesus is perfectly capable of walking on water and commanding the seas. Jesus could have walked out a bit from the shore and started teaching. Or, he could have commanded the waters to be still as He sat in the boat. Can you imagine that?

I know what I would have been thinking about if I had been on that shore. I would not have heard a word Jesus was saying. I would have been too busy trying to figure out how He was doing that! Was He really standing on the water, or was there something underneath that was supporting Him? Did He throw an anchor that I had not noticed before? Straining my eyes, I would have been looking for evidence of a natural explanation for the supernatural sight before my eyes. I just bet you would have too. Jesus knows the way we think. For whatever reason, Jesus needed some separation between himself and the crowds. Peter's boat and his rowing skills provided a grand solution to the problem.

---

267   Kenneth E. Bailey, *Jesus Through Middle Eastern Eyes: Cultural Studies in the Gospels* (Downer's Grove, IL: InterVarsity Press, 2008), 140.
268   See Luke 4:38-39.
269   Bailey, *Middle Eastern Eyes*, 140.

Scripture records that "When he had finished speaking, he said to Simon, "Put out into deep water, and let down the nets for a catch" (Luke 5:4).[270] How would you have responded to such a request? There was a reason that the men fished at night. The fish were swimming around looking for food in the dark hours but hid under rocks during the day.[271] The night was not only prime fishing time but the only time one would be likely to catch any in their nets. Moreover, fish were not caught in the deep, but in the shallow waters.[272] As a professional, Peter was well aware of this. Jesus was from Nazareth, a landlocked town. He was a carpenter. He knew about wood but not about the habits of fish. By then, Peter would have been very tired.

Peter is polite. A student would never disrespect their rabbi and expect to remain a student. He replies to Jesus, "Master, we've worked hard all night and haven't caught anything. But because You say so, I will let down the nets" (Luke 5:5). Let me paraphrase. He is essentially saying, "Look, we worked hard during the prime fishing hours when the fish were actually hungry and caught nothing. There is no point in throwing our nets when the fish are asleep and they are not in out in the deep anyway. This is pointless. But, because You are asking me to do it, I will do it anyway." I cannot help but wonder if this was said with a mental eye roll. Remember, Peter knows fish and he has got to be exhausted at this point.

He obeys. Jesus had, after all, just healed his mother-in-law and he was the rabbi. Here's what Peter got for his troubles: more fish than he had likely ever caught before in one night. Scripture records "they caught such a large number of fish that their nets began to break. So they signaled their partners in the other boat to come and

---

270   Peter's name was originally Simon and had not yet been changed.
271   Bailey, *Middle Eastern Eyes*, 141.
272   Dr. Tom Litter mentioned this in his comments to me regarding my paper, Craving Life, May 23, 2023.

help them, and they came and filled both boats so full that they began to sink" (Luke 5:6-7).

Peter becomes undone with himself. Falling to his knees, he exclaims, "Go away from me, Lord; I am a sinful man!" (Luke 5:8) Scholars debate the meaning of Peter referring to himself as a sinful man. Joel Green makes the astute point that "Peter recognizes the vast difference between Jesus and himself and so recoils in 'the terror experienced in the presence of the revelation of the Holy One (cf. Exod 3:5– 6; Isa 6:1ff.).'"[273] Peter may not have completely understood who Jesus was in that moment, but he certainly recognized that He had come into the presence of someone through whom God was working. By allowing himself to "help" Jesus, Peter was changed. His submission to a request that seemed ridiculous did more to help him than it helped Jesus.

During the journey through these pages, you have been asked to do some tough things. Forgiving those who have hurt us can feel as if we are being asked to needlessly row a boat when our muscles are full of pain from the strain. It can seem cruel. Setting aside pride can feel like we are being asked to fish while the fish are sleeping. It can seem pointless and even a bit embarrassing. But, when we submit to God and do things that we do not understand, we are changed, and the process produces more abundance in our lives than we can imagine. Jesus has been calling us through these pages to let down our nets. He is calling us to break agreements with man's reason and embrace God's truth. He is calling us to fish.

---

273   Joel B. Green, *The Gospel of Luke* (Grand Rapids: Wm. B. Eerdmans Publishing Co., 1997), 250.

People Fishing

Peter's life was not the only life transformed that day. His business partners' lives were changed as well. It says that they left everything and followed Jesus. Suddenly, their greatest riches did not seem so grand after all. Jesus had captured their hearts. He said to Peter, "Don't be afraid; from now on you will fish for people" (Luke 5:10). Green makes two keen observations about this text. First, the term fish for people uses a word that implies to "capture alive."[274] Jesus is saying that they will no longer catch something that is sold into death in the marketplace but will catch living souls and release them into liberty. This powerful imagery warms my soul all the way down to my toes.

Green's next observation is that Jesus used the words *from now on*. This implies putting the past behind you. When I was in my mid to late twenties and made that first phone call to get inner healing, there was a thought that had formed in my mind: just because the first 20-something years of my life were awful did not mean that the next 50 years had to be terrible too.[275] We have learned some amazing tools to put to death those deadly agreements we have made and choose life. These tools are powerful. Throughout these pages, we have practiced admitting the truth about ourselves, repenting, forgiving those who have hurt us, even when that person is ourselves, and accepting the grace of God to wash us clean through the shed blood of Jesus Christ of Nazareth

---

274   Green, *Luke*, 250.

275   Today, I would revise that statement to say that the next 90 or so years would not have to be terrible because I plan on living a very long and fruitful life. I often remind God that I got a late start, have appeared to be a slow learner, and therefore need the extra time!

No longer will we partner with death and live suffocatingly impotent lives. If you have read this far, you desire to follow hard after God. You desire to fish. You desire to embrace God's call to make disciples who make disciples.

> *"Then Jesus came to them and said, 'All authority in heaven and on earth has been given to me. Therefore go and make disciples of all nations, baptizing them in the name of the Father and of the Son and of the Holy Spirit, and teaching them to obey everything I have commanded you. And surely I am with you always, to the very end of the age.'"*
> *Matthew 28:18–20*

He is sending you out. But He is not sending you out alone. He will never leave you. He will never turn His back on you. He has given you the Holy Spirit to empower you to row His boat. He has given us each other that we may support one another in brotherly love. Go fish.

Preparing to Pray

Before we go to our final prayer together on this journey, I would like to pray over you. I encourage you to also pray for the Holy Spirit to reveal to you any partnerships you may have with fear.

My Prayer for You

Father, I lift up this beautiful soul created in your image. I ask that You empower them to love like Jesus loves. I pray that You empower them to love You with all of their body, soul, and spirit. I pray that You empower them to love themselves and to love others. I ask that they may be filled with the Spirit of Wisdom to know how to wield that love well.

Lord, I ask that You bless this soul with abundant life and release upon them now an impartation of love, wisdom, and healing. You know what You have called them to do, and I ask that You release an impartation that is specific to their call, their time, and their circumstance. Bless them Lord, and please, continue to teach them to fish.

Now, let's go to the Lord and ask Him to reveal any ways that we have come into partnership with fear and why. I encourage you to ask the Lord for a willingness to hear what He is saying to your heart and make note of it for the upcoming prayer.

Prayer to Embrace Love

Father, I thank You for leading me to and through this journey. I thank You that Your love for me empowers me to release any agreements I have made with death and choose life. I affirm my choice to choose life and celebrate the life You have given to me. I ask that You empower me to love You even more.

I no longer want to wear fig leaves. I want the courage to be vulnerable to You and to those who I am doing life with. I ask You to help me continue to walk in the freedom I have received and to slay giants as they come against me. Help me discern the identities of these giants and how to defeat them. Help me to discern whether the giant is a new thing that looks familiar or an old thing trying to regain access to my life and my thoughts.

Lord, I no longer want to live in fear. I choose to repent for the ways that I have embraced fear. (List the things that the Holy Spirit brought to your mind.) I renounce fear and all the underlings associated with it. I forgive any and all of my ancestors who embraced fear and released an attachment of it upon my bloodline. I come into agreement with every legitimate claim the enemy has against me and my bloodline regarding fear and ask for Your forgiveness in the name of Jesus. Wash me and my bloodline free of the defilement and effects of fear by the blood of Jesus. I renounce fear!

Holy Spirit, come fill me now with the Father's love and with his peace that surpasses all understanding. I receive Your cleansing, Your healing, and Your filling now, in the name of Jesus. Amen.

Alternate Prayer A

Father, I thank You for this journey and ask that You continue to pour out Your love upon me to empower me to walk out the freedom Jesus purchased for me on Calvary. I ask You to help me to love You more because I want to know You and to follow You. I am scared but trust that You will help me because You are good. I want to break agreements with fear and am grateful that You have been showing me the steps to take to live an abundant life. I will not despise the small steps that I have taken because they are preparing me to begin a deeper journey into intimacy with You. In the name of Jesus, I pray. Amen.

Alternate Prayer B

Lord, I have journeyed through this book and struggled mightily with doubt and unbelief. I ask that You set me free to love You and to receive Your love for me. I am not sure, yet, that You really love me, but if You do, please help me to embrace it. I need Your help but I am still scared. In the name of Jesus, I pray. Amen.

Walking It Out

- *Submit to Soul Checks.* Ask the Lord to search your heart and reveal to you any wicked way that is setting up shop within it. Ask Him to create within you a clean and pure heart.

- *Do not naval gaze!* We do not need to pick ourselves apart. We can trust the Holy Spirit's timing to bring conviction. He will show us what issues we need to deal with if we trust Him and leave ourselves open to His leading. Remember, God is the author of our sanctification process. He will heal our hurts and transform us into the person he created us to be. We do not need to continually dissect ourselves trying to make ourselves more holy.

- *Pray Often.* Stay connected to the Lord through prayer and worship.

- *Read the Word.* Stay connected to God through his Word. Ask the Holy Spirit to give insight to you as you read.

- *Meditate Upon the Word.* Sometimes less is more. Reading copious amounts of words without thinking about what they mean will not transform your heart. Take a small verse and think about it throughout the day.

- *Repent Quickly.* Do not make excuses for bad behavior. Admit it and ask for forgiveness and move on.

- *Choose Love.* When we feel those grumblings of things like offense, pride, jealousy, or unforgiveness, we must run to the Lord and ask Him to help us choose love. There is a very good chance the person we are ready to annihilate is someone Jesus died for, no matter how awful they appear to us.

- *Stay Connected.* We are not called to do this alone. We need each other. Connect with others, especially when you are sure that you are the only person in the world.

- *Bless.* Create a culture of blessing, determining to be a blessing to others.

- *Practice loving the Lord your God with all your might!*

Additional Resources

Paradox Lost by Catherine Skurja with Jen Johnson

Restoring the Soul by Geoffrey Wattoff

Epilogue

I am honored to have made this journey with you out of the wilderness into abundant life. It has been a journey, hasn't it? I pray you have fared well and will continue to practice what you have learned. If you continue to struggle in any of these areas, please reach out for help. Remember we are not islands and we are not made to do this thing called life in isolation. Feel free to reach out to me through www.ezekieltree.com or beth@EzekielTree.com and I will help you get connected.

In the name of our Lord and Savior,
Jesus Christ of Nazareth, be blessed.

Beth

ACKNOWLEDGEMENTS

This endeavor was made possible through the help of good and faithful friends. I would like to offer my most sincere gratitude to those who selflessly gave their time and talent to help make this manuscript free of typos and errors that I never can seem to notice on my own. Any that may remain would purely be an oversight on my part.

I would first like to thank each person through whom I have practiced working out these principles in my own life. I am sure I have been taxing at times, and I appreciate each of you, whether or not you have found a place in your hearts to forgive me. If you have forgiven me, thank you. If you have not, I pray you can because it will bless you more than you can imagine. Please know that I am sorry for each of the times I have not looked much like Jesus in our fellowship.

It is with a heart full of gratitude that I acknowledge Dr. Tom Litteer with Global Awakening Theological Seminary who agreed to this project and made sure that I stayed on solid theological ground. There will always be a special place in my heart for your willingness to accept this task.

Next, I would like to thank Charlene Holland who faithfully read every word and found mistakes no one else noticed. I took every one of your suggestions because they were good. You are amazing and I am so glad you called me out of the blue one day. I have loved getting to know you.

Ty and Cindy Snyder were generous with their time to read over manuscripts and offer suggestions. This book is better because of your input.

Big shout out to Tony Vismor of Grace Fellowship Athens for first introducing me to the term "acedia" and pointing me to a very good resource for study.

Behind every good project is a team, and I am honored to have such an amazing team of prayer warriors by my side. The Ezekiel Tree Intercessor Team is the best. Thank you to Memory Watson, Connie Hood, Cheryl Hafner, Linda Maynard, Charlene Holland, and Tina Dupree. You guys helped me through some battles during this project. Thank you from the bottom of my heart.

This project could not have been possible without the love and ministry I received from Marcia McWhorter, founder of New Beginnings Counseling Center. Marcia has dumped her earth suit and is awaiting her glorified body. I know she is full of joy because she is with the One whom she loves: Jesus.

Finally, my man. Scott Erwin, you are the best. Thank you for never complaining about the hours I spent at the computer typing away and not hearing a thing that was said to me. Thank you for proofing texts when I know that you were tired and would have preferred not to read. I wub, wub, wub you!

APPENDIX

How to Hear God's Voice – By Dr. Mark Virkler

She had done it again! Instead of coming straight home from school like she was supposed to, she had gone to her friend's house. Without permission. Without our knowledge. Without doing her chores.

With a ministering household that included remnants of three struggling families plus our own toddler and newborn, my wife simply couldn't handle all the work on her own. Everyone had to pull their own weight. Everyone had age-appropriate tasks they were expected to complete. At fourteen, Rachel and her younger brother were living with us while her parents tried to overcome lifestyle patterns that had resulted in the children running away to escape the dysfunction. I felt sorry for Rachel, but, honestly my wife was my greatest concern.

Now Rachel had ditched her chores to spend time with her friends. It wasn't the first time, but if I had anything to say about it, it would be the last. I intended to lay down the law when she got home and make it very clear that if she was going to live under my roof, she would obey my rules.

But…she wasn't home yet. And I had recently been learning to hear God's voice more clearly. Maybe I should try to see if I could hear anything from Him about the situation. Maybe He could give me a way to get her to do what she was supposed to (i.e. what I wanted her to do). So I went to my office and reviewed what the

Lord had been teaching me from Habakkuk 2:1,2: "I will stand on my guard post and station myself on the rampart; And I will keep watch to see what He will speak to me…Then the Lord answered me and said, 'Record the vision….'"

Habakkuk said, "I will stand on my guard post…" (Hab. 2:1). **The first key to hearing God's voice is to go to a quiet place and still our own thoughts and emotions.** Psalm 46:10 encourages us to be still, let go, cease striving, and know that He is God. In Psalm 37:7 we are called to "be still before the Lord and wait patiently for Him." There is a deep inner knowing in our spirits that each of us can experience when we quiet our flesh and our minds. Practicing the art of biblical meditation helps silence the outer noise and distractions clamoring for our attention.

I didn't have a guard post but I did have an office, so I went there to quiet my temper and my mind. Loving God through a quiet worship song is one very effective way to become still. In 2 Kings 3, Elisha needed a word from the Lord so he said, "Bring me a minstrel," and as the minstrel played, the Lord spoke. I have found that playing a worship song on my autoharp is the quickest way for me to come to stillness. I need to choose my song carefully; boisterous songs of praise do not bring me to stillness, but rather gentle songs that express my love and worship. And it isn't enough just to sing the song into the cosmos – I come into the Lord's presence most quickly and easily when I use my godly imagination to see the truth that He is right here with me and I sing my songs to Him, personally.

"I will keep watch to see," said the prophet. To receive the pure word of God, it is very important that my heart be properly focused as I become still, because my focus is the source of the intuitive flow. If I fix my eyes upon Jesus (Heb. 12:2), the intuitive flow comes from Jesus. But if I fix my gaze upon some desire of my heart, the intuitive flow comes out of that desire. To have a pure flow I must become still and carefully fix my eyes upon Jesus. Quietly worshiping the King and receiving out of the stillness that follows quite easily accomplishes this.

So I used **the second key to hearing God's voice: As you pray, fix the eyes of your heart upon Jesus, seeing in the Spirit the dreams and visions of Almighty God.** Habakkuk was actually looking for vision as he prayed. He opened the eyes of his heart, and looked into the spirit world to see what God wanted to show him.

God has always spoken through dreams and visions, and He specifically said that they would come to those upon whom the Holy Spirit is poured out (Acts 2:1-4, 17).

Being a logical, rational person, observable facts that could be verified by my physical senses were the foundations of my life, including my spiritual life. I had never thought of opening the eyes of my heart and looking for vision. However, I have come to believe that this is exactly what God wants me to do. He gave me eyes in my heart to see in the spirit the vision and movement of Almighty God. There is an active spirit world all around us, full of angels, demons, the Holy Spirit, the omnipresent Father, and His omnipresent Son, Jesus. The only reasons for me not to see this reality are unbelief or lack of knowledge.

In his sermon in Acts 2:25, Peter refers to King David's statement: "I saw the Lord always in my presence; for He is at my right hand, so that I will not be shaken." The original psalm makes it clear that this was a decision of David's, not a constant supernatural visitation: "I have set (literally, I have placed) the Lord continually before me; because He is at my right hand, I will not be shaken" (Ps.16:8). Because David knew that the Lord was always with him, he determined in his spirit to *see* that truth with the eyes of his heart as he went through life, knowing that this would keep his faith strong.

In order to see, we must look. Daniel saw a vision in his mind and said, "I was looking...I kept looking...I kept looking" (Dan. 7:2, 9, 13). As I pray, I look for Jesus, and I watch as He speaks to me, doing and saying the things that are on His heart. Many Christians will find that if they will only look, they will see. Jesus is Emmanuel, God with us (Matt. 1:23). It is as simple as that. You can see Christ present with you because Christ *is* present with you. In fact, the vision may come so easily that you will be tempted to reject it, thinking that it is just you. But if you persist in recording these visions, your doubt will soon be overcome by faith as you recognize that the content of them could only be birthed in Almighty God.

Jesus demonstrated the ability of living out of constant contact with God, declaring that He did nothing on His own initiative, but only what He saw the Father doing, and heard the Father saying (Jn. 5:19,20,30). What an incredible way to live!

Is it possible for us to live out of divine initiative as Jesus did? Yes! We must simply fix our eyes upon Jesus. The veil has been torn, giving access into the immediate presence of God, and He calls us to draw near (Lk. 23:45; Heb. 10:19-22). "I pray that the eyes of your heart will be enlightened...."

When I had quieted my heart enough that I was able to picture Jesus without the distractions of my own ideas and plans, I was able to "keep watch to see what He will speak to me." I wrote down my question: "Lord, what should I do about Rachel?"

Immediately the thought came to me, "She is insecure." Well, that certainly wasn't my thought! Her behavior looked like rebellion to me, not insecurity.

But like Habakkuk, I was coming to know the sound of God speaking to me (Hab. 2:2). Elijah described it as a still, small voice (I Kings 19:12). I had previously listened for an inner audible voice, and God does speak that way at times. However, I have found that usually, God's voice comes as spontaneous thoughts, visions, feelings, or impressions.

For example, haven't you been driving down the road and had a thought come to you to pray for a certain person? Didn't you believe it was God telling you to pray? What did God's voice sound like? Was it an audible voice, or was it a spontaneous thought that lit upon your mind?

Experience indicates that we perceive spirit-level communication as spontaneous thoughts, impressions and visions, and Scripture confirms this in many ways. For example, one definition of *paga*, a Hebrew word for intercession, is "a chance encounter or an accidental intersecting." When God lays people on our hearts, He does it through *paga*, a chance-encounter thought "accidentally" intersecting our minds.

So **the third key to hearing God's voice is recognizing that God's voice in your heart often sounds like a flow of spontaneous thoughts.** Therefore, when I want to hear from God, I tune to chance-encounter or spontaneous thoughts.

Finally, God told Habakkuk to record the vision (Hab. 2:2). This was not an isolated command. The Scriptures record many examples of individual's prayers and God's replies, such as the Psalms, many of the prophets, and Revelation. I have found that obeying this final principle amplified my confidence in my ability to hear God's voice so that I could finally make living out of His initiatives a way of life. The **fourth key, two-way journaling or the writing out of your**

prayers and God's answers, brings great freedom in hearing God's voice.

I have found two-way journaling to be a fabulous catalyst for clearly discerning God's inner, spontaneous flow, because as I journal I am able to write in faith for long periods of time, simply believing it is God. I know that what I believe I have received from God must be tested. However, testing involves doubt and doubt blocks divine communication, so I do not want to test while I am trying to receive. (See James 1:5-8.) With journaling, I can receive in faith, knowing that when the flow has ended I can test and examine it carefully.

So I wrote down what I believed He had said: "She is insecure."

But the Lord wasn't done. I continued to write the spontaneous thoughts that came to me: "Love her unconditionally. She is flesh of your flesh and bone of your bone."

My mind immediately objected: She is not flesh of my flesh. She is not related to me at all – she is a foster child, just living in my home temporarily. It was definitely time to test this "word from the Lord"!

There are three possible sources of thoughts in our minds: ourselves, satan and the Holy Spirit. It was obvious that the words in my journal did not come from my own mind – I certainly didn't see her as insecure *or* flesh of my flesh. And I sincerely doubted that satan would encourage me to love anyone unconditionally!

Okay, it was starting to look like I might have actually received counsel from the Lord. It was consistent with the names and character of God as revealed in the Scripture, and totally contrary to the names and character of the enemy. So that meant that I was hearing from the Lord, and He wanted me to see the situation in a different light. Rachel was my daughter – part of my family not by blood but by the hand of God Himself. The chaos of her birth home had created deep insecurity about her worthiness to be loved by anyone, including me and including God. Only the unconditional love of the Lord expressed through an imperfect human would reach her heart.

But there was still one more test I needed to perform before I would have absolute confidence that this was truly God's word to me: I needed confirmation from someone else whose spiritual discernment I trusted. So I went to my wife and shared what I had received. I knew if I could get her validation, especially since she was the one most wronged in the situation, then I could say, at least to myself, "Thus sayeth the Lord."

Needless to say, Patti immediately and without question confirmed that the Lord had spoken to me. My entire planned lecture was forgotten. I returned to my office anxious to hear more. As the Lord planted a new, supernatural love for Rachel within me, He showed me what to say and how to say it to not only address the current issue of household responsibility, but the deeper issues of love and acceptance and worthiness.

Rachel and her brother remained as part of our family for another two years, giving us many opportunities to demonstrate and teach about the Father's love, planting spiritual seeds in thirsty soil. We weren't perfect and we didn't solve all of her issues, but because I had learned to listen to the Lord, we were able to avoid creating more brokenness and separation.

The four simple keys that the Lord showed me from Habakkuk have been used by people of all ages, from four to a hundred and four, from every continent, culture and denomination, to break through into intimate two-way conversations with their loving Father and dearest Friend. Omitting any one of the keys will prevent you from receiving all He wants to say to you. The order of the keys is not important, just that you *use them all*. Embracing all four, by faith, can change your life. Simply quiet yourself down, tune to spontaneity, look for vision, and journal. He is waiting to meet you there.

You will be amazed when you journal! Doubt may hinder you at first, but throw it off, reminding yourself that it is a biblical concept, and that God is present, speaking to His children. Relax. When we cease our labors and enter His rest, God is free to flow (Heb. 4:10).

Why not try it for yourself, right now? Sit back comfortably, take out your pen and paper, and smile. Turn your attention toward the Lord in praise and worship, seeking His face. Many people have found the music and visionary prayer called "A Stroll Along the Sea of Galilee" helpful in getting them started. You can listen to it and download it free at www.CWGMinistries.org/Galilee.

After you write your question to Him, become still, fixing your gaze on Jesus. You will suddenly have a very good thought. Don't doubt it; simply write it down. Later, as you read your journaling, you, too, will be blessed to discover that you are indeed dialoguing with God. If you wonder if it is really the Lord speaking to you, share it with your spouse or a friend. Their input will encourage your faith and strengthen your commitment to spend time getting to know the Lover of your soul more intimately than you ever dreamed possible.

Is It *Really* God?

Five ways to be sure what you're hearing is from Him:

1. Test the Origin (1 Jn. 4:1)

Thoughts from our own minds are progressive, with one thought leading to the next, however tangentially. Thoughts from the spirit world are spontaneous. The Hebrew word for true prophecy is *naba,* which literally means to bubble up, whereas false prophecy is *ziyd* meaning to boil up. True words from the Lord will bubble up from our innermost being; we don't need to cook them up ourselves.

2. Compare It to Biblical Principles

God will never say something to you personally which is contrary to His universal revelation as expressed in the Scriptures. If the Bible clearly states that something is a sin, no amount of journaling can make it right. Much of what you journal about will not be specifically addressed in the Bible, however, so an understanding of biblical principles is also needed.

3. Compare It to the Names and Character of God as Revealed in the Bible

Anything God says to you will be in harmony with His essential nature. Journaling will help you get to *know* God personally, but knowing what the Bible says *about* Him will help you discern what words are from Him. Make sure the tenor of your journaling lines up with the character of God as described in the names of the Father, Son and Holy Spirit.

4. Test the Fruit (Matt. 7:15-20)

What effect does what you are hearing have on your soul and your spirit? Words from the Lord will quicken your faith and increase your love, peace and joy. They will stimulate a sense of humility within you as you become more aware of Who God is and who you are. On the other hand, any words you receive which cause you to fear or doubt, which bring you into confusion or anxiety, or which stroke your ego (especially if you hear something that is "just for you alone – no one else is worthy") must be immediately rebuked and rejected as lies of the enemy.

5. Share It with Your Spiritual Counselors (Prov. 11:14)

We are members of a Body! A cord of three strands is not easily broken and God's intention has always been for us to grow together. Nothing will increase your faith in your ability to hear from God like having it confirmed by two or three other people! Share it with your spouse, your parents, your friends, your elder, your group leader, even your grown children can be your sounding board. They don't need to be perfect or super-spiritual; they just need to love you, be committed to being available to you, have a solid biblical orientation, and most importantly, they must also willingly and easily receive counsel. Avoid the authoritarian who insists that because of their standing in the church or with God, they no longer need to listen to others. Find two or three people and let them confirm that you are hearing from God!

The book *4 Keys to Hearing God's Voice* is available at www.CWGMinistries.org.

Shame Test – by Robert S. McGee

Excerpt from The Search for Significance: Book and Workbook by Robert S. McGee

Read each of the following statements; then, from the top of the test, choose the term that best describes the frequency of your typical response. Put the number above that term in the blank beside each statement.

1	2	3	4	5	6	7
always	very often	often	sometimes	seldom	very seldom	never

___ 1. I often think about past failures or experiences of rejection.

___ 2. There are certain things about my past that I cannot recall without experiencing strong, painful emotions (for example, guilt, shame, anger, fear, and so on).

___ 3. I seem to make the same mistakes over and over again.

___ 4. There are certain aspects of my character that I want to change, but I don't believe I can ever successfully do so.

___ 5. I feel inferior.

___ 6. There are aspects of my appearance that I cannot accept.

___ 7. I am generally disgusted with myself.

___ 8. I feel that certain experiences have basically ruined my life.

___ 9. I perceive myself as an immoral person.

___ 10. I feel that I have lost the opportunity to experience a complete and wonderful life.

___ Total (Add up the numbers you have placed in the blanks.)

If your score is:

57-70: God has apparently given you a very strong appreciation for His love and unconditional acceptance. You seem to be freed from the shame that plagues most people. (Some people who score this high either are greatly deceived or have be- come callous to their emotions as a way to suppress pain.)

47–56: Shame controls your responses rarely or only in certain situations. Again, the only major exceptions are those who are not honest with themselves.

37–46: When you experience emotional problems, they may relate to a sense of shame. Upon reflection, you will probably relate many of your previous decisions to feelings of worthlessness. Many of your future decisions will also be affected by low self-esteem unless you take direct action to overcome it.

27–36: Shame forms a general backdrop to your life. There are probably few days that you are not affected in some way by shame. Unfortunately, this robs you of the joy and peace your salvation is meant to bring.

0–26: Experiences of shame dominate your memory and have probably resulted in a great deal of depression. These problems will remain until some definitive action is taken. In other words, this condition will not simply disappear; time alone can- not heal your pain. You need to experience deep healing in your self-concept, in your relationship with God, and in your relationships with others.[276]

---

276   McGee, *Search for Significance*, 105-106.

BIBLIOGRAPHY

Allan, A., and D. McKillop. "The Health Implications of Apologizing after an Adverse Event." International Journal for Quality in Health Care 22, no. 2 (2010): 126–31. doi:10.1093/INTQHC/MZQ001.

Assembly at Edinburg, "Westminster Shorter Catechism." Assembly at EDINBURGH, July 28, 1648. Sess. 19. https://prts.edu/wp-content/uploads/2013/09/Shorter_Catechism.pdf.

Bailey, Kenneth E.. *Jesus Through Middle Eastern Eyes: Cultural Studies in the Gospels.* Downers Grove, IL: InterVarsity Press, 2008.

Bevere, John. *The Bait of Satan.* Lake Mary, FL: Charisma House, 2014. Scribd.

Blackburn, Dr. Elizabeth and Dr. Elissa Epel. *The Telomere Effect: A Revolutionary Approach to Living Younger, Healthier, Longer.* New York: Grand Central Publishing, 2018. Kindle.

Bixler, Heather. *Breaking Pride: Tearing Down Walls, Walking in Grace.* Indianapolis, IN: Becoming Press, 2021.

Boling, Robert G, ed. *Judges.* 1st ed. The Anchor Bible, 6a. Garden City, N.Y.: Doubleday, 1975.

Casting Crowns. "Thrive (Official Lyric Video)," December 18, 2013. YouTube Music Video, 5.09, https://www.youtube.com/watch?v=qQ71RWJhS_M

Clark Randy. *The Essential Guide to the Power of the Holy Spirit : God's Miraculous Gifts at Work Today.* Shippensburg, PA: Destiny Image, Inc, 2015

Clark Randy. *There is More! The Secret to Experiencing God's Power to Change Your Life.* Grand Rapids, MI: Chosen Books, 2013.

DeYoung, Patricia A. *Understanding and Treating Chronic Shame: Healing Right Brain Relational Trauma* (version Second edition.) New York, NY: Routledge, 2022. https://doi.org/10.4324/9780367814328.

DeVries, Simon. *1 Kings, Volume 12: Second Edition.* Grand Rapids: HarperCollins Christian Publishing, 2015.

Edwards, James R.. *The Gospel According to Luke.* Grand Rapids: William B. Eerdmans Publishing Company, 2015.

Federal Bureau of Investigation: Crime Data Explorer. October 5, 2022. https://cde.ucr.cjis.gov/LATEST/webapp/#/pages/explorer/crime/crime-trend. (accessed January 26, 2023)

Freed, Sandra. *Breaking the Threefold Demonic Cord: How to Discern and Defeat the Lies of Jezebel, Athaliah and Delilah.* Grand Rapids, MI: Chosen Books, 2008.

Gilbertson, Tina LPC. "The Paradox of Self Pity," Psychology Today, April 3, 2015, Tina Gilbertson, LPC., "The Paradox of Self Pity," Psychology Today, April 3, 2015, https://www.psychologytoday.com/us/blog/constructive-wallowing/201504/the-paradox-self-pity

Garland, David E.. *1 Corinthians (Baker Exegetical Commentary on the New Testament).* Grand Rapids: Baker Academic, 2003. Accessed May 26, 2023. ProQuest Ebook Central.

Gorrell, Dr. Stanley J.. *The Spirit of Offense: Breaking Free.* Pennsauken, NJ: Book Baby Publishing. 2020.

Graham, Billy. *Storm Warning.* Nashville, TN: Thomas Nelson, 2011. Scribd.

Green, Joel B.. *The Gospel of Luke*. Grand Rapids: Wm. B. Eerdmans Publishing Co., 1997. Accessed May 18, 2023. ProQuest Ebook Central.

Haenchen, Ernst, Robert W. Funk, and Ulrich Busse. *John 1: A Commentary on the Gospel of John, Chapters 1-6*. Augsburg Fortress Publishers, 2016. https://muse-jhu-edu.dtl.idm. oclc.org/book/45980.

Hartley, John E.. *The Book of Job*. Grand Rapids: Wm. B. Eerdmans Publishing Co., 1988. Accessed May 2, 2023. ProQuest Ebook Central.

Hodges, Pastor Chris. "Week Five: Pastor Chris Hodges – Overflow of the Heart" Church of the Highlands, Birmingham, AL, https://freedom.churchofthehighlands.com/curriculum.

Hogue, Rodney. *Forgiveness*. Collierville, TN: InstaPublisher, 2008.

Hotchkin, Robert. *Leviathan Exposed*. Maricopa, AR: XP Publishing, 2015.

Hunter, Jonathan. *Breaking Free from the spirit of death*. Maitland, FL: Xulon Press, 2012. Kindle.

Hutchings, Mike. *Supernatural Freedom from the Captivity of Trauma: Overcoming the Hindrance to Your Wholeness*. Shippensburg, PA: Destiny Image Publishers, 2021.

Irenaeus. "Against Heresies" *Ante Nicene Fathers, Volume 1*. Revised and Edited by Alexander Roberts, James Donaldson, and A. Cleveland Coxe and Translated by Alexander Roberts and William Rambaut. Buffalo NY: Christian Publishing Co. 1885. https://www.newadvent.org/fathers/0103.htm Book III, Chapter 23 (Irenaeus) (newadvent.org), Accessed February 23, 2023

Kass, Leon R.. *The Beginning of Wisdom: Reading Genesis*. Chicago IL: Chicago University Press, 2003.

Keener, Craig S. *The IVP Bible Background Commentary: New Testament*. 2nd ed. Downers Grove: IL. InterVarsity Press, 2014.

Keener, Craig S. *Romans: A New Covenant Commentary*. 1st ed. The Lutterworth Press, 2009.

Keller, W. Phillip. *A Shepherd Looks at Psalm 23*. Grand Rapids, MI: Zondervan, 2015.

Kendall, R.T.. *Jealousy the Sin that Nobody Talks About: How to Overcome Envy and Live a Life of Freedom*. Lake Mary FL: Charisma House, 2010. Kindle.

Kraft, Charles H.. *Defeating Dark Angels: Breaking Demonic Oppression in the Believers Life*. Bloomington MN: Chosen Books, 2016.

Kruse, Colin G.. *John: An Introduction and Commentary*. Vol. Revised edition. Tyndale New Testament Commentaries. Downers Grove, Illinois: IVP Academic, 2017.

LeClair, Jennifer. *The Spiritual Warrior's Guide to Defeating Water Spirits: Overcoming Demons that Twist, Suffocate, and Attack God's Purposes for Your Life*. Shippensburg, PA: Destiny Image, 2018. Kindle.

Leithart, Peter J.. *1 and 2 Kings (Brazos Theological Commentary on the Bible)*. Grand Rapids: Brazos Press, 2006.

Lewis, C. S.. *Mere Christianity*. Durham: HarperCollins Publishers, 2015.

Lewis, C.S.. *The Screwtape Letters*. San Francisco CA: HarperOne Publishers, 2013.

Louth, Andrew, ed. *Genesis 1-11*. Westmont, IL: InterVarsity Press, 2001.

McCall, Anita. *Overcoming the Spirit of Offense: Understanding How Offense Operates, in Order to Be Able to Overcome It.* Bloomington, IN: iUniverse, 2016. Kindle.

McGee, Robert S.. *The Search for Significance: Book & Workbook.* Houston, TX: Rapha Publishing, 1985.

Myles, Dr. Francis. *The Battle of the Altars: Spiritual Technology for Divine Encounters!.* Stockbridge, GA: Francis Miles International, 2020.

Moore, George F.. *A Commentary on the Book of Judges: A Critical and Exegetical Commentary on Judges.* London: Bloomsbury T&T Clark, 1958.

Norris, Kathleen. *Acedia & Me: A Marriage, Monks, and a Writer's Life.* New York: Riverhead Books, 2008. Kindle.

Harini Natarajan, "How to Tell if Someone is Jealous of You – 14 Signs," reviewed by Dr. Nancy B. Irwin, PsyD, Stylecraze, March 6, 2023, https://www.stylecraze.com/articles/signs-of-jealousy/

Olson, Roger E.. *The Mosaic of Christian Belief: Twenty Centuries of Unity and Diversity.* 2nd ed. Downers Grove Il, InterVarsity Press, 2016.

Oswalt, John N.. *The Book of Isaiah, Chapters 1-39.* Grand Rapids: Wm. B. Eerdmans Publishing Co., 1986. Accessed March 12, 2023. ProQuest Ebook Central.

Pooley, Simon. "When and where to Nile crocodiles attack? Here is what we found," The Conversation, Simon Pooley, July 15, 2019, https://theconversation.com/when-and-where-do-nile-crocodiles-attack-heres-what-we-found-119037

Potter-Efron, Ronald T, and Patricia S Potter-Efron. *Letting Go of Shame: Understanding How Shame Affects Your Life.* San Francisco: Harper & Row, 1989.

Prince, Derek. *Pride versus Humility.* New Kensington, PA: Whittaker House, 2016. Kindle.

Protasi, Sara. "What Is Envy?" In *The Philosophy of Envy*, 6-25. Cambridge: Cambridge University Press, 2021.

Richards, E. Randolph, and Richard James. *Misreading Scripture with Individualist Eyes: Patronage, Honor, and Shame in the Biblical World.* Downners Grove, IL: IVP Academic, 2020.

Russell, Stephen C and Esther J. Hamori. *Mighty Baal.* Leiden, The Netherlands: Brill, 2020. Accessed May 4, 2023, https://brill-com.dtl.idm.oclc.org/view/book/edcoll/9789004437678/front-5.xml

Rustad, Martha E.H.. *Pythons.* North Mankato, MN: Pebble, 2021. Scribd.

Sampson, Steve. *Discerning and Defeating the Ahab Spirit: The Key to Breaking Free from Jezebel.* Grand Rapids, MI: Chosen Books, 2010. Kindle.

Sandford, John Loren and Paula. *Transforming the Inner Man.* Lake Mary, FL: Charisma House, 2007.

Scott, Michael. "ORACLE." In *Delphi: A History of the Center of the Ancient World*, 9–30. Princeton University Press, 2014. https://doi.org/10.2307/j.ctt5vjv8t.6.

Seamands, David A.. *Healing for Damaged Emotions: Recovering from the Memories that Cause Our Pain.* Colorado Springs, CO: Victor Publishing, 1991.

Selner, Marissa. "What is Failure to Thrive?," Healthline, July 25, 2012, https://www.healthline.com/health/failure-to-thrive.

Shatner Method. "Gomer Pyle's "Citizen's Arrest!" of Barney Fife - The Andy Griffith Show – 1963" September 30, 2021. YouTube Video, 3.25, https://www.youtube.com/watch?v=A1D78Y60gvo

Simon, Paul and Art Garfunkel. "I Am a Rock (Lyrics)" May 16, 2020. YouTube Music Video, 2.53, https://www.youtube.com/watch?v=hTKcqOWprRc.

Snell, R.J.. *Acedia and Its Discontents: Metaphysical Boredom in an Empire of Desire.* Kettering, OH: Angelico Press, 2015. Kindle.

Solomon, Andrew. *The Noonday Demon: An Atlas of Depression.* New York: Scribner Publications, 2011.

Souza, Katie. *Be Revived: Defeat the Spirit of Death With the Power of Life.* Lake Mary FL: Charisma House, 2020.

Stott, John R.W.. *The Message of Ephesians.* Downers Grove, IL: InterVarsity Press, 1979.

Stuart, Douglas. *Hosea-Jonah, Volume 31.* Word Biblical Commentary. Grand Rapids, MI: Zondervan Academic, 2017.

Taylor, *The Ethics of Authenticity.* Cambridge MA: Harvard University Press, 1991. Scribd.

Taylor, Charles. *A Secular Age.* Gifford Lectures, 1999. Cambridge, MA.: Belknap Press of Harvard University Press, 2007.

Townsend, John Sims. *Hiding from Love: How to Change the Withdrawal Patterns That Isolate and Imprison You.* Grand Rapids, MI: Zondervan Pub. House, 1996.

Warren, Rick. *The Purpose Drive Life: What on Earth am I Here For?.* Grand Rapids, MI: Zondervan, 2012. Scribd.

Wenham, Gordon John. *Genesis 1-15, Volume 1.* Word Biblical Commentary. Grand Rapids, Michigan: Zondervan Academic, 2014.

White, Thomas Joseph Op. *Exodus (Brazos Theological Commentary on the Bible).* Grand Rapids: Brazos Press, 2016.

Williams, Jr. Hank. "Hank Williams jr. Family Tradition (Music Video)," September 20, 2010. YouTube Music Video, 4.00, https://www.youtube.com/watch?v=xd0TGfZSACI.

Wright, Christopher J.H.. *New International Biblical Commentary: Deuteronomy.* Peabody MA: Hendrickson Publishers, 1996.

Wright, N.T.. *Surprised by Hope : Rethinking Heaven, the Resurrection, and the Mission of the Church.* 1st ed. (New York: HarperOne, 2008), 214. Kindle

USA Facts. "Homicides increased by 25% but overall crime rates fell in 2020." July, 14, 2021. https://usafacts.org/articles/homicides-increased-by-25-but-overall-crime-rate-fell-in-2020/. (accessed January 26, 2023)

Vallotton, Kris and Bill Johnson. *The Supernatural Ways of Royalty: Discovering Your Rights and Privileges of Being a Son or Daughter of God.* Shippensburg, PA: Destiny Image: 2006.

Made in the USA
Columbia, SC
25 November 2023

26636441R00191